UMB Bank and Trust Company
Rockefeller Center
630 Fifth Avenue
New York, New York 10020

**UMB
BANK**
and Trust Company

_May 2, 1978_

With compliments of
**UNITED MIZRAHI BANK LTD.**
on the occasion of the opening of
**UMB BANK AND TRUST COMPANY**
in New York.

_Autographed by the Author_

# WHO STANDS ACCUSED?

# Chaim Herzog

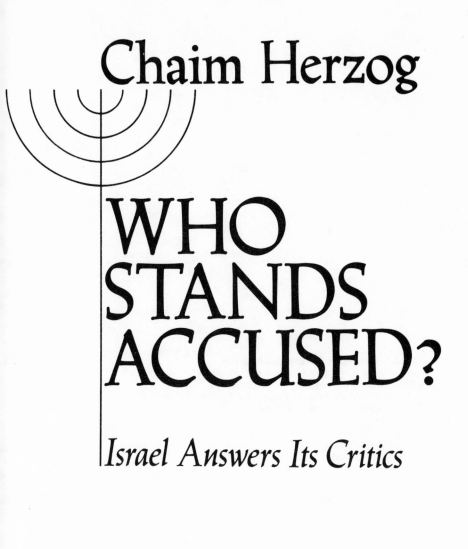

# WHO STANDS ACCUSED?

*Israel Answers Its Critics*

Random House  New York

All royalties from this book have been
donated by the author to the
Israel Defense Fund.

Library of Congress Cataloging in Publication Data

Herzog, Chaim, 1918–
   Who stands accused?

   Includes index.
   1. Jewish-Arab relations—Addresses, essays,
lectures.   2. United Nations—Israel—Addresses,
essays, lectures.   I. Title.
DS119.7.H43      327.5694′017′4927      77–90235
ISBN 0–394–50132–2

Manufactured in the United States of America

9 8 7 6 5 4 3 2

FIRST EDITION

# Foreword

THE material in this volume was never intended to be a book, nor does it represent a detailed academic analysis of the Middle East conflict. For over two years at the United Nations I have listened to a continuous outpouring of attacks and accusations against Israel on every conceivable subject. Indeed, the paranoiac obsession of the world organization with Israel has reached such heights of absurdity that something like 50 percent of the time of each General Assembly session is devoted to condemnations of this one small Jewish democracy, as though there were no other problems in the world today. In that Orwellian atmosphere it has fallen to my lot, time and again, to present Israel's case and to answer our critics.

All too frequently I have found myself alone. In these situations what has alarmed me most has been to see nations which once fought in defense of values and principles against totalitarian dictatorships compromise those same values for reasons of political and economic expediency. The prospect of civilized nations bowing to the forces of oil blackmail which have brought much of the developing world to the verge of bankruptcy is a somber one indeed. It recalls the theme of the last volume of Winston

Churchill's *Second World War:* "How the Great Democracies triumphed and so were able to resume the follies which had so nearly cost them their life."

Now, politics does not always take place in an atmosphere of reasoned objectivity. So what follows frequently reflects the heat of the debate, with all the resultant advantages and drawbacks. It also recalls such historic events as the infamous resolution equating Zionism with racism, an episode which represented the most concentrated international attack on the Jewish people since the days of Hitler. It evokes memories of the tense and emotion-laden atmosphere in a packed General Assembly Hall as all present sensed the profound significance of that event and as Israel once again in history faced its accusers. It further evokes memories of the brilliant rescue operation at Entebbe as a tense Security Council debated Israel's action in striking the first major blow against international terror.

The material also represents Israel's case on many other issues affecting both Israel and the Jewish people: the prospects for peace, the administered territories, relations with the Arab states, human rights, anti-Semitism, the UN, to mention but a few.

The material in this book predates the great moments of history when President Anwar el-Sadat made his historic visit to Jerusalem and was received with open arms by the government, Parliament and population of Israel. Prime Minister Menachem Begin's equally historic visit to Ismailia has now also taken place, and as this book goes to press, arduous negotiations at the ministerial level are under way. The first step has been taken; indeed, more than a step. It was an act of courage and imagination on both sides, and a challenge that has transcended the rivalries and maneuverings of the past to create a new vista that promises the first real hope for peace in our region.

A momentous and historic series of events has taken place in the Middle East. The world watched spellbound as old suspicions and barriers were broken down, as rhetoric gave way to dialogue, and the limits of what seemed possible were suddenly expanded to new horizons.

The recent historic developments are a vindication of the case put forth in these pages. They are indeed a vindication of Israel's position over the years that only face-to-face negotiations can move our war-torn area towards peace. For President Sadat came to Jerusalem as he did because he could not reach Jerusalem by any other route.

One can but hope and pray that the leaders of the other Arab states bordering on Israel will follow in President Sadat's footsteps. Indeed, if the historic events in Jerusalem, Cairo and Ismailia have proved anything, it is that the common people of the region yearn for nothing more than an end to war and a life of peace and cooperation.

The idea was conceived of taking many of the speeches and statements I have made during my period of service at the United Nations and encapsulating the main points in a form which would enable the concerned reader to understand Israel's case. Hence, this book.

I am indebted to many, but above all to Mr. Dan Abraham of Netanya and New York, who suggested this book and whose practical support was so invaluable.

My thanks are due Miss Susan Bolotin, an editor whose professional guidance has been so constructive, and Miss Raquel Lederman, who has tirelessly typed both the original speeches and their adaptation as presented in this book.

C. H.

*January 1978*
*United Nations*
*New York*

# *Contents*

I

The
State
of Israel

# Zionism and Racism

*Speech to the General Assembly of the United Nations,*
*November 10, 1975*

Mr. President,

It is symbolic that this debate, which may well prove to be a turning point in the fortunes of the United Nations and a decisive factor in the possible continued existence of this organization, should take place on November 10. Tonight, thirty-seven years ago, has gone down in history as *Kristallnacht*, the Night of the Crystals. This was the night in 1938 when Hitler's Nazi stormtroopers launched a coordinated attack on the Jewish community in Germany, burned the synagogues in all its cities and made bonfires in the streets of the Holy Books and the Scrolls of the Holy Law and Bible. It was the night when Jewish homes were attacked and heads of families taken away, many of them never to return. It was the night when the windows of all Jewish businesses and stores were smashed, covering the streets in the cities of Germany with a film of broken glass which dissolved into the millions of crystals which gave that night its name. It was the night which led eventually to the crematoria and the gas chambers, Auschwitz, Birkenau, Dachau, Buchenwald, Theresienstadt and others. It was the night which led to the most terrifying holocaust in the history of man.

It is indeed befitting, Mr. President, that this debate, conceived in the desire to deflect the Middle East from its moves towards peace and born of a deep pervading feeling of anti-Semitism, should take place on the anniversary of this day. It is indeed befitting, Mr. President, that the United Nations, which began its life as an anti-Nazi alliance, should thirty years later find itself on its way to becoming the world center of anti-Semitism. Hitler would have felt at home on a number of occasions during the past year, listening to the proceedings in this forum, and above all to the proceedings during the debate on Zionism.

It is sobering to consider to what level this body has been dragged down if we are obliged today to contemplate an attack on Zionism. For this attack constitutes not only an anti-Israeli attack of the foulest type, but also an assault in the United Nations on Judaism—one of the oldest established religions in the world, a religion which has given the world the human values of the Bible, and from which two other great religions, Christianity and Islam, sprang. Is it not tragic to consider that we here at this meeting in the year 1975 are contemplating what is a scurrilous attack on a great and established religion which has given to the world the Bible with its Ten Commandments, the great prophets of old, Moses, Isaiah, Amos; the great thinkers of history, Maimonides, Spinoza, Marx, Einstein, many of the masters of the arts and as high a percentage of the Nobel Prize-winners in the world, in the sciences, in the arts and in the humanities as has been achieved by any people on earth? . . .

The resolution against Zionism was originally one condemning racism and colonialism, a subject on which we could have achieved consensus, a consensus which is of great importance to all of us and to our African colleagues in particular. However, instead of permitting this to happen, a group of countries, drunk with the feeling of power inherent in the automatic majority and without regard to the importance of achieving a consensus on this issue, railroaded the UN in a contemptuous maneuver by the use of the automatic majority into bracketing Zionism with the subject under discussion.

I do not come to this rostrum to defend the moral and historical values of the Jewish people. They do not need to be defended. They speak for themselves. They have given to mankind much of what is great and eternal. They have done for the spirit of man more than can readily be appreciated by a forum such as this one.

I come here to denounce the two great evils which menace society in general and a society of nations in particular. These two evils are hatred and ignorance. These two evils are the motivating force behind the proponents of this resolution and their supporters. These two evils characterize those who would drag this world organization, the ideals of which were first conceived by the prophets of Israel, to the depths to which it has been dragged today.

The key to understanding Zionism is in its name. The easternmost of the two hills of ancient Jerusalem during the tenth century B.C.E. was called Zion.* In fact, the name Zion, referring to Jerusalem, appears 152 times in the Old Testament. The name is overwhelmingly a poetic and prophetic designation. The religious and emotional qualities of the name arise from the importance of Jerusalem as the Royal City and the City of the Temple. "Mount Zion" is the place where God dwells.† Jerusalem, or Zion, is a place where the Lord is King,‡ and where He has installed His king, David.§

King David made Jerusalem the capital of Israel almost three thousand years ago, and Jerusalem has remained the capital ever since. During the centuries the term "Zion" grew and expanded to mean the whole of Israel. The Israelites in exile could not forget Zion. The Hebrew Psalmist sat by the waters of Babylon and swore: "If I forget thee, O Jerusalem, let my right hand forget her cunning." ** This oath has been repeated for thousands of years by Jews throughout the world. It is an oath which was made

* II Sam. 5:6–9.
† Isa. 8:18, Psalm 74:2.
‡ Isa. 24:23.
§ Psalm 2:6.
** Psalm 137:5.

over seven hundred years before the advent of Christianity and over twelve hundred years before the advent of Islam, and Zion came to mean the Jewish homeland, symbolic of Judaism, of Jewish national aspirations.

While praying to his God every Jew, wherever he is in the world, faces towards Jerusalem. For over two thousand years of exile these prayers have expressed the yearning of the Jewish people to return to their ancient homeland, Israel. In fact, a continuous Jewish presence, in larger or smaller numbers, has been maintained in the country over the centuries.

Zionism is the name of the national movement of the Jewish people and is the modern expression of the ancient Jewish heritage. The Zionist ideal, as set out in the Bible, has been, and is, an integral part of the Jewish religion.

Zionism is to the Jewish people what the liberation movements of Africa and Asia have been to their own people.

Zionism is one of the most dynamic and vibrant national movements in human history. Historically it is based on a unique and unbroken connection, extending some four thousand years, between the People of the Book and the Land of the Bible.

In modern times, in the late nineteenth century, spurred by the twin forces of anti-Semitic persecution and of nationalism, the Jewish people organized the Zionist movement in order to transform their dream into reality. Zionism as a political movement was the revolt of an oppressed nation against the depredation and wicked discrimination and oppression of the countries in which anti-Semitism flourished. It is no coincidence that the co-sponsors and supporters of this resolution include countries who are guilty of the horrible crimes of anti-Semitism and discrimination to this very day.

Support for the aim of Zionism was written into the League of Nations Mandate for Palestine and was again endorsed by the United Nations in 1947, when the General Assembly voted by overwhelming majority for the restoration of Jewish independence in our ancient land.

The re-establishment of Jewish independence in Israel, after centuries of struggle to overcome foreign conquest and exile, is a vindication of the fundamental concepts of the equality of nations and of self-determination. To question the Jewish people's right to national existence and freedom is not only to deny to the Jewish people the right accorded to every other people on this globe, but it is also to deny the central precepts of the United Nations.

As a former Foreign Minister of Israel, Abba Eban, has written:

> Zionism is nothing more—but also nothing less—than the Jewish people's sense of origin and destination in the land linked eternally with its name. It is also the instrument whereby the Jewish nation seeks an authentic fulfillment of itself. And the drama is enacted in the region in which the Arab nation has realized its sovereignty in twenty states comprising a hundred million people in 4½ million square miles, with vast resources. The issue therefore is not whether the world will come to terms with Arab nationalism. The question is at what point Arab nationalism, with its prodigious glut of advantage, wealth and opportunity, will come to terms with the modest but equal rights of another Middle Eastern nation to pursue its life in security and peace.*

The vicious diatribes on Zionism voiced here by Arab delegates may give this Assembly the wrong impression that while the rest of the world supported the Jewish national liberation movement the Arab world was always hostile to Zionism. This is not the case. Arab leaders, cognizant of the rights of the Jewish people, fully endorsed the virtues of Zionism. Sherif Hussein, the leader of the Arab world during World War I, welcomed the return of the Jews to Palestine. His son, Emir Feisal, who represented the Arab world in the Paris Peace Conference, had this to say about Zionism:

> We Arabs, especially the educated among us, look with deepest sympathy on the Zionist movement . . . We will wish the Jews a hearty welcome home . . . We are working together for a reformed and revised Near East, and our two movements complement one another. The movement is national and not imperialistic. There is room in Syria for us both. Indeed, I think that neither can be a success without the other.†

It is perhaps pertinent at this point to recall that when the question of Palestine was being debated in the United Nations in

* "Zionism and the UN," New York *Times* (November 3, 1975).
† Letter from Emir Feisal to Felix Frankfurter, sent by Délégation Hedjazienne, Paris, March 3, 1919.

1947, the Soviet Union strongly supported the Jewish independence struggle. It is particularly relevant to recall some of Andrei Gromyko's remarks:

> As we know, the aspirations of a considerable part of the Jewish people are linked with the problem of Palestine and of its future administration. This fact scarcely requires proof. . . . During the last war, the Jewish people underwent exceptional sorrow and suffering. Without any exaggeration, this sorrow and suffering are indescribable. It is difficult to express them in dry statistics on the Jewish victims of the fascist aggressors. The Jews in the territories where the Hitlerites held sway were subjected to almost complete physical annihilation. The total number of Jews who perished at the hands of the Nazi executioners is estimated at approximately six million. . . .
>
> The United Nations cannot and must not regard this situation with indifference, since this would be incompatible with the high principles proclaimed in its Charter, which provides for the defense of human rights, irrespective of race, religion or sex. . . .
>
> The fact that no Western European State has been able to ensure the defence of the elementary rights of the Jewish people and to safeguard it against the violence of the fascist executioners explains the aspirations of the Jews to establish their own State. It would be unjust not to take this into consideration and to deny the right of the Jewish people to realize this aspiration.*

How sad it is to see here a group of nations, many of whom have but recently freed themselves of colonial rule, deriding one of the most noble liberation movements of this century, a movement which not only gave an example of encouragement and determination to the peoples struggling for independence but also actively aided many of them either during the period of preparation for their independence or immediately thereafter.

Here you have a movement which is the embodiment of a unique pioneering spirit, of the dignity of labor, and of enduring human values, a movement which has presented to the world an example of social equality and open democracy being associated in this resolution with abhorrent political concepts.

We in Israel have endeavored to create a society which strives to implement the highest ideals of society—political, social and

* United Nations General Assembly, First Special Session, May 14, 1947. UN Document A/PV 77.

cultural—for all the inhabitants of Israel, irrespective of religious belief, race or sex.

Show me another pluralistic society in this world in which despite all the difficult problems, Jew and Arab live together with such a degree of harmony, in which the dignity and rights of man are observed before the law, in which no death sentence is applied, in which freedom of speech, of movement, of thought, of expression are guaranteed, in which even movements which are opposed to our national aims are represented in our Parliament.

The Arab delegates talk of racism. What has happened to the 800,000 Jews who lived for over two thousand years in the Arab lands, who formed some of the most ancient communities long before the advent of Islam. Where are they now?

The Jews were once one of the important communities in the countries of the Middle East, the leaders of thought, of commerce, of medical science. Where are they in Arab society today? You dare talk of racism when I can point with pride to the Arab ministers who have served in my government; to the Arab deputy speaker of my Parliament; to Arab officers and men serving of their own volition in our border and police defense forces, frequently commanding Jewish troops; to the hundreds of thousands of Arabs from all over the Middle East crowding the cities of Israel every year; to the thousands of Arabs from all over the Middle East coming for medical treatment to Israel; to the peaceful coexistence which has developed; to the fact that Arabic is an official language in Israel on a par with Hebrew; to the fact that it is as natural for an Arab to serve in public office in Israel as it is incongruous to think of a Jew serving in any public office in an Arab country, indeed being admitted to many of them. Is that racism? It is not! That, Mr. President, is Zionism.

Zionism is our attempt to build a society, imperfect though it may be, in which the visions of the prophets of Israel will be realized. I know that we have problems. I know that many disagree with our government's policies. Many in Israel too disagree from time to time with the government's policies . . . and are free to do so because Zionism has created the first and only real democratic state in a part of the world that never really knew democracy and freedom of speech.

This malicious resolution, designed to divert us from its true purpose, is part of a dangerous anti-Semitic idiom which is being insinuated into every public debate by those who have sworn to block the current move towards accommodation and ultimately towards peace in the Middle East. This, together with similar moves, is designed to sabotage the efforts of the Geneva Conference for peace in the Middle East and to deflect those who are moving along the road towards peace from their purpose. But they will not succeed, for I can but reiterate my government's policy to make every move in the direction towards peace, based on compromise.

We are seeing here today but another manifestation of the bitter anti-Semitic, anti-Jewish hatred which animates Arab society. Who would have believed that in this year, 1975, the malicious falsehoods of the "elders of Zion" would be distributed officially by Arab governments? * Who would have believed that we would today contemplate an Arab society which teaches the vilest anti-Jewish hate in the kindergartens? . . . We are being attacked by a society which is motivated by the most extreme form of racism known in the world today. This is the racism which was expressed so succinctly in the words of the leader of the PLO, Yassir Arafat, in his opening address at a symposium in Tripoli, Libya: "There will be no presence in the region other than the Arab presence . . ." † In other words, in the Middle East from the Atlantic Ocean to the Persian Gulf only one presence is allowed, and that

---

* *The Protocols of the Elders of Zion* was a notorious anti-Semitic forgery concocted in Paris in the last decade of the nineteenth century by an unknown author working for the Russian secret police (Okhvana). It was probably intended to influence the policies of Czar Nicholas II. For his purpose the anonymous forger adopted an old French political pamphlet by Maurice Joly, attributing ambitions of world domination to Napoleon III, which does not contain the slightest allusion to Jews or to Judaism. This "dialogue" was transformed into the "protocols" of an alleged conference of world Jewry. The first Russian public edition of the *Protocols* appeared in 1905, but they were widely circulated as from 1919 by anti-Semitic groups. In 1934 the Jewish community of Switzerland brought the publishers of the *Protocols* to trial, establishing in court that the work was a forgery. This did not deter its propagators. In World War II the *Protocols* became an implicit justification by the Nazis for the genocide of the Jews. The *Protocols* have been reissued in numerous Arab states and President Nasser of Egypt publicly vouched for their authenticity.

† Reported by the Libyan News Agency, May 16, 1975.

is Arab presence. No other people, regardless of how deep are its roots in the region, is to be permitted to enjoy its right to self-determination.

Look at the tragic fate of the Kurds of Iraq. Look what happened to the black population in southern Sudan. Look at the dire peril in which an entire community of Christians finds itself in Lebanon. Look at the avowed policy of the PLO, which calls in its Palestine Covenant of 1964 for the destruction of the State of Israel, which denies any form of compromise on the Palestine issue and which, in the words of its representative only the other day in this building, considers Tel Aviv to be occupied territory. Look at all this, and you see before you the root cause of the pernicious resolution brought before this Assembly. You see the twin evils of this worlc at work, the blind hatred of the Arab proponents of this resolution, and the abysmal ignorance and wickedness of those who support them.

The issue before this Assembly is neither Israel nor Zionism. The issue is the fate of this organization. Conceived in the spirit of the prophets of Israel, born out of an anti-Nazi alliance after the tragedy of World War II, it has degenerated into a forum which was this last week described by [Paul Johnson] one of the leading writers in a foremost organ of social and liberal thought in the West as "rapidly becoming one of the most corrupt and corrupting creations in the whole history of human institutions. . . . almost without exception those in the majority came from states notable for racist oppression of every conceivable hue." He goes on to explain the phenomenon of this debate.

> Israel is a social democracy, the nearest approach to a free socialist state in the world; its people and government have a profound respect for human life, so passionate indeed that, despite every conceivable provocation, they have refused for a quarter of a century to execute a single captured terrorist. They also have an ancient but vigorous culture, and a flourishing technology. The combination of national qualities they have assembled in their brief existence as a state is a perpetual and embittering reproach to most of the new countries whose representatives swagger about the UN building. So Israel is envied and hated; and efforts are made to destroy her.

The extermination of the Israelis has long been the prime objective of the Terrorist International; they calculate that if they can break Israel, then all the rest of civilisation is vulnerable to their assaults. . . .

The melancholy truth, I fear, is that the candles of civilisation are burning low. The world is increasingly governed not so much by capitalism, or communism, or social democracy, or even tribal barbarism, as by a false lexicon of political clichés, accumulated over half a century and now assuming a kind of degenerate sacerdotal authority. . . . We all know what they are . . .*

Over the centuries it has fallen to the lot of my people to be the testing agent of human decency, the touchstone of civilization, the crucible in which enduring human values are to be tested. A nation's level of humanity could invariably be judged by its behavior towards its Jewish population. Persecution and oppression have often enough begun with the Jews, but it has never ended with them. The anti-Jewish pogroms in Czarist Russia were but the tip of the iceberg which revealed the inherent rottenness of a regime that was soon to disappear in the storm of revolution. The anti-Semitic excesses of the Nazis merely foreshadowed the catastrophe which was to befall mankind in Europe. . . .

On the issue before us, the world has divided itself into good and bad, decent and evil, human and debased. We, the Jewish people, will recall in history our gratitude to those nations who stood up and were counted and who refused to support this wicked proposition. I know that this episode will have strengthened the forces of freedom and decency in this world and will have fortified the free world in their resolve to strengthen the ideals they so cherish. I know that this episode will have strengthened Zionism as it has weakened the United Nations.

As I stand on this rostrum, the long and proud history of my people unravels itself before my inward eye. I see the oppressors of our people over the ages as they pass one another in evil procession into oblivion. I stand here before you as the representative of a strong and flourishing people which has survived them all and

* Paul Johnson, "The Resources of Civilization," in the *New Statesman* (October 31, 1975), p. 532.

which will survive this shameful exhibition and the proponents of this resolution.

The great moments of Jewish history come to mind as I face you, once again outnumbered and the would-be victim of hate, ignorance and evil. I look back on those great moments. I recall the greatness of a nation which I have the honor to represent in this forum. I am mindful at this moment of the Jewish people throughout the world wherever they may be, be it in freedom or in slavery, whose prayers and thoughts are with me at this moment.

I stand here not as a supplicant. Vote as your moral conscience dictates to you. For the issue is neither Israel nor Zionism. The issue is the continued existence of this organization, which has been dragged to its lowest point of discredit by a coalition of despots and racists.

The vote of each delegation will record in history its country's stand on anti-Semitic racism and anti-Judaism. You yourselves bear the responsibility for your stand before history, for as such will you be viewed in history. We, the Jewish people, will not forget.

For us, the Jewish people, this is but a passing episode in a rich and event-filled history. We put our trust in our Providence, in our faith and beliefs, in our time-hallowed tradition, in our striving for social advance and human values, and in our people wherever they may be. For us, the Jewish people, this resolution based on hatred, falsehood and arrogance, is devoid of any moral or legal value.*

---

* At this point I tore up the draft text of the resolution before the General Assembly.

# 2

# The New
# Anti-Semitism and
# Israel's Response

TODAY, a few years after the Zionism debate, it is possible to look back and see two distinct results of that shameful episode. On the one hand it sounded a warning, the clearest since the days of Hitler, that the anti-Semitic hatred which a generation ago killed one third of our people continues to thrive. Indeed, the hatred is now worse, for the bigotry of despots has been given official sanction and respectability by the United Nations itself. On the other hand the denunciation of Zionism also created a renewed awareness of the meaning of the State of Israel, and reaffirmed the unbreakable link between Zion and the eternal values of the Jewish people. It is therefore fitting that we examine both the hatred and the reaffirmation in the light of recent history.

Forty years ago Nazism was on the rise and the anti-Semitic rantings of Hitler echoed across Europe, sounding a warning note to humanity. Alas, the warning went unheeded until the world was plunged into a bloodbath which was to lead to a holocaust such as humanity had not yet witnessed. Sadly, the world has not learned its lesson. Today we are approaching a new Munich as the free nations of the world make their peace with the despots of the 1970s. The same disturbing signs of appeasement exist today as in

1938, the same alarming indications that many Western nations are prepared to turn a blind eye, to by-pass the problem, to pretend it does not exist.

Our experiences in the United Nations in the last three years should have sounded the alarm for all decent and freedom-loving people throughout the world. In 1974 a gun-toting terrorist leader, Yassir Arafat, was received with adulation and a standing ovation at the United Nations, and with honors normally accorded a head of state. Then, without so much as a demur on the part of the representatives of the West, Idi Amin, himself a racist murderer responsible for the deaths of hundreds of thousands of his countrymen, appeared on the podium of the General Assembly to demand the elimination of a member state, Israel. When this can happen, when an abomination such as the Zionism resolution can be accepted by the World Assembly, when such examples of cynical expediency occur daily, then we have a clear indication of the direction in which the world is moving.

Many of the Third World countries which Israel itself has aided, and which are prepared today to receive Israeli assistance in the various fields of technology and agriculture, have been swept up unwillingly by the automatic majority that evinces little concern for their national interests. And the West, succumbing to the power of oil and commercial interests, has turned a blind eye to the behavior of dictatorships and despotisms while it ingratiates itself with petty tyrants. When Israel is accused of terror by terrorists, of police tactics by police states, of torture by torturers, of racism by racists, the free nations stand in silence today as they did forty years ago when Hitler leveled his own accusations against the Jewish people. The alarm has been sounded, and again it has gone unheeded.

For us, the Jewish people, it has not been so easy to dull the memories of the Holocaust, and we have learned from the past that we cannot ignore the modern anti-Semitism we have witnessed in recent years. If we, as one people all over the world, do not today speak out against this new international outburst of anti-Semitism, this medieval attack on our religion which masquerades under a condemnation of Zionism, then we shall sin towards the future generations of Jews who will ask where we were when this occurred. In the past we did sin, for we thought that if we kept our heads down, the storm would blow over. We were wrong, and it is a moot point now to ask how many we could have saved if we had stood up as one and fought with all we had.

But I believe we have learned our lesson, for I have seen that the ordinary Jew in the street is not going to be pushed around. When he hears today the same outbursts of vile prejudice and anti-Semitic hatred which, a generation ago, led to Auschwitz, he is prepared to stand up and fight, to look his enemies defiantly in the eye and give the answer of a united and proud Jewish people. He draws his inspiration today from those who rose in the Warsaw Ghetto thirty-five years ago and proclaimed that man's spirit is stronger than the arms of the oppressors. He remembers that handful of desperate, outnumbered and doomed rebels fighting through the sewers of Warsaw to the last bullet and the last breath and dying in the crumbling masonry of the ghetto.

The Jew today recalls the streets of that ghetto in Warsaw whose very names are part of Jewish folklore, streets in which so many of the great figures in Jewish history lived, wrote, created and died, and from which so many departed to enrich Jewry in Israel and in the Diaspora.

These streets, which were once the powerhouse of the Jewish nation, in 1943 lay covered in ruins, the silence of death broken only by the moaning of the wounded and the trampling of jack-boots.

Each Passover the Jew reads from the Haggadah the words "B'chol dor vador." And in every generation we should see ourselves as having participated in the Exodus from Egypt. So should we in every generation see ourselves as having stood up as a people, and as in the Exodus or in the Warsaw Ghetto, having proclaimed, "Enough, we are not prepared to compromise our dignity as a free people." When we remember the Holocaust we must also renew the vow "Never again" so that those heroes who announced in Warsaw that the Jewish people had risen against the forces of evil did not die in vain.

We are frequently accused of having a Holocaust complex; the Holocaust is not a complex. It is a very awesome and realistic experience of our generation. When the same Nazi philosophy calling for the destruction of our people is the basic philosophy of an organization such as the PLO, which is given Observer status in the UN, then what are we to say? Who can challenge us in a world in which mass slaughter in nations such as Lebanon and Iraq, a major invasion of an independent country such as Ethiopia, and other horrifying developments throughout the world and similar catastrophes do not merit the attention of the United Nations? Who can challenge us if we feel that this world is still capable of cynically ignoring the massacre and destruction of nations? Who can challenge us if our security takes precedence over other nations' political expediency?

Rarely in our long history has a united and determined Jewish reaction been so capable of deterring enemies and encouraging friends. Time and again it has become clear to us that both friendly and hostile governments are influenced by the degree of support they feel that Israel is receiving from world Jewry, and especially from American Jewry. They follow it closely, because what Jews say and do is a measure of the degree to which the Jewish people is prepared to stand up and fight. When we stood united against our enemies on the Zionism issue, we saw that we were not alone. The United States, the Europeans, indeed the whole Western world, stood up and were counted with us on that occasion, fighting at our side in a most impressive manner. The continent of Africa split down the middle on this issue, and for the first time in years the majority of black African countries refused to support an anti-Israeli resolution. The vast majority of Latin American countries also refused to go along.

We represent principles and values which are distasteful to so many regimes in the world that we must continue to expect the outpouring of calumnies against the Jewish people and Israel to which we have become accustomed. The question is whether the voice of our enemies is the only one to be heard. The task of Jewish people is to stand united against the new wave of international anti-Semitism, and to speak out proudly and defiantly to defend our heritage, our tradition and our values. We owe it to our forebears to do so, and we owe it to our children and to the generations to come.

When I tore up the document containing the pernicious resolution equating Zionism with racism, I was giving expression to the

revolt of the Jewish people against any attempt to revive the curse
of anti-Semitism in the world. But that moment also represented
a profound reaffirmation of the unity and values of the Jewish
people, for I was acting on behalf of a people who had given
much of the eternal values of mankind to the world. I also
knew that I was not acting alone. At that moment the Jewish
heart was beating as one throughout the world—from the great
Jewish community of America to the windswept prison camps of
Siberia, from my brothers and sisters in Israel to the hell on earth
that is the Jewish ghetto in Damascus. At that moment we as a
people were one as we have never been before, reaffirming our
belief in Judaism, in Zionism, in the State of Israel and in the
eternal values of the Jewish people.

It is crucial to our survival that Zionism never become a mere
political slogan, and that it never lose its intimate connection with
the principles of Judaism. Indeed, it was evident to the founding
fathers of modern Zionism that in the political rebirth of Israel
the concrete achievements without the spiritual ideals would be
meaningless. In debates at the United Nations it is only natural,
therefore, that I invoke the Bible and the Prophets, not only as the
moral underpinnings of our own actions but as a testament of our
contribution as a people to mankind. No religious document, for
example, has exercised a greater influence on the moral and social
life of man than the Divine Proclamation of Human Duty known
as the Decalogue—the Ten Commandments. These few brief
words—only 120 Hebrew words in all—cover the whole sphere of
conduct and lay down the fundamental rules of worship and of
rights for all time and for all men. Our sages describe how as the
Divine Commandments rang out from Sinai's heights, no bird
sang, no ox lowed, the ocean did not roar and no creature stirred:
all nature was rapt in breathless silence at the sound of the Divine
Voice asserting the supremacy of Conscience and Right in the
Universe. The rabbis held the sixth of Sivan, the day of the
Revelation at Mount Sinai, to be as momentous as the day of
Creation itself, for without the coming into existence of Moral
Law, the creation of the material universe would have been incom-
plete, even meaningless.

With these principles, over three thousand years old, we set
forth as a nation into the modern world. These are the principles

which have preserved us through ages of adversity, trial and struggle, and which sustain us today. The Jewish people today is a nation which has survived some four thousand years, with the same religion, the same language, the same country, the same identity and culture—the only such nation in the world, with the possible exception of the Chinese. Today it is the vital task of Jewish education to make sure that Jewish children will maintain our sacred traditions and strengthen the chain of immortality which binds us as a nation.

In Israel today the great immortal teachings which we have given to the world are being practiced, not only preached. During the terrible slaughter which took place in the Lebanese war, the only island of human kindness in the scene of death, destruction and misery was the so-called good fence between Lebanon and Israel. There Israel opened its doors to its proclaimed enemies, setting up centers for medical treatment, taking refugees into hospitals and giving them work, buying their produce and selling them supplies. As we contemplate the slaughter in the Lebanon and the silence of the Christian world while their coreligionists were massacred, we can take pride in the commitment of the Jewish people to their oppressed brothers. Every year, thousands of Jewish gatherings are held throughout the world with the single purpose of helping our fellow Jews. But perhaps the most significant achievement in our generation has been the fate of the 800,000 Jewish refugees from Arab lands. They were saved, transported, absorbed and trained to be useful citizens by the Jewish people in Israel and elsewhere. By contrast, 500,000 Arab refugees are still maintained by international charity in camps—thirty years after the War of Independence—kept there as pawns by their Arab brethren, who are too busy gambling away billions of petrodollars at the gaming tables of Monte Carlo or Las Vegas to care for them.

Our dedication one to the other received its highest form of expression on July 4, 1976. On that date the Israeli government ordered the Israel Defense Forces to rescue over a hundred Jewish hostages at Entebbe Airport who had been separated from the non-Jewish passengers and were threatened with death by the forces of international terror. For the Jewish people, this was more than a brilliant rescue operation. The separation of the Jewish passengers recalled the selection process of the Nazi concentration camps and evoked the determination to ensure that never again would there be another Auschwitz or Dachau. The Israeli soldiers who took part in the hazardous rescue risked their lives to save their fellow Jews. Consciously or unconsciously they realized that we as a people stand or fall as one, and not one of them hesitated to do his duty. For the Jewish people, Entebbe symbolized one of the great principles of our people, the principle of oneness, the principle of our readiness to sacrifice ourselves for our fellow Jews.

As I pointed out earlier, the Zionism resolution simultaneously produced a new wave of anti-Semitism and a positive reaffirmation of Jewish values and Zionist ideals. In a very real sense, this dual awareness has been a microcosm of our whole generation, which has been chosen to witness both the greatest holocaust in history and the rebirth of the Jewish commonwealth.

This, then, is the moment to recall those historic days in 1948 when the Zionist dream became a reality. Those who wish an objective account of what occurred must seek it elsewhere, for I cannot look back on those days without vivid personal memories of the deeds and the individuals who made the dream a reality. In retrospect, I believe that our strength lay in the fact that we did not know how utterly hopeless our situation was. I recall a small but closely knit population of 600,000 struggling against unbelievable odds. I recall the youngsters going out to fight inadequately armed, obliged to avoid the watchful eyes of the British Mandatory authorities before entering into combat with the Arab gangs and later with the Arab armies. I recall the ominous silhouettes of the Royal Navy's vessels patrolling in the distance off the shores of the country, to prevent the arrival of arms and refugees. I recall the struggle of Tel Aviv against the neighboring city of Jaffa with its 70,000 Arabs, and the nightmare of a trip in armored buses from Tel Aviv to Jerusalem through a series of hostile towns such as Azur and Ramle, and then the gamble of a trip up through the Arab-infested hillsides of Bab el-Wad on the road to Jerusalem. I recall the long and circuitous trip from Tel Aviv to Haifa bypassing the Mount Carmel range. I recall the sole link by sea which existed between Haifa and the Jewish settlements in west-

ern Galilee, such as Naharia. I recall the dastardly explosions in
Ben Yehuda Street, and in the Jewish Agency, at both of which I
was present. I recall the siege in Jerusalem, the Holy City, when
we were pounded by the British-directed artillery of the Arab Legion, when we had to bury our dead in the back gardens, when
unsung heroes distributed one pint of water per day to every family, under this hail of death, when people lived on three slices of
bread per day and cooked the weeds from the backyards as food.
I recall one trip to Jerusalem through the Arab blockade with a
convoy of food and supplies, only to learn that at the other end of
the city the Arabs had closed in and set fire to the remnants of
the Hadassah convoy to Mount Scopus—seventy doctors, employees and nurses—who were already in their final death throes.
I recall the desperate and hopeless battles at Latrun as the 7th
Brigade, composed of immigrants from the refugee camps in Cyprus, with little or no training, desperately tried to break through
on the road to Jerusalem. I recall the small handful of us in the
hills of Jerusalem reconnoitering the Burma Road, which was to
be the life line to besieged Jerusalem. I recall the spirit of the
people, a spirit so magnificent as to defy description. I recall the
Jews from the Orthodox sector of Jerusalem, with their rabbis by
their sides, working on the Sabbath digging trenches, participating
in the struggle. I recall the little schoolchildren dodging among
the hail of bullets and the explosion of shells carrying messages
and manning the communications services. I recall in the battles
of Latrun against the Arab League the expletives of Micky Mar-
cus, an American Jewish colonel who had come to join us—and to
fight with us—as he saw the incredible barrage of Arab fire mow-
ing down our troops. And I can still remember the death of a
communications operator, a young girl of nineteen called Hadassah, who was in an armored half-track that had succeeded in
breaking through the Arab lines and reaching the police station at
Latrun, only there to come under fire. Her last words—cut short
by death—still re-echo in my ears.

As I recall all this I realize that these experiences of mine were
multiplied 600,000 times, when a small determined people stood
and fought. By the very nature of things, I saw only a minute part
of the bravery, devotion and sacrifice. I did not see Bet Eshel,
outside Beersheba, besieged for months. I did not see Yad Mor-

dechai struggling against the Egyptian army as it broke through along the coast, and I did not see all the strike forces of the Palmach: in the south in the desert, in the north in the Jerusalem hills. But we did feel our strength as one family, and were conscious of the fact that we were being led at the time by one of the greatest leaders to have arisen in Jewish history.

We emerged victorious from the War of Independence. We lost 1 percent of our population—a youth which has stood the test of all the years and has never failed us in time of crisis. We emerged conscious of the historical significance of the events surrounding us. We looked forward with hope to a great and new future of our people. In our Declaration of Independence we held forth our hand to our Arab neighbors and to the Arab people. We signed armistice agreements with Egypt, Jordan, Syria and Lebanon, confident that the final peace treaty specified in the preamble to the agreements would be effected within six months, as was indeed laid down in the agreements. But this was not to be. We faced a bitter struggle for our independence, but we have faced perhaps an even more bitter struggle to maintain that independence.

As is their wont, the media tend to emphasize the adverse and ignore the positive. Yet the meaning of Zionism is reflected above all in the very nature of Israel's society and in the unusual achievements of that society in the space of less than thirty years. For one thing, Israel is a democracy in a world in which democracy is on the wane. In the United Nations there are some 30 democracies out of 149 member states. In the Middle East there is only one—Israel. We live at a time when those spiritual values which have inspired the United States for two hundred years and which were brought to the world by the Prophets of Israel are endangered. When we see that pandering to expediency and to the whims of dictators has become the norm, it is time for all those who believe in a system guaranteeing freedom and human values to stand up and be counted.

When we look at the Middle East, therefore, and see one stable country in the area, Israel, practicing democracy and giving freedom to all its citizens, that is a matter for pride. We have created a free society in which the dignity of man is enshrined as a supreme value, a society with a free and independent judiciary, a democratically elected Parliament and a free press.

When elections were recently held in Israel, it was disturbing to note the degree of incredulity with which the process of democracy was greeted in the United States and elsewhere. One detected a feeling of frustration and even annoyance that Israel had to engage in such a luxury, thereby upsetting calculations and timetables, and disturbing planned moves and projections. The question mark of elections, accepted as inevitable in such a process and as something that goes without saying in day-to-day life in the United States, tended to be regarded as superfluous and even tiresome when applied to Israel.

This rather strange and primitive reaction to our elections was compounded by a mass-media reaction both vile and uncivilized. Thinly veiled anti-Semitic overtones, such as *Time* magazine's remark that Begin "rhymes with Fagin," * left one dumfounded. We were regaled with an outpouring of slander and innuendo such as has rarely been used when referring to the leader elect of a hostile country, let alone to a close ally. A mass hysteria gripped the media in the United States, in Britain and in other countries, and they immediately labeled Begin a terrorist. Menachem Begin is a patriot who led an underground movement against the British in Palestine. Not all agreed with him, but he fought as a guerrilla and Jewish resistance leader against regular British forces. At no time did he call for the destruction of a nation or a people. Nobody today would call Eamon De Valera of Ireland, Jomo Kenyatta of Kenya or Archbishop Makarios of Cyprus a terrorist, yet all fought against the British.

The media further suggested that Begin's election had arrested the advance towards peace. Our enemies and some friends now bewail the passing of the Labor-led coalition. For nineteen years, they forget, Israel was ruled by such a coalition—moderate, willing to make concessions, so-called doves if one can use such a characterization. The Arab states, which now bemoan the fate of the Middle East, had thirty years in which to move towards accommodation, thirty years in which they refused to negotiate, refused to make peace, refused to recognize Israel. The issue of war and

* *Time* (May 30, 1977).

peace in the Middle East is not related to the elections in Israel. Some political parties are willing to concede more than others, but all want to sit down and negotiate peace in face-to-face talks.

In the midst of all this sordid reaction to free elections in a world in which such a phenomenon is a comparative rarity, one very positive element emerged. That bright spot was the proud and upstanding reaction of American Jewry to the media's hypocritical raising of hands in horror. The American Jewish leadership refused to allow a wedge to be driven between Israel and American Jewry and solemnly reaffirmed the American Jewish commitment to Israel. Of course, there were those who had and have their doubts, but they were never confused about the basic commitment of Jews the world over one to others, and especially of American Jewry to Israel. American Jewry made it clear that its dedication is not to political parties, but to the State of Israel.

But it is not only the democratic process that distinguishes Israel's society, important though that is. We have absorbed our fellow brethren from all over the world, from countries where Jews traditionally suffered discrimination, and made them useful citizens. We have created a system of universal education in which no child has to want for education, however poor his circumstances. We have created one of the most highly developed systems of agriculture in the world, which dozens of nations have come to study. We have created a system of social equality, including such original forms as the kibbutz and the moshav.*

We have created an industry which is capable of producing the most sophisticated equipment—supersonic planes, missile boats and missiles—and also some of the best fashionable apparel in the world. Our small country is one of the ten nations in the world that produce a modern supersonic jet fighter. Our Kfir fighter attracted world-wide attention at the international Paris air show. Israel's pavilion displaying the Kfir, the Arava, the Westwind, missile-carrying speed boats, missiles and electronic tech-

---

* The kibbutz (plural: kibbutzim) is a communal settlement in which property is held in common, and work organized on a collective basis. The moshav is a village based on the cooperative principle, in which ownership is private but produce is sold and supplies bought through central cooperatives. Some farm equipment is owned collectively.

nology was the biggest hit of the show.* Thousands crowded to
view with disbelief the products of Israeli technology. We are
one of six countries today producing a major battle tank. Our
"Chariot" is, I believe, the best tank in the world. I mention these
products because they indicate the existence of a highly advanced
industrial basis which has grown up over the years.

We have also become one of the more advanced countries in
the world in the production of sophisticated electronics. Israeli-
manufactured components are used in U.S. space ships on the
moon and on Mars. We are among the leaders in the world in
desalination of sea water and in harnessing solar energy. We have
made deserts bloom. Our deserts today are some of the principal
daily suppliers of agricultural products to the markets of Europe,
and we are gradually becoming the food supplier of Europe in the
winter months. A million stem flowers are exported from Israel
every night. We are a medium-sized maritime nation with a strong
and growing merchant marine.

We have it in our power to join together with Arab wealth to
create an area of prosperity, of technical advance and of cultural harmony in the Middle East. For our part, we will move
slowly but surely towards this goal—surely because we long for
nothing more than peace; slowly because we want to be sure of a
real and sincere peace. In this we shall succeed if we are strong
enough to maintain a firm posture in our defense and diplomacy,
and if our economic and social fabric remains strong and united.

Our small country with only 3 million inhabitants exported
goods and services in 1977 for approximately $4.5 billion. This
figure itself is worth contemplating, for since the establishment of
the State of Israel, the total contribution of the United Jewish
Appeal to Israel as part of the American Jewish commitment to
world Jewry has been $5.3 billion. In 1978 Israel's exports in goods
and services will reach $5.4 billion. In other words, parallel to the
great efforts of world Jewry, Israel has been making massive advances in its own development. Had we not been burdened by
huge defense expenditures, Israel would today be a new Switzer-

---

* The Kfir is an Israeli-produced supersonic jet fighter, the Arava is a short-
takeoff-and-landing transport and supply plane, and the Westwind is a sophisticated executive jet plane.

land economically. As vast quantities of arms from the Soviet Union and the Western countries pour into the Middle East we have no option but to turn to our friends for help. The $3.5 million deficit in our budget is a function of the steps we have to take to counter the vast rearmament going on in the Arab countries, particularly from the Soviet Union. Our economic problems are great and we are attempting to solve them through measures which are inevitably painful. Few countries in the world have taken such drastic steps as Israel in order to cut down on expenses and at the same time to develop our economic infrastructure. Despite the almost insuperable problems which face us, we have succeeded in creating an average per capita income equivalent to the average West European income.

But Israel's achievements cannot be summarized in figures and material goods alone, important though these are as a measure of a society's vitality and viability. We Israelis must look also at the quality of our life and take pride in the fact that we have become a center of learning, study and culture in the Jewish world. We have achieved, at least in part, Isaiah's prophecy that ". . . for out of Zion shall go forth the law, and the word of the Lord from Jerusalem." * Our musicians, our actors, our artists bring us renown. Despite the many problems that exist, we have created one of the most successful multiracial societies in the world today. Our Arab population has achieved political equality, personal freedom and economic advance even in circumstances of a continuous threat on the part of the Arab world against our very existence. Five million people have crossed the bridges between us and the Arab world—both ways—in the past few years. Indeed, 50 percent of the children treated in the Hadassah Hospital in Jerusalem are Arab children from throughout the region. We are similarly proud of our liberal administration of the territories where the Arab population continues to enjoy the benefits of a free society.

In short, we have endeavored to behave in a manner befitting our tradition as Jews. Sometimes I look at those representatives in the United Nations who have made a practice of maligning Israel, and I contemplate the sum total of human misery, lack of

* Isa. 2:3.

freedom, lack of expression, hunger, disease, despotism, arbitrary imprisonment and callous disregard of human rights which they represent. At those moments I cannot help but compare this with what a small country like Israel has accomplished in terms of both human dignity and technological advance, under the most adverse conditions possible but in an atmosphere of true freedom. As I contemplate our maligners it strikes me that I represent a people which over an unbroken period of four thousand years has remained committed to the moral values which are the basis of civilization. It is then that I am especially proud of the Jewish heritage that I represent.

# 3

# *Jerusalem*

THE city of Jerusalem is a city of unique character. It is a Holy City, sacred to millions of members of the three large religions, and its holy shrines and traditions are the heritage of mankind. It is this unique character of Jerusalem that makes all considerations affecting it so difficult to limit and delineate. The demographic and the urban, the cultural and the legal, the historical and the religious, the aesthetic and the economic, the parochial and the international—all are inextricably associated in the city of Jerusalem.

In the course of history Jerusalem has known many rulers, but only for Jews has it been the capital of our nation. At all other times Jerusalem was ruled by foreigners, who treated it as a provincial town. The Jews of Jerusalem today are the inhabitants with the longest unbroken historical association with it. Before the capital cities we know today even existed, Jerusalem was the capital city of the Jewish commonwealth. Wild herds roamed on the sites of what are today the great capital cities of the world while the Prophets of Israel were walking in the streets of Jerusalem and proclaiming in their immortal words the great principles of humanity for the first time. When many of the great civilizations of today were primitive societies, the judges of Israel were dispensing justice in Jerusalem on the basis of one of the most advanced and enlightened codes of law in history. Even when the city was under alien domination, the story of Jewish attachment to Jerusalem was an unremitting struggle to preserve a Jewish presence in it, never allowing the link to be broken.

Since the days of King David's rule (1010–970 B.C.E.) when the city was established as the capital of Israel, Jerusalem has continued to be the center of Jewish life, hope and yearning. Three times a day for thousands of years Jews have prayed, "To Jerusalem, thy city, shall we return with joy." And for thousands of years Jews have re-echoed the Psalmist's oath, "If I forget thee, O Jerusalem, let my right hand forget her cunning."

With the rebirth of Israel in modern times, it was possible for Jerusalem to reassume its rightful place at the center of Jewish experience, and Jews throughout the world saw the return to Mount Zion as an event of profound spiritual and historical significance. These hopes were shattered in 1947, for when the Jewish community accepted the United Nations decision dividing what was then Palestine into two states, one Jewish and the other Arab, the Arab states rejected that decision and chose instead to try to destroy the infant State of Israel by force of arms.

In defiance of the United Nations Charter, Jordan attacked the city of Jerusalem in 1948, placed it under siege and opened indiscriminate fire on its inhabitants and on its historical and religious sites. Jordan became the first country in modern history to bombard the Holy City. Colonel Abdullah al-Tal, who commanded part of the Jordanian forces in 1948, described the attack on the Jewish Quarter of the Old City of Jerusalem as follows:

> The operations of calculated destruction were set in motion. I knew that the Jewish Quarter was densely populated with Jews who caused their fighters a good deal of interference and difficulty. I embarked, therefore, on the shelling of the quarter with mortars, creating harassment and destruction. Only four days after our entry into Jerusalem the Jewish Quarter had become a graveyard. Death

and destruction reigned over it . . . As the dawn of Friday, May 28, 1948, was about to break, the Jewish Quarter emerged convulsed in a black cloud—a cloud of death and agony.*

The French consul in Jerusalem at the time, M. Neuville, sent a cable to the President of the UN Security Council:

The Arab Legion has heavily shelled the New City and the Jewish Quarter in the Old City during the night. The shelling, which started again this morning, has been going on for about two hours. The destruction of the city is proceeding at an ever-increasing rate.†

As a result of this bombardment, the Jordanian army was able to seize the eastern half of Jerusalem and the historic walled Old City, which contains religious shrines sacred to Christians, Jews and Moslems.

Until 1967, Jerusalem remained a city cut in half by barbed wire and ugly walls. For nineteen years the Jordanian rule in the eastern half of the city constituted a record of deliberate desecration of Holy Places and complete disregard for an international agreement to provide free access to religious shrines. In 1949 Jordan had signed an armistice agreement with Israel. Article 8 of that agreement prescribed "free access to the Holy Places and to cultural institutions and use of the Jewish cemetery on the Mount of Olives." The Jordanian government never honored its undertaking. For the first time in centuries, Jews were completely barred from the Old City of Jerusalem and its Holy Places. They had no access to the cemetery on the Mount of Olives or to their cultural institutions on Mount Scopus. The functioning of these institutions stopped until June 1967. Jordan also prevented Moslem residents of Israel from visiting Islam's Holy Places in East Jerusalem.

But the Jordanian government was not content to divide the city in two and ban all movement of Israelis—Jews and Moslems —to the part which it had annexed by force. It began to eliminate systematically every trace of the city's Jewish past. The Jewish Quarter was laid waste. Fifty-eight synagogues, some of great antiquity, were destroyed or desecrated. For seven centuries, since

---

* Memoirs of Abdullah al-Tal, published in Arabic (Cairo, 1959).
† Security Council, 301st meeting (May 22, 1948), p. 28.

1267, the Hurva Synagogue had stood as a landmark in Jerusalem—until it was wantonly destroyed at the behest of the Jordanian authorities. Those synagogues that were not razed to the ground were converted into toilets, stables and henhouses filled with dung heaps, garbage and carcasses. In the process, hundreds of holy scrolls and books, reverently preserved for generations, were plundered and burned to ashes. On the Mount of Olives, a hallowed spot to Jews for centuries, 38,000 of the 50,000 tombstones in the ancient Jewish burial ground were torn up, profaned, broken into pieces and used as flagstones, steps and building materials for public latrines and Jordanian army barracks. Large areas of the cemetery were leveled and converted into parking areas and gas stations. Through the devastated remains of the graves, the Jordanian government cut an asphalt road to provide a shortcut to a new hotel built incongruously on the top of the Mount of Olives. In June 1967 I myself found the graves of my grandparents and my great-grandmother desecrated on the Mount of Olives, with the tombstones destroyed. In May 1967 the Temple Mount itself became a military camp for the Jordanian national guard.

During the entire period, as these foul acts of desecration were being perpetrated against places holy to the Jewish people, the world remained silent. There was no Security Council meeting when Jewish synagogues were burned, Jewish graves defiled and Jewish shrines closed off. One month after the war, on July 12, 1967, Israel's Foreign Minister, Abba Eban, addressed the United Nations:

> I heard not one expression of dismay across the entire human scene when Jordan destroyed ancient synagogues in the old city in an orgy of hate. No United Nations organ expressed any dismay when Jordan for 20 years refused access to the oldest and most revered of all holy places, the Western Wall. Nor was there any expression of dismay when tombstones of the Mount of Olives were uprooted to build walls and secular buildings.*

This shameful silence is even more remarkable when one considers that the Jordanian government, in its attempt to "Arabize"

* UN Document A/PV 1550.

the city, not only sought to erase its Jewish identity but took action against the Christian inhabitants of Jerusalem as well. For example, the Amman Parliament passed a law requiring all members of the Brotherhood of the Holy Sepulcher to adopt Jordanian citizenship. Since the fifth century, members of this brotherhood had invariably been Greek. In 1965 the Jordanian legislature passed a law restricting the development of Christian institutions by canceling their right to acquire land in or near Jerusalem. In 1958 Christian schools were compelled to close on Fridays, the Moslem day of rest, Christian education was restricted, and previously enjoyed privileges of Christian religious institutions were abolished.

The reunification of Jerusalem in 1967 was the fulfillment of a dream for which the Jewish people had prayed for centuries. On June 7 we entered the Old City and were reunited with the symbol of Jewish yearning and prayer for two thousand years, the holiest site of the Jewish people, the Western Wall. This section of the western supporting wall of the Temple Mount has remained intact since the destruction of the Second Temple in the year 70 C.E. It is the most hallowed spot in Jewish religious and national consciousness and tradition by virtue of its proximity to the Western Wall of the Holy of Holies in the Temple, from which, according to Jewish tradition, the Divine Presence never departed.

Only eleven years have passed since those historic moments, yet they are as vivid now as the day they occurred. But of all the dramatic events of June 1967, the moment I recall with greatest pride is the gathering of the heads of all the religious denominations in Jerusalem which I—as the first Jewish Governor of Judea and Samaria in two thousand years—convened in my new headquarters. Assembled in one room were the Greek, Armenian and Latin Patriarchs, the Apostolic Delegate of the Vatican, the Anglican Archbishop, the Lutheran Bishop, and the Syrian, Coptic, and Ethiopian religious leaders, along with many others. (The Moslems were to be convened the next day.)

I stood before them and told them how proud I was—not only as the representative of the State of Israel on this unique occasion but as the son of my late father, who had been Chief Rabbi of Israel—that it had fallen to my lot to undertake the historic task of informing them that from now on under a Jewish government they would be guaranteed freedom of worship and conscience, and that they would enjoy freedom of religion and belief such as Jerusalem had not known for two thousand years. I reminded them of the Jordanian destruction which they had witnessed and assured them that our own actions would be very different.

When I had finished, the Greek Patriarch expressed the gratitude of all those assembled for Israel's humane approach and policy. And the Anglican Archbishop rose to place on historic record the general appreciation of the fact that the Israeli command consciously endangered the lives of its own soldiers in order not to direct fire against the Holy Places and to effect as little damage as possible to the Holy City of Jerusalem.

One other personal recollection bears repetition, for it tells the entire story of the contrast between Jordanian and Israeli rule in Jerusalem. It was the Friday evening of that historic week in 1967 when the Jordanian governor of Jerusalem District, Anwar el-Khatib, came to call on me to pay his respects. He began to talk to me about the entry of our soldiers into Beit Hanina, his village outside Jerusalem. And as he talked about it he broke down and cried like a child. I became very worried, wondering God knows what had happened in the village. I said to him, "What did they do?" He replied, "Nothing," crying, and then I understood. I asked him, "You expected them to behave towards you as you would have behaved towards us?" He nodded his head in assent.

While the Jordanian government destroyed the ancient Jewish Quarter in the Old City and barred Jews from entering, even as tourists, Jerusalem today is an open city, as President Sadat discovered when he visited the Al-Aqsa Mosque for prayers and the Church of the Holy Sepulcher on his historic visit to Jerusalem. Open to all its citizens—Jews, Moslems and Christians—and to members of all faiths from all nations, it is open even to those who claim to be Israel's enemies. To date, millions of tourists from all over the world, including hostile Arab states, have visited Jerusalem and have been afforded freedom of access to and worship at their respective Holy Places.

In this regard it is relevant to recall that for nineteen years, between 1948 and 1967, the gates of the mosques on the Temple Mount in Jerusalem were closed to Israeli Moslems by Jordanian order. These gates were opened to Israeli Moslems only in 1967 when the city was reunified. Indeed, to this day Saudi Arabia prevents Israeli Moslems from carrying out the precept of *hajj* (the pilgrimage to Mecca), one of the five basic precepts of Islam.

Israel's policy with regard to Jerusalem's Holy Places is governed by the Protection of Holy Places Law 5272-1967, enacted after the Six-Day War, on June 28, 1967. According to this law, unrestricted access to the respective Holy Places is guaranteed to members of all faiths. For the record, it is worth reproducing the relevant sections of the law:

1. The Holy Places shall be protected from desecration and any other violation and from anything likely to violate the freedom of access of the members of the different religions to the places sacred to them or their feelings with regard to those places.

2. (A) Whosoever desecrates or otherwise violates a holy place shall be liable to imprisonment for a term of seven years.

(B) Whosoever does anything likely to violate the freedom of access to the members of different religions to the places sacred to them of their feelings with regard to those places shall be liable to imprisonment for a term of five years.

3. This law shall add to and not derogate from any other law.

The Israeli government recognizes, for example, the sensitivity of the Temple Mount area, which also contains the Al-Aqsa Mosque—the third most important Moslem holy site after the mosques of Mecca and Medina. Therefore, in order to protect Moslem interests and in order not to offend the susceptibilities of the Moslem population while preventing disturbances between the religious communities, the government has to this day refrained from issuing regulations for Jewish prayer on the Temple Mount.

Israel is, therefore, confronted with a paradoxical situation in which Jews have not only refrained from exercising their inherent right to worship where and how they please, but the Israeli government has even arrested those who have attempted to pray on the Temple Mount. An interesting corollary of this situation is that in accordance with Israel's policy of leaving the protection and control of Holy Places in the hands of the appropriate religious authorities, the guards on the Temple Mount who are responsible for preventing Jewish prayer in that area are Muslim police appointed by the Islamic Waqf [religious holdings] Bureau.

The former Qadi of Jaffa and Jerusalem, Tawfiq Mahmoud Asaliya, had this simple comment to make on the situation prevailing on the Temple Mount:

> . . . how good it would be if those who have heard unfounded rumors of desecration and interference . . . could come to witness the peace and tranquillity which prevail in this Holy Place during the prayers that are regularly held there.*

But Jerusalem is more than a conglomeration of Holy Places. It is a city, a living and breathing entity, a human community engaged in all the traffic and commerce of everyday life. It is home to 250,000 Jews, 62,000 Moslems and 11,500 Christians of all denominations—Armenians, Copts, Greek Orthodox, Syrians, Roman Catholics and Protestants. To all these people Jerusalem is a city in which they live and work, raise families and acquire their education. The unusual and the everyday are deeply mingled in the life of the people of Jerusalem, and it is the first time in history that Jerusalem has reached such a level of harmony and peaceful coexistence among its various communities.

In view of Jerusalem's special universal significance it was only natural that many distinguished personalities from all over the world should either volunteer or be sought out to give advice on the city's future character. In 1969 Mayor Teddy Kollek gave form and organization to this idea when he invited some seventy outstanding international personalities—religious leaders, intellectuals, architects, statesmen, and men and women of letters—to join together as members of the Jerusalem Committee, to advise Mayor Kollek on the restoration of this ancient historic committee.

In December 1975 the committee passed the following resolutions:

> In a world of distressing frictions and intolerance, Jerusalem observes and encourages religious and communal freedom, full

---

* Statement issued January 1, 1970.

access to its Holy Places and shrines of worship, a deep respect for the cultural and historical heritage of all its citizens, and beyond that, for all mankind. Attempts to break the peace through acts of terror or civil disturbance that have recently occurred or may recur should not deflect or deter the responsible guardians of this universal city from the continued policy and practice of ever-increasing inter-communal cooperation.

The Committee would like to acknowledge the successful efforts made in the field of education. Everywhere we observed the building of new schools, appropriately located, serving all ethnic and religious groups. Especially does the Committee applaud the action within the educational system of Jerusalem, permitting schools, Christian and Moslem alike, to allow their students to choose a curriculum that gives them the opportunity of choice to continue their education in Israeli universities as well as universities in Arab countries. . . .

The Committee acknowledges the energy, imagination and sensitivity which Mayor Kollek and his colleagues are applying to the problems as well as the opportunities to be found in the now unified city. Especially it is impressed by the dedication, objectivity and sophistication being brought to bear on the excavation and restoration of the relics and the rich past of the city, carried out with due respect for the integrity of all the existing holy and historical places. Recognizing their unique and heavy responsibility, a group of highly qualified archaeologists is uncovering heretofore unsuspected and important physical aspects of all of the great cultures and faiths—Judaism, Christianity and Islam—to which Jerusalem has been home for thousands of years. It is already evident that when these projects are completed, investigation, excavation and restoration will have become revelation and historical clarification. The commitment of the Government and the skill of its archaeologists have put the civilized world in their debt. . . .

The Committee is impressed by the extraordinary and careful efforts of the municipality in bringing the walled Old City to its former charm and splendor. . . .

The Committee finds it necessary to express its conviction that Jerusalem is and should remain a united City, humane and universal. In the views of the Committee, those at present responsible for administering the City have proved themselves conscious of the trust to serve the best interests not only of its inhabitants but of all mankind.

Finally, the Committee calls upon the peoples of the world and on all international organizations to recognize their responsibility to assist those engaged in planning and executing the restoration and development of this universal city, Jerusalem, by intensifying their interest and concern and providing support for this important work.*

Israel offers no excuse for its presence in Jerusalem; it owes no apologies. Israel is there as a right—a right which has been hallowed by the Bible, a right which has been sanctified by history, by sacrifice, by prayer, by yearning, a right which has been strengthened and vindicated by virtue of the creation of the only liberal administration in two thousand years.

Israel is proud of Jerusalem and all that it stands for. It is proud of the trust it holds in respect to the two other great religions in the capital city. It is proud of the manner in which it carries out its trust before history.

Our sages say that ten measures of beauty were given to the world. Nine of them belong to Jerusalem. Under Mayor Kollek's dynamic and imaginative leadership, the city has become a place of beauty in which the cultural, religious and aesthetic mingle together to give Jerusalem its character.

And Jerusalem cannot be allowed to revert from its present condition of beauty and of human purpose to a death-haunted minefield, a no man's land strewn with barbed wire and reeking with the decaying corpses of stray animals blown up on the mines, in which the voice of hatred reigns, in which the laughter is not that of children but of hyenas and jackals, and in which the voice of human intercourse is replaced by the stutter of the machine gun. Israel will not allow this beautiful, immortal city to become again a city torn, divided, at war. It will not allow the freedom for all religions which has been the pride of the Israeli administration to be replaced by the restrictions, the discrimination, the anti-Jewish and anti-Christian laws of the Jordanian regime.

The purveyors of hate and discrimination will not deflect Israel from continuing on the road towards peace in the Middle East with the inspiring model of Jerusalem today as its example.

The prayers of Jews, the call of the muezzin and the pealing of the church bells will resound above the majestic mountains of Jerusalem and combine in a prayer for peace in the City of Peace.

* Resolutions of the Third Plenary Meeting of the Jerusalem Committee, December 19, 1975, Jerusalem, Israel.

# II

# Israel and Its Neighbors

# 4

## The Arab-Israeli Conflict and the Road to Peace

AFTER World War I the League of Nations confirmed the ancient historic and religious rights of the Jewish people in the Holy Land. The re-establishment of a Jewish homeland in Palestine (under a British Mandate) was welcomed by, among others, leaders of the Arab resurgence, who recognized that there was room for one small Jewish state, within the total area of 4.5 million square miles in which the Arab nation has since realized its sovereignty in the form of twenty Arab states.

After World War II the General Assembly of the United Nations confirmed the inalienable right of the Jewish people to a state of its own in its ancient homeland, which would be divided into two states, one Jewish and one Arab. The Jewish people formally accepted the famous resolution adopted by the General Assembly on November 29, 1947; the Arab nations rejected it out of hand. On May 15, 1948, with the conclusion of the British Mandate, seven Arab armies invaded Palestine with the avowed purpose of destroying the State of Israel in its infancy. Those Arab military operations were described in the Security Council by the then Soviet delegate to the United Nations, Andrei Gromyko, as "aimed at the suppression of a National Liberation Movement."

A small Jewish population, outnumbered and outgunned, fought back desperately and successfully, losing 1 percent of its total population in the process, and the State of Israel was secured. The groundless allegations, repeated again and again, by Arab spokesmen, about the expulsion of Palestinian Arabs constitute nothing but a series of falsehoods. The Palestinian Arabs, as everybody who takes the trouble to read about those tragic days discovers, left their homes on the specific instructions of their leaders, who, incidentally, were the first to leave. They were promised that they would return in the wake of victorious Arab armies and inherit the spoil and the loot of the Jewish population, which would be annihilated and thrown into the sea.

A vivid description of that period appears in the memoirs of Trygve Lie, the first Secretary-General of the United Nations. He described the Arab assault on May 15, 1948, in unequivocal terms:

> During the next hours and days, events crowded upon us. The Arab states launched their invasion of Palestine with the end of the Mandate. This was clear aggression, and that failure to meet it could easily lead to the ultimate downfall of the United Nations, just as the mishandling of the Manchurian and Ethiopian cases in the 1930's had led to the collapse of the League of Nations.*

It is obvious to all how the Arab-Israeli conflict started and which side was the aggressor in 1947–1948. There would not have been one single Arab refugee—not even one—had the Arab states not chosen to go to war in defiance of a United Nations resolution with the declared aim of destroying the newly reborn State of Israel.

The Palestinians themselves have written an entire literature describing those tragic days and the callous advice given by their leaders. For example, in the memoirs of Haled al-Azm, the Prime Minister of Syria in 1948 and 1949, which were published in Beirut, one can read his analyses of the reasons for the Arab failure in 1948:

> Since 1948 we have been demanding the return of the refugees to their homes. But we ourselves are the ones who encouraged them to leave. Only a few months separated between our call to them to

* In the Cause of Peace (New York, Macmillan, 1954).

leave and our appeal to the United Nations to resolve on their
return.

(Vol. I, pp. 386–87)

And writing in *Falastin al-Thawra* (an official publication of the
PLO) in March 1976, Abu Mazer, a member of the PLO executive committee, noted:

> The Arab armies entered Palestine to protect the Palestinians . . .
> but, instead, they abandoned them, forced them to emigrate and to
> leave their homeland, imposed upon them a political and ideological
> blockade and threw them into prisons similar to the ghettos in
> which the Jews used to live in Eastern Europe.

Time and again, over the years, Israel offered to help rehabili-
tate the refugees, but the Arab states refused because they wanted
to perpetuate the conflict and did not want to lose this invaluable
political pawn. For instance, Israel offered compensation for the
refugees' property, but the Arab states would not hear of it, since
this would have implied recognition of the State of Israel. Every
proposal that Israel made over the years indicating a willingness
for compromise was turned down by the Arabs.

However, there was also a second group of refugees which, together with the Palestinian Arab refugees, comprised the so-called
Middle East refugee problem.

During the United Nations debate on the Partition Resolution
of 1947, Arab leaders warned that the Jews in Arab countries
would be used as hostages to prevent the establishment of Israel.
With the passage of the resolution and the establishment of Israel,
these dire threats were carried out in Aden, in Egypt, in Iraq, in
Syria, and elsewhere. Riots and pogroms, together with mass ar-
rests and legislation confiscating the property of Jews, restricting
their employment and limiting their education and freedom of
movement, were the order of the day in many Arab lands. As a
result, more than 800,000 Jews fled those countries to Israel between 1948 and 1967.

Israel could have approached the question of the Jewish refugees in the same manner as the Arabs approached their part of the
refugee problem. After all, the two populations displaced by

the war were of approximately equal size. It could have kept the Jewish refugees as political pawns in camps financed by the United Nations. Instead, the Jewish people throughout the world cared for its refugees, transported them, rehabilitated them and re-established them as useful citizens and productive human beings.

The fundamentally different approach of Israel on the one hand and the Arab states on the other was also described at length by Trygve Lie:

> Israel's approach to its problem of Jewish refugees was strikingly in contrast. Hundreds of Jews were arriving daily, especially now from Arab lands. . . . The organization for receiving immigrants was most impressive. . . . I was impressed in Israel, both by the accomplishments and by the spirit behind them.*

Arab sources have also documented Arab responsibility for having expelled their Jewish citizens. In an article published in *al-Nahar* (Beirut) on May 15, 1975, Sabri Jiryis, a researcher with the Institute of Palestinian Studies in Beirut, observed:

> This is hardly the place to describe how the Jews of the Arab states were driven out of the countries in which they lived for hundreds of years, and how they were shamefully deported to Israel after their property had been confiscated or taken over at the lowest possible price.
>
> . . . Since 1948, you Arabs have caused the expulsion of just as many Jews from the Arab states, most of whom settled in Israel after their properties had been taken over in one way or another. Actually, therefore, what happened was only a kind of "population and property exchange," and each party must bear the consequences. Israel is absorbing the Jews of the Arab states; the Arab states, for their part, must settle the Palestinians in their own midst and solve their problems.
>
> There is no doubt, at the first serious discussion of the Palestinian problem in an international forum, Israel will put these claims forward.

The Arab refugee problem does not differ from the many other refugee problems in our world, except for the fact that it is the only major one that has not been solved. In virtually all cases other refugee problems, infinitely larger in scope, have been solved

*Lie, *op. cit.*

through the resettlement and rehabilitation of the refugees with the help of suitable financial arrangements. This is what happened, for example, after the Greek-Turkish conflict following World War I, after World War II in West Germany and elsewhere, after the Indian-Pakistan conflict of the early 1960s. None of these refugee problems, involving tens of millions of human beings, was resolved by attempting to repatriate the refugees, en masse, to the countries and homes from which they had fled.

The Arabs have deliberately kept the problem of the refugees alive for thirty years in order to use it as a political weapon in the struggle against Israel. The Arab world today disposes of an unprecedented glut of assets and resources which are employed for such purposes as the purchase of arms instead of the benefit of their kin—the Palestine Arab refugees. The time has therefore come for the United Nations to approach this problem by taking both sides into consideration.

Throughout the years when the Arabs demanded the return of the Arab refugees, they did not even bother to hide their true intentions. To cite one example, the following resolution was adopted by the "Refugee Conference" in Homs, Syria, on July 15, 1957:

> Any discussion aimed at a solution of the Palestine problem which will not be based on ensuring the refugees' right to annihilate Israel will be regarded as a desecration of the Arab people and an act of treason.

In contrast, Israel recently helped over six thousand Arab families to move out of refugee camps in Gaza, out of squalid, inhuman conditions into decent housing, which they acquired with their own earnings, supplemented by mortgages and loans from the Israeli government.

Other refugees in Gaza are clamoring, cash in hand, to enter such housing. Nevertheless, the United Nations General Assembly promptly adopted—by a vote of 119 to 1 with 4 abstentions—an Arab-inspired resolution calling on Israel to put the refugees back in the camps, to return them from homes with running water, electricity and gardens, to primitive, disease-infested hovels! *

* Resolution 32/90C on the Gaza Strip, passed December 13, 1977. Israel voted against; the United States, Canada, Costa Rica and Liberia abstained.

It is important to remember again that 800,000 Jewish refugees were driven out of Arab countries where their ancestors had lived for thousands of years, contributing to the culture, the commerce, the science, the literature and the well-being of the countries of which they were part. The refugees left behind considerable wealth. Yet not one word of their rights, of their properties, is mentioned in any United Nations statement or resolution. In light of this, Israel cannot and will not, at any stage, consider valid any discussion of the refugee problem in the Middle East, if half of that problem, the Jewish refugee problem, is ignored.

Israel has always maintained that the solution to the problem of the Palestinian Arabs must be sought through direct negotiations between Israel and Jordan. Indeed, the mechanism for peace already exists. The United Nations Security Council has produced two resolutions which, in the view of the Israeli government, form the framework for negotiations towards a just and lasting peace. On the basis of these resolutions, which have been accepted by the states which are party to the conflict, the Geneva Peace Conference was established.

On November 22, 1967, the Security Council passed Resolution 242, which affirms

> that the fulfilment of Charter principles requires the establishment of a just and lasting peace in the Middle East which should include the application of both the following principles:
> (i) Withdrawal of Israel armed forces from territories occupied in the recent conflict;
> (ii) Termination of all claims or states of belligerency and respect for and acknowledgement of the sovereignty, territorial integrity and political independence of every state in the area and their right to live in peace within secure and recognized boundaries free from threats or acts of force.

The resolution further affirms the necessity

> for guaranteeing the freedom of navigation through international waterways in the area . . . and also the necessity for guaranteeing the territorial inviolability and political independence of every state in the area through measures including the establishment of demilitarized zones.

This resolution was adopted unanimously by all members of the Security Council at its 1382nd Meeting.

On October 22, 1973, Security Council Resolution 338 was also adopted unanimously. It called upon the states involved in the 1973 conflict to

> start immediately after the cease fire the implementation of Security Council resolution 242 (1967) in all its parts.

This resolution decided further:

> Negotiations shall start between the parties concerned under appropriate auspices aimed at establishing a just and durable peace in the Middle East.

The Geneva Peace Conference was thus convened under the auspices of the United States of America and the Soviet Union, and as a result the process of negotiation in the Middle East, designed to bring about a peaceful solution, was initiated.

In 1975 most members of the United Nations applauded the Israel-Egypt agreement on Sinai and expressed the hope, as is indeed envisaged in the agreement itself, that it will be the forerunner of an ongoing process towards peace in the Middle East. In that context, it is worth recapitulating a few excerpts from the agreement itself:

> The Government of the Arab Republic of Egypt and the Government of Israel have agreed that . . . the conflict between them and in the Middle East shall not be resolved by military force but by peaceful means . . .
> The parties hereby undertake not to resort to the threat or use of force or military blockage against each other . . .
> This agreement is regarded by the parties as a significant step toward a just and lasting peace. It is not a final peace agreement.
> The parties shall continue their efforts to negotiate a final peace agreement within the framework of the Geneva Peace Conference in accordance with Security Council resolution 338. . . .

These excerpts reflect the framework envisaged by Security Council resolutions 242 and 338, which constitutes the approach holding out most hope for an advance towards peace.

Within the framework of the Geneva Peace Conference an

agreement was reached earlier, in May 1974, for a disengagement between Israeli and Syrian forces. The text of this agreement was reported to the Security Council on May 30, 1974. This agreement of disengagement between Israeli and Syrian forces sets out in paragraph A that

> Israel and Syria will scrupulously observe the cease-fire on land, sea and air and will refrain from all military actions against each other, from the time of the signing of this document, in implementation of United Nations Security Council resolution 338 dated 22 October 1973.

Paragraph H reads:

> This agreement is not a peace agreement. It is a step towards a just and durable peace on the basis of Security Council resolution 338 dated October 22, 1973.

The annex to the agreement reads as follows:

> Israel and Syria will support a resolution of the United Nations Security Council which will provide for the U.N.D.O.F. (United Nations Disengagement Observer Force) contemplated by the agreement. The initial authorization will be for six months subject to renewal by further resolution of the Security Council.

The Israeli government therefore regards the presence of the UNDOF as an integral part of the disengagement of forces agreement between Israel and Syria entered into freely by both governments in May 1974. Israel will continue to observe, on a basis of strict reciprocity, this disengagement agreement in all its components and implications, including the prevention of terrorist acts. The agreements entered into freely between Israel on the one hand and Egypt and Syria on the other are the first fruits of the mechanism for peace created by the Security Council. It is a mechanism which can continue to move our strife-torn area towards peace and accommodation.

Israel has made it clear to the United Nations and to the world that it is prepared to go to Geneva any time for a resumption of the peace conference of December 1973 in accordance with the invitation from the Secretary-General dated December 18, 1973, which the parties to the conflict then received.

Suggestions that the PLO be included in the Geneva negotiations attempt to impose preconditions as to participation in the Geneva Peace Conference and are irreconcilable with the letters of the co-chairmen of the conference dated December 18, 1973, and signed by Ambassador Yakob Malik for the USSR and Ambassador W. Tapley Bennett, Jr., for the United States. Their two letters, communicated by the Secretary-General to the President of the Security Council, state:

> The parties have agreed that the Conference should proceed under the joint chairmanship of the Soviet Union and the United States. The parties have also agreed that the question of other participants from the Middle East area will be discussed during the first stage of the Conference.

This mechanism could have been activated at any time so that Israel could have commenced negotiations with the Arab States. Israel's position has always been crystal-clear: it desires and is prepared to compromise for peace, real peace between countries as the ordinary man in the street understands the word "peace."

Today we are told that President Sadat wants peace, and indeed, the logic of his situation militates for peace. He is urgently in need of development, of foreign investment, of economic and social consolidation. He can choose either war or development and investment, but he can't have both and he knows it. Sadat has said that if he considers that war is in Egypt's interest, he will go to war, and if peace is in Egypt's interest, he will make peace. In November 1977 President Sadat by his visit to Jerusalem chose to try peace, opening a period of long and difficult negotiations.

Israel's problem is, however, that nobody knows which is the true voice representing the Arab world. Do the soothing statements made by President Sadat to visiting congressmen and the American media represent the true voice of the Arabs today? Or should one rather believe those Arab statements which call for an imposed solution rather than negotiations, and for war if Israel does not accept such an imposed solution?

For his part, the President of Egypt has subtly spelled out what he meant by the Geneva Peace Conference. He has pointed out in a number of interviews with Western correspondents that in his view, successful negotiations at the Geneva Peace Conference would of course entail an Israeli withdrawal, but would not mean a renewal of diplomatic relations between Israel and its neighbors, the opening of borders, establishment of commercial relations, tourist traffic, and so forth. All this, he thought, should be left over to the next generation. Have we not waited long enough? Have not enough generations suffered that Israel must wait for yet another generation? Why can we not negotiate for peace now?

At the same time, a sinister process has evolved in the UN to destroy the existing mechanism for peace. In furtherance of this purpose, all the one-sided and baseless resolutions submitted by Arab and hostile delegations to the General Assembly have specifically eliminated the principles enumerated in Security Council resolutions 242 and 338, and above all, have eliminated any mention of the word "negotiation." This is in flagrant violation of Article 33 of the Charter of the United Nations, which requires that "the parties to any dispute . . . shall . . . seek a solution by negotiation, enquiry, mediation, conciliation, etc. . . ." It is a terrifying, tragic and sobering thought to contemplate the fact that not one General Assembly resolution on the Middle East issue calls for the process of negotiation between the states which are parties to the conflict. The reason is obvious: negotiations imply Israel's right to exist, and this would run counter to the Arab policy on the issue, the soothing sounds emanating from various capitals in the Middle East notwithstanding. The Egyptian Foreign Minister, Ismail Fahmy, openly threatened war as recently as September 28, 1977, in the General Assembly, vilified Zionism and launched a new move to isolate Israel in the international arena. He went so far as to make peace conditional on an end to Jewish immigration to Israel. That is not the way to make peace.*

If the purpose of United Nations debates is to develop a process of negotiation and maintain the momentum of negotiation with-

---

* This statement, seen against the historic visit of President Sadat to Jerusalem and his statement to the Knesset, emphasizes the revolutionary change which has occurred in the Middle East. Foreign Minister Fahmy resigned in protest at President Sadat's initiative.

out preconditions, the Israeli government will cooperate in every way as befits a self-respecting sovereign nation. If, however, the purpose is merely to pass one-sided resolutions and create a situation whereby the United Nations will attempt to impose a solution and dictate to one or other parties, then Israel will have no part in such a process.

The issue before the world today is whether or not it is going to allow the elements of violence, hate and intransigence to set the tone in the Middle East, or whether it will maintain the momentum which has been achieved on the basis of resolutions reached in the Security Council towards negotiation, accommodation and peace in the Middle East.

In the course of the protracted struggle in the Middle East, nothing has been achieved without negotiation. On the other hand, no negotiation has taken place without something positive being achieved. Why not, therefore, encourage the process of negotiation which has already achieved results?

Nobody has better summed up this issue than a former representative of the Soviet Union to the United Nations, Deputy Foreign Minister Andrei Vyshinsky, who on March 29, 1954, addressed the Security Council as follows:

> You can submit whatever resolutions you like. But life does not call for resolutions: it calls for decisions which can promote the settlement of important international questions which are still outstanding.
>
> What is the proper method for this? The method is that of direct negotiation between the interested parties. On the one side we have the representative of Israel and on the other the representative of Egypt; they are sitting opposite one another. Let them sit down together at one table and try to settle the questions which the Security Council cannot settle now. I am deeply convinced that they can find a better solution. That is why certain representatives and States show a stubborn disinclination to permit direct negotiations between the interested parties and are trying to interfere in and, unfortunately, to hinder those negotiations.*

I have declared again and again that I am prepared to sit down with each and every one of the UN ambassadors from the Arab

* United Nations Document S/PV 664.

countries in an atmosphere of mutual respect. Yet they have persistently refused even to talk to me, thereby providing an ominous indication of their real intentions. As long as the Arab representatives refuse to talk to us, it means that they do not recognize our right to exist. If they don't recognize our right to exist, then we are not disposed to accommodate them by sitting still in the territories and awaiting their pleasure.*

Israel is prepared to enter into negotiations at any moment without any preconditions whatsoever, and in such negotiations, all states will be free to make whatever proposals they wish to make. But we will negotiate only on the basis of a recognition of Israel's sovereign rights. We will not negotiate our own suicide, for that is what withdrawal without concrete moves towards peace means.

Peace can be achieved as soon as it is recognized that while the question of the Palestinian Arabs is an important part of the Middle East conflict, it is not its core. At the heart of an Arab-Israeli conflict lies not the question of finding a satisfactory solution to the problem of territories that came under Israeli administration as a result of Arab aggression in 1967.

You may solve all of the problems raised publicly today and not yet solve the Arab-Israeli conflict, because at the core of the conflict lies the Arab refusal to recognize the right of the Jewish nation to self-determination and national sovereignty in at least a part of its ancient homeland—a homeland that was never in history considered a homeland by any other people; a homeland that the Jewish people has inhabited continuously and without interruptions for the last four millennia. Unless and until the Arabs recognize Israel's right—and I repeat, right—to exist (rather than, as one Arab leader declared, as a fact because it is not in their reach to destroy Israel militarily), durable peace will not come in the Middle East.

This is not only an Israeli opinion. Some learned Arabs have come to recognize this to be the underlying problem in our conflict. One such leader is the internationally respected former

---

* On Sunday, November 27, 1977, I met with Ambassador A. Esmat Abdel Meguid, Egypt's Permanent Representative to the United Nations, when he transmitted to me Egypt's invitation to Israel to send a delegate to the Cairo Conference in December 1977. The barriers between us had broken down.

president of the General Assembly, Dr. Charles Malik. In an interview Dr. Malik stated:

"The main essential for peace—indeed the quintessential—is the need for the Arab world to accept Israel's existence." He [Malik] felt that this is the ultimate issue. Unless and until the Arab peoples have a genuine change of heart on this question, the Middle East will be vibrated from one crisis to the next. He [Malik] repeated "change of heart" in order to emphasize his belief that what is required is not just a temporary accommodation or an expedient political maneuver, but a genuine acceptance of Israel as a State.*

Israel seeks no legitimization of its right to sovereignty. It seeks no confirmation of this right. It makes no apologies for its statehood and it owes no explanation for the exercise of its rights. The recognition by its neighbors of these rights and of its place as an integral element in the Middle East lies at the heart of the problem, and only when this fact is acknowledged by the world community will the Middle East once again become a center in which the great cultures of Judaism and Islam will combine, as they have in the past, to contribute to the elevation of mankind, for the benefit of humanity in general and of the Middle East in particular.

* *Saturday Review* (March 22, 1975).

# 5

---

# The PLO

ISRAEL'S critics, often well-meaning, have demanded that we negotiate with the PLO. In order to understand Israel's refusal to do so, one must examine the nature of this organization. It is, in fact, an umbrella for several disparate and feuding terrorist groups which do not represent the vast majority of Palestinian Arabs and which seek the destruction of the State of Israel. The PLO has never been democratically elected, and it was founded not on the initiative of Palestinians, but by the League of Arab States meeting in Cairo in January 1964. Among the terrorist groups that make up the PLO are the following:

- Al-Fatah, founded in 1957 under Egyptian sponsorship, and responsible for numerous raids into Israel in which scores of innocent civilians were killed. Al-Fatah is also the parent body of Black September, the organization that murdered eleven Israeli athletes at the Munich Olympics in 1972 and killed the American ambassador to the Sudan.
- The Popular Front for the Liberation of Palestine (PFLP), under George Habash, a violent and rigidly Marxist organization responsible for numerous hijackings of civilian aircraft.

- Al-Saiqa, formed by the Syrian government and one of the most active forces in the destruction of Lebanon.
- The Popular Democratic Front for the Liberation of Palestine (PDFLP), a Marxist-Maoist offshoot of the PFLP, responsible, among other things, for the massacre of twenty-four Israeli school-children at Ma'alot.

Several other, smaller terrorist groupings and splinter organizations which have at various times claimed responsibility for hijackings, bombings and attacks on civilians also belong to the PLO. The different groups, financed by Egypt, Syria, Libya and Iraq, are usually at loggerheads depending on the policies of their respective sponsors at any given time. They frequently engage in armed clashes among themselves and have killed dozens of their own members in Lebanon during 1976 and 1977. The PFLP and other "rejectionists" regularly accuse al-Fatah of "selling out" to the Egyptians, while al-Fatah itself claims to be "the summit of rejection" of all settlement with the Zionists (Algiers, "Voice of Palestine," July 14, 1977). In fact, the only consensus among the various groupings is on the destruction of Israel.

The PLO is governed by the Palestinian Covenant of 1964, as amended in 1968. Article 19 of this covenant declares that "the establishment of Israel is fundamentally null and void." In Article 20 it makes the preposterous assertion that "the claim of historical or spiritual ties between the Jews and Palestine does not tally with historical realities." In other words, the PLO rejects four thousand years of one of the most ancient histories in the world. The Palestinians reject any link between Judaism and the Holy Land, and treat the Bible as if it never were. They also imply that Christianity was born in a never-never land to a people that did not exist, nurtured on a religion which existed only in mythology. The PLO, bent on the destruction of the Israeli state and people, therefore has no interest in a peace agreement. Other sections of the covenant call for the elimination of Zionism (Article 15) and, in effect, for the expulsion of the bulk of the Jewish population from Israel (Article 6). Article 21 declares that they

reject all plans that aim at the settlement of the Palestine issue. . . .

And the Palestinians give short shrift to United Nations Resolution 242.* For instance, the first of the ten points adopted by the Palestine National Council on June 8, 1974, specifically declares that

> dealing with this resolution [242] is rejected at any level of Arab and international dealings including the Geneva Conference.

Point Number 3, adopted by that council, specifies that

> the PLO will struggle against any plan for the establishment of a Palestinian entity, the price of which is recognition [of Israel], conciliation [with it], secure borders, etc. . . .

Or in Point Number 8:

> "The Palestine National Authority . . . will struggle for the liberation of all Palestine soil . . ."

Farouh al-Kaddoumi, the chief political officer of the PLO, speaking at a UN press conference, later clarified what was meant by "all Palestine soil," confirming that he considered Tel Aviv to be occupied territory.

Is this the basis on which Israel is expected to approach the Geneva Conference? Is there any self-respecting country that would agree to deal with a body whose sole declared purpose is to destroy it and whose aim is to draw concessions so that its destruction will be so much easier?

The policy of the PLO has been affirmed and reaffirmed by all its leaders. Kaddoumi stated unequivocally in a magazine interview: "This Zionist ghetto of Israel must be destroyed." † Now he is a little more circumspect. According to *Newsweek* of March 14, 1977, Kaddoumi said:

> "There are two [initial] phases to our return. The first phase to the 1967 lines, and the second to the 1948 lines . . . The third stage is the democratic State of Palestine. So we are fighting for these three stages. . . ."

* See Chapter 4 for an explanation of Resolution 242.
† *Newsweek* (November 17, 1975).

This is now the authoritative program of the PLO—the destruction of Israel by stages. As to how this program is to be implemented, PLO leader Yassir Arafat has been quite explicit:

> "I am not a man of settlements and concessions. I will struggle till the last inch of Palestine is returned . . . Our struggle in the occupied land will be violently and bitterly escalated. We will start with the stepping up of our suicide strikes against the Zionist enemy . . . I foresee a new war, the fifth, in the Middle East . . . Our revolution is a revolution of liberation, not a revolution of concessions." *

And Salah Khalaf, better known as Abu Ayad, the second in command of al-Fatah, said:

> "There is something the world must know. Let us all die, let us all be killed, let us all be assassinated, but we will not recognize Israel." †

Is this the group to which Israel is supposed to talk and make concessions—a group whose basic creed and main tenet of faith is our destruction?

Since 1976 Israel has been subjected to a barrage of tendentious reports in much of the Western media designed to prove to the world that the PLO is now adopting a more moderate policy and approach. What the Middle East hears is, unfortunately, in stark contrast to the smooth statements published in the Western press. The following comment, for example, was broadcast over Radio Damascus in the Palestine Corner:

> The Arabs intend to demand that Israeli retreat not only from Sinai, Golan, Jerusalem and Gaza, but primarily from Tel Aviv, Haifa and Nazareth.
>
> (December 29, 1976)

And a few weeks later:

> The first article of the unwritten Palestinian constitution will be a call for a struggle to return the Palestinian territories on which

* *Al-Yakza*, Kuwait Weekly (April 11, 1977).
† New York *Times* (February 17, 1976).

Israel rests . . . from Rosh Hanikra to Rafiah, and from Bet She'an and Jericho in the Jordan Valley to Haifa and Jaffa on the coastal plain—that is, all of Palestine, from the Galilee to the Negev, and from the Jordan to the Mediterranean.

(February 15, 1977)

For those who continued to indulge in wishful thinking, the Palestine National Council, which met in Cairo in March 1977, should have dispelled such doubts. By a vote of 194 to 13—the 13 thought that the resolution was not extreme enough—the PLO National Council voted for a continuation of "the armed struggle" against Israel and rejected recognition of the State of Israel or the signing of a peace agreement.

One of the more popular misconceptions today is that there was a moderate element in the PLO which tried to bring about a change but was outvoted by the extremists. Nothing is further from the truth. True, there are moderates and extremists in the PLO, but these moderates and extremists are completely identical in their attitude towards Israel or towards a change in the Palestine Covenant. Another popular fallacy maintains that there is a debate in the PLO on the basic approach to Israel. In that debate the moderates agree, as it were, to some form of coexistence with Israel, while the extremists oppose such coexistence. This is completely and absolutely untrue. The negation of Israel's right to exist is a principle accepted by all groupings within the PLO. Not one delegate to the Palestine National Council raised even the slightest doubt as to that thesis.

The division between extremists and moderates, in fact, relates to secondary issues, to tactics and to modes of operation. The extremists emphasize the importance of the armed struggle and maintain that participation in the Geneva Conference or acquiescence in interim agreements can lead to a cessation of the struggle against Israel and thereby to a continuance of the existence of Israel. Those extremists criticize the PLO surrender to Syria. They oppose discussions with Jordan that run counter to the traditional PLO stand, which calls for the removal of the present Jordanian leadership and the royal Hashemite house and opposes contacts of any form with Israelis.

As opposed to them, the moderates are willing to adopt a political approach as a tactic, on condition that such an approach will lead ultimately to the destruction of Israel. Thus the decision of the Palestine National Council was in the spirit of the so-called moderates.

The "moderate" approach, for example, rejects UN Security Council Resolution 242 because it recognizes Israel's right to exist and refers instead to General Assembly Resolution 3236, which Yassir Arafat described to a Lebanese weekly newspaper in the following words: "This resolution comprises the liquidation of Zionist existence." *

Not only was the Palestine Covenant not changed at the Cairo meeting; on the contrary, the council reaffirmed the covenant and declared that all resolutions are based on that covenant. Nothing changed in the PLO's basic approach and it remains the only example in the world of an organization calling for the actual destruction of a nation and a people.

The illusion of PLO moderation appears to have spread even to certain Jewish and Israeli individuals who have advocated a dialogue with the organization. I do not doubt the sincerity of those who seek to establish those contacts, but they should realize that insofar as the PLO meets with them, it does so in furtherance of a political propaganda offensive, and they are nothing more than an integral part of that offensive, wittingly or unwittingly. The fact remains that the PLO is committed to the elimination of 3 million Jews and is bound by the doctrine of destruction and annihilation enunciated in the Palestine Covenant.

We, in Israel, look to the Geneva Conference and the process of negotiations with one purpose, and one purpose only, in mind: to achieve peace. We do not contemplate it as a step in the direction of national suicide for Israel, which is the PLO's avowed purpose.

The PLO proposes a so-called democratic secular state in which Moslems, Christians and Jews would live in amity and equality. If it believes so strongly in democracy and secularism, why is there not a single democratic secular state anywhere in the Arab world? For nineteen years the Jordanians controlled the West

---

* *Al-Balagh* (January 5, 1975).

Bank, and the Egyptians controlled the Gaza Strip. Jordan and Egypt today talk about a Palestine homeland and independence in the West Bank and Gaza. But in all this time the Jordanians and Egyptians did not even set up a local Palestinian administration. In fact, the Palestinian Arabs achieved greater control of their domestic affairs under Israel's administration, which authorized free and open elections in the West Bank, than at any time in the nineteen years of Arab rule before 1967.

If the Arab governments really support the Palestinian cause, why is it that the major pitched battles carried out by the PLO have been waged against Arab governments and Arab authority, in 1970 in the so-called Black September against the Hashemite kingdom of Jordan and, more recently, as a major element in the destruction of the Lebanese state? The reason is that the PLO, despite the hypocritical lip service paid to it by the Arab governments, is discredited in the Middle East, and is, in fact, today fighting for its own survival.

It is clear today from the behavior of the Arab leaders in the Middle East that they are considerably disenchanted with the PLO. What they say about this organization is one thing, and what they do is another. Egypt keeps the most stringent control on its members. They are not even admitted to Jordan, let alone permitted to operate from there. They are under the strictest control in Syria. They are not even allowed to fly on Syrian commercial flights without special permission, and now that Syria has converted Lebanon into a vassal state, their freedom of operation has been very considerably curtailed, even in Lebanon. Indeed, of late, the Lebanese authorities have begun to ban the entry of Palestinians into Lebanon.

The attitude of the Arab states towards the PLO is understandable in light of PLO threats to their own sovereignty. In 1974 Yassir Arafat announced:

> Jordan is ours, Palestine is ours, and we shall build our national entity on the whole of this land after having freed it of both the Zionist presence and the reactionary traitor presence [King Hussein].*

* Arafat in a letter to the Jordanian Student Congress in Baghdad, as reported in the Washington *Post* (November 12, 1974).

Other PLO leaders have reiterated this threat, and the Ten Points of the Palestine National Council of June 8, 1970, call, in effect (in points 5 and 8), for a struggle against the Jordanian regime.

That this was not idle rhetoric was demonstrated after PLO terrorists executed, in the most cowardly manner, Wasfi Tal, Prime Minister of Jordan, during a visit to Cairo. One of the assassins, not content with shooting Tal in the back, felt obliged to drink his blood on the steps of the Sheraton Hotel in Cairo.*

It is hardly surprising, then, that King Hussein, in an interview with the German magazine *Der Stern* spoke of the PLO's claim to act as spokesman for the Palestinians in these words: "Ridiculous! How can a half-dozen disunited organizations, partly dominated by criminals, disunited by radical ideologies, make this claim?" President Sadat of Egypt echoed these sentiments when he described Zuheir Muhsein, leader of the Syrian-controlled PLO faction al-Saiqa, as "a common car thief."

During the Lebanese war Syria attempted to assume complete control of the PLO, a process which led to bitter bloodshed in pitched battles between the Syrian army and PLO units. Indeed, more PLO casualties were inflicted by the Syrian army, or by Syrian-controlled units, in a few weeks than by the Israel Defense Forces in thirty years since Israel's establishment.

As the clashes escalated, the PLO took its terror campaign into the heart of Syria. On September 26, 1976, Radio Damascus announced:

> Before dawn [today] three PLO terrorists, captured after they attacked the Semiramis Hotel in Damascus, were hanged in a public square of that city, where their bodies remained suspended for hours.
> The terrorists admitted under interrogation that they belonged to the al-Fatah wing of the PLO.

Commenting on the attack, President Hafez al-Assad declared on Radio Damascus the next day: "We condemn this act of terror, committed by a gang of traitors and criminals. We refuse to

* The murder took place on November 28, 1971. Four members of Black September, arrested after the incident, were freed by Egyptian authorities in January 1973.

bargain with them." Referring to those who sent the terrorists to Damascus, he added: "The only thing these PLO leaders wanted was to attack Syria, despite its sacrifices on behalf of the Palestinians."

On September 10, 1976, an article appeared in *Tishrin*, the official Syrian army newspaper, signed by General Mustafa T'lass, the Syrian Defense Minister, which bitterly attacked the PLO:

> My Palestinian comrades, the Moslems of Lebanon have begun to hate you because you are interfering in their daily life and their personal liberty. What, then, is the aim of your liberation? Is your sublime target the massacre of Lebanon? Or perhaps your grand design was to slaughter the residents of the Semiramis Hotel in Damascus? You are mistaken, Palestinian comrades, because you arouse nothing but disgust among all honest Arab citizens.

And in a statement with which Israel is completely in accord and which reflects its position, too, the general concluded: ". . . no regime will ever accept the illegal acts of the PLO within its borders."

The slogan of a democratic and secular Palestinian state was finally discredited by the Lebanese war. Before the civil war, Lebanon was the only country where the PLO was free to operate, and Yassir Arafat boasted in 1975: "We have in the Lebanese experience a significant example that is close to the multi-religious state we are trying to achieve." *

What has happened to Lebanon should be an important lesson to the world about so-called Arab unity and the effectiveness of Arab action. This Arab nation, which has been held up to the world as an example of the secular democratic state that the PLO wishes to establish in Palestine, was torn apart literally, limb by limb, and the Arab world, with its Arab League and its summit conferences, was incapable of doing anything to save Lebanon because it was directly involved in the process of dismemberment.

Lebanon's Ambassador to the United Nations described his country's plight in these words:

> . . . Lebanon's tragedy should be a warning—and indeed a stern one—that the security, nay, the survival, of Member States cannot

* Quoted in the *Economist* (April 12, 1975).

be viewed with lethargy and indifference . . . Furthermore, we believe that small States should draw the proper conclusion and realize that they must be ever more vigilant and efficient in protecting their higher interests and national rights. They must principally rely on their national means to safeguard their independence and sovereignty . . .

About the PLO, he said the following:

> . . . They committed all sorts of crimes in Lebanon and also escaped Lebanese justice in the protection of the camps. . . . It is difficult to enumerate all the illegal activities committed by those Palestinian elements. . . . It became apparent that the Palestinians had designs on becoming a major factor in the battle for political power in Lebanon. They openly allied themselves, and continue to do so at this very hour, with one group of Lebanese against another. . . .*

The PLO not only pitted one Lebanese group against another but also busily engaged themselves in killing one another in the streets of the cities of Lebanon. The many groups within the PLO have not stopped feuding to this day, and one is constrained to ask of those who want Israel to talk to the PLO—with which PLO is Israel supposed to talk? With al-Saiqa or with al-Fatah? The various elements of the PLO have labeled each other as traitors to the Arab cause, and in 1976 daily killed each other by the dozen in Lebanon. The PLO is no more than an uneasy coalition of a varying number of feuding terrorist organizations torn among themselves and unable to achieve any consensus on any problem apart from a vicious and nightmarish fate for every man, woman and child in Israel.

Israel has for years described the nature of the PLO and the destructiveness of its policy. But those disinclined to accept its evaluation should heed the words of Arab leaders in the wake of the tragic war in Lebanon. Here are but a few examples:

The former President of Lebanon, Suleiman Franjieh, at the height of the war:

---

* Ambassador E. Ghorra to the UN General Assembly, October 14, 1976 (in UN Document A/31/PV 32).

Assad has woken up. Kuwait has awakened, and Jordan awoke before them. We woke up too late and others still sleep . . . This is a
war of the Palestinians against us . . . This is a crime which dwarfs
the other crimes.*

King Hussein of Jordan:

The Palestine Liberation Organization has weakened, perhaps ir-
reparably, its argument that Jews, Muslims and Christians could live
in harmony, side by side, in a future greater Palestine. It can now
be seen that Arabs themselves, citizens of the same country, not
only cannot coexist but collide day and night.†

Sheik Muhammad Ali al-Jaabari of Hebron:

As long as there is a body called the PLO which behaves in the
way it does, there will be no solution to the Palestine Question. I
think that the Arab people of the West Bank should be brave
enough to admit this, courageous enough to know what is in its true
interest. . . . The PLO wrought havoc in Jordan and now it is destroying Lebanon. It would do the same thing here, given the
chance.‡

And Israel recalls the more than 800,000 Jews who left, or were
driven out of, the Arab countries of the Middle East and North
Africa since 1948, and observes the tortured existence of the
roughly 4,000 hostages left in Syria today, as it conjures up what
the fate of the Jews of Israel would be if the PLO nightmare were
to be realized. The PLO gave an example of this nightmare in a
broadcast over Radio Damascus on July 7, 1975: "Not a single
house must remain standing in Safed. This city must be burned
down, and not a Jew remain to live there . . ." I will not burden
readers with other gory details in which PLO spokesmen have
described Israel's fate should they have their way. It is too horrifying for civilized people to contemplate. Yet the Jewish people is
only too aware of the fact that such horrors are not beyond modern
man, in our present-day world.

Yassir Arafat has left no doubt as to his conception of the

* Radio Beirut (September 19, 1976).
† Interview with *Newsweek* senior editor, Arnaud de Borchgrave, 1976.
‡ Statement to Tawfiz Khoury, Israeli Arab journalist, published in *Yediot
Aharonot* (October 14, 1976).

Jewish fate in a Palestinian state. Opening a symposium on Palestine in Tripoli, Libya, in May 1976, he said:

> The revolution is struggling to establish a democratic state in which we all will live in peace . . . There will be no presence in the region other than the Arab presence since this is the historic truth which no one, no matter how powerful, can change.

It is necessary at this time, when it is becoming fashionable to proclaim in a facile and superficial manner that the solution to all the problems in the Middle East lies in the invitation of the PLO to Geneva, to examine the record of this organization on which so many spokesmen of countries unfriendly to Israel, and also friendly to Israel, place their hopes for a future peace in the Middle East.

The PLO's policy is a matter of record. It is one based on the most brutal terrorism, in the course of which attacks have been made upon innocent people, including women and children. These gangs have cut down pregnant women in cold blood in Kiryat Shmona, have shot Olympic athletes bound hand and foot, have hijacked planes, have engaged in open assassination, have attacked innocent tourists in Tel Aviv, have held small schoolchildren hostage in Ma'alot and caused the death there of over twenty children, with sixty more wounded. These are the same terrorists who killed innocent passers-by, both Jew and Arab alike, in bomb outrages in Zion Square in Jerusalem. These are the same individuals who have imposed a reign of terror on the Palestinian people in the West Bank and in Gaza, killing cold-bloodedly those suspected of not agreeing with them.

Their activities have not only been directed against Israel. Seventeen PLO terrorists were arrested in Rabat and in Spain when they planned to assassinate the heads of five Arab states attending the Arab summit conference in Rabat in 1974.

These are the same people who on January 31, 1974, sabotaged the oil installations in Singapore. These are the same people who gained control of the Egyptian embassy in Madrid and held hostage three members of the staff, including the ambassador.

These are the same people who in cold blood murdered American and Belgian diplomats, bound hand and foot, on Arafat's orders, in Khartoum in 1973. These were the people who were instrumental in destroying the Lebanese state, killing tens of thousands and wounding thousands of others. These are the terrorists who kidnapped and held hostage the ministers attending the OPEC conference in Vienna and were then released by the government of Algeria in an act which constituted a blatant condoning of the criminal terror acts of that group. From there they proceeded to Libya, where they were greeted and embraced by Prime Minister Abdel Salarn Jailoud—the same terrorists who had shot one of Libya's citizens a day before in Vienna. These are the same terrorists who have attacked hotels in Amman and Damascus, and who invaded Syrian embassies abroad. The Japanese Red Army and other international terrorist groups that have hijacked planes at Arab airports, as well as the kidnappers and murderers of public figures in Germany, are graduates of PLO courses and maintain close associations with Palestinian terror groups.

The PLO has brought misery, murder and assassination to the area of the Middle East and has introduced terrorism as a form of international idiom—terrorism which affects innocent people wherever they may be.

The stark reality is that the PLO is today synonymous with the scourge of international terror which the United Nations does not have the courage to condemn.

The leaders of these terrorists take care to be well removed from what they call the area of battle. In their time-honored tradition these leaders stay behind in the comparative security of their bases in Lebanon and elsewhere, sending others to carry out their nefarious activities. In pursuance of their cowardly policy, the terrorists have endangered civilian lives by locating their bases and camps next to civilian concentrations. Those who would regard the PLO as a so-called liberation organization would do well to recall that it is the only such organization in the world whose leadership does not live among the people it is purporting to liberate.

There are two clear choices: one is a negotiating process leading towards peace; the other is the PLO policy calling for the destruction of Israel, and rejecting any process of negotiation or compromise out of hand.

Many countries blithely express themselves on the question of the representation of the PLO at Geneva or even at meetings of the Security Council. The PLO has made it quite clear that it does not accept the basis of the Geneva Conference, which, after all, is based on recognition of Israel, compromise with Israel, secure and recognized borders, and so on. The Security Council has created the Geneva Conference on the basis of resolutions 242 and 338. It is inconceivable that the United Nations should propose inviting an organization to Geneva that refers to the resolutions which the Security Council has laid down as a framework for that conference.

As for Israel, it will not negotiate with a representative of a body which, in principle, rejects compromise as a basis of solving international problems and which avowedly sees the destruction of Israel as the only solution of the Middle East problem, not to mention the destruction of other societies in the region as well. Israel will negotiate only on the basis of a recognition of its sovereign rights. It will not negotiate its own suicide.

# 6

# The Territories: Gaza and the West Bank

To SOLVE the Middle East conflict, our critics maintain, all that is necessary is for Israel to withdraw to the pre-1967 borders. This approach, which sees the 1967 borders as a magic formula for peace, is based on a fundamental misconception. It focuses all attention on the consequences of the Six-Day War and, in effect, ignores the events which led up to the conflict. Therefore, before we examine the situation in the West Bank and Gaza, we must ask how these territories fell into Israel's hands and whether the pre-1967 lines in fact constituted any real guarantee of peace.

In mid-May of 1967, President Gamal Abdel Nasser announced that "Egypt, with all her resources—human, economic and scientific—is prepared to plunge into a total war that will be the end of Israel." [*] On May 17, Egypt instructed the UN Emergency Force to withdraw immediately from its positions along the front line with Israel, and UN Secretary General U Thant acquiesced. Nasser ordered 100,000 troops into Sinai, and these swiftly replaced the departing UNEF troops on the Israeli border.

[*] "Voice of the Arabs," Radio Cairo, May 17, 1967.

One Arab nation after another committed its forces until 250,000 Arab troops, 2,000 tanks and 700 first-line aircraft encircled Israel—at a time when Tel Aviv and Jerusalem were within range of Arab guns. Tel Aviv was fifteen miles' distance from Jordanian troops and Israel's "waist" at Netanya was ten miles wide.

On May 22 Nasser declared the Straits of Tiran closed to Israeli shipping—an action which amounted to a declaration of war.

On May 19 Radio Cairo announced: "This is our chance, Arabs, to deal Israel a mortal blow of annihilation to blot out its entire presence in our holy land," and added, on May 25: "The Arab people is firmly resolved to wipe Israel off the map."

On May 26 President Nasser stated:

> The Arab people wants to fight. We have been waiting for the right day when we would be fully prepared . . . Recently, we have felt strong enough to triumph, with God's help, if we enter into battle with Israel. On that basis, we have decided to take the actual measures. Sharm el-Sheikh implies a confrontation with Israel. Taking this step makes it imperative that we be ready to embark on a total war with Israel.*

And on May 28 Nasser told a press conference that "Israel's existence in itself is an act of aggression . . . We accept no kind of coexistence with Israel."

For three weeks the world looked on as the entire population of Israel faced destruction, and valedictory articles were published in the Western press about the great democracy that was Israel.

The world may now have conveniently forgotten the trauma through which Israel and the entire Jewish people lived during those three weeks as the massed Arab armies ringed Israel and prepared to attack. But Israel has not forgotten the promises made over all the Arab media of massacre, annihilation and destruction. It has not forgotten that all the leaders of the Arab world who today appear so moderate in the Western press promised to throw all Israelis, man, woman and child, into the sea.

* *Ibid.*

Israel has also not forgotten how the world looked on petrified at this time, utterly incapable of taking action. The Great Powers vacillated and hesitated, and held conferences to discuss the problem of the opening of the Straits of Tiran. Two American aircraft carriers, a British aircraft carrier and a French warship were in the area at the time. None acted, yet in the final analysis it took only two Israeli torpedo boats to open the Straits, without a shot being fired.

And unlike those who would have us again rely on United Nations guarantees, Israel has also not forgotten how that world community reacted when danger of war was imminent. The Secretary-General of the United Nations withdrew UN forces without demur on Nasser's instructions, leaving Egypt free to go to war. And then, as long as the Arab claims of victory were believed, no action was taken to stop the fighting. The Soviet Ambassador to the United Nations, Nikolai Fedorenko, stated at the time that there was no urgency to the problem. (The next day, however, when news of the Israeli successes broke, the entire United Nations was galvanized into action.)

That was the background to the Six-Day War, and these were the reasons Israel took its fate into its own hands and made a pre-emptive strike on June 5. As a result of the hostilities, the territories which are the subject of so much discussion today—Sinai, the Golan Heights, the West Bank and Gaza—fell into Israeli hands. But it must be remembered that Israel sought no aggression in 1967, it sought no war.

Immediately after the Six-Day War, Israel again called for direct negotiations between the parties towards a state of peaceful coexistence between Israel and the Arab nations. On June 19, 1967, the Israeli Cabinet, which at that time included Menachem Begin, unanimously voted to hand back the whole of Sinai to Egypt and the whole of the Golan Heights to Syria in return for peace and demilitarization. The only reply received came on September 1, 1967, from the Khartoum Conference: no negotiation, no recognition, no peace with Israel. This Arab position becomes more comprehensible when one recalls the urgent message sent on June 11 by the Soviet leadership to the Arab governments in Egypt and Syria, guaranteeing them the wherewithal to recover their lost land if they would not move toward accommodation with Israel.

For nineteen years Israel was not in the territories and for nineteen years it sat along the pre-1967 borders, which today are held up as the panacea for all evils. But this did not prevent the mobilization of a quarter of a million Arab troops around Israel, threatening it with annihilation. If there is one lesson the world must learn from the Six-Day War, it is that the 1967 lines were an invitation to war and would constitute a renewed invitation to war were Israel ever to return to them.

A standard tactic in Arab political warfare against Israel has been to accuse it in every international forum of violations of human rights in the administered areas. Before examining these allegations, one would do well to examine the credentials of two of its primary accusers—Egypt and Jordan.

For nineteen years Egypt kept the people of Gaza oppressed and virtually imprisoned in their refugee camps, subjecting them to every form of human disability, denying them the most elemental freedoms and violating one human right after another.

For nineteen years Egypt did not allow residents of Gaza to work in Egypt. Today, thousands of Gaza inhabitants move daily into Israel to work. One of the first decrees of the Military Governor of Gaza when the Egyptians took over was the imposition of a curfew, from 9 P.M. to dawn. This curfew lasted for nineteen years and violators were put to death. Highways were closed to all but military traffic after dusk. A strict censorship was imposed. Locally published newspapers were prohibited and all newspapers came from Cairo. For nineteen years under the Egyptians no elections were ever held. The Governor was the executive, the legislature and the judiciary rolled into one, and his decree was final.

In October 1961 Radio Damascus announced that "Egypt [was] exercising tyranny in the Strip." It reminded one of the description that appeared in a Jordanian newspaper:

> The shabbily-clothed and undernourished refugees said that they were ill-treated by the Egyptian authorities. Every refugee had a

card issued by the Egyptians which said: Bearer is prohibited from employment with or without wages . . . We must admit that thousands of young Gazaites flee under cover of the Haj pilgrimage to Mecca in the hope of finding work in Saudi Arabia and escaping the disgrace of living under Egyptian domination in the Strip.*

Radio Jidda in Saudi Arabia, on March 10, 1962, described the Egyptian occupation in this way:

Let us now examine the Cairo rulers' attitude to the Palestinians. Saudi Arabia opened its doors wide to the people of Palestine at a time when Egypt shut its door in their faces. We are aware of the laws which prohibit all Palestinians from working in Egypt with or without pay, a condition which is stamped on the passport of every Arab who enters Cairo. On this occasion, we would like to ask Cairo what is this Iron Curtain which Abdel Nasser and his cohorts have lowered around Gaza and the refugees there? The Military Governor in Gaza has prohibited any Arab from travelling to Cairo by air without a military permit, which is valid for 24 hours. Imagine, Arabs, how Nasser, who claims to be the pioneer of Arab nationalism, treats the Arab people of Gaza, Gaza and its miserable people who starve while the Egyptian Governor of Gaza and his officers and soldiers bask in the wealth of the Strip . . . These are the very methods which the dictator Hitler used in the countries that he occupied during the world war 2.

The inhabitants of Gaza, like those of the West Bank, have varying views as to their fate in a future settlement. They are free to express their opinions and conduct open debates on the subject. But it is significant that not once has an Egyptian solution for Gaza ever been proposed in Gaza.

Jordan's record in the West Bank is no better. During the nineteen years that the Jordanians occupied the West Bank, they did not even create a central administration for the area. Instead, they oppressed the Arab population and brutally suppressed the riots which broke out every few months. During those nineteen years, dozens of West Bank Arabs were killed and wounded by the Jordanian army.

A chronology of these clashes would take pages. Suffice it to

* *Falastin,* Jerusalem (May 19, 1950), interviewing 510 refugees from Gaza.

recall therefore just some of the events in the West Bank during 1966, several months before the Israeli administration began.

In January 1966 the Jordanian authorities arrested two hundred persons in Jericho; in April they arrested two thousand in the West Bank. In May, mass demonstrations took place in East Jerusalem, Hebron and Ramallah. The police, using force, closed down schools, and arrested hundreds of persons. In July, disturbances and mass demonstrations broke out in Nablus. The Jordanian police wounded twelve people and arrested two hundred and fifty.

That November saw a series of stormy clashes between civilians, police and army forces, with numerous casualties. On November 21, shop and business strikes broke out in the Ramallah area. The army, called in to intervene, employed tanks to restore order. The Jordanian authorities imposed a curfew and closed all schools. Similar events recurred through November and December in most other towns. On November 24 the Jordanian army again employed tanks and tear gas. Twenty demonstrators were killed and many more wounded. On December 8, 1966, a general business strike was forcibly suppressed by the police and the Jordanian army.

On January 13, 1967, the population of Nablus revolted and barricades were put up in the streets. The Jordanian army had to surround the city and suppress resistance by force.

With an army composed mainly of Bedouins from the East Bank, the Jordanian government succeeded in retaining its military hold over the West Bank. The Jordanian authorities knew, however, that the West Bank was at best only a stepchild, not a member of the family; they knew well that the heart of the Arab inhabitants of the West Bank was not with them. The Amman government treated the West Bank accordingly.

On April 23, 1971, the Beirut daily, *al-Hawadith*, carried an interview with Arab inhabitants of the West Bank who were visiting Lebanon:

Those arriving from the West Bank define the situation thus: We have not forgotten nor will we ever forget the type of rule which degraded our honour and trampled the human feelings within us, a rule which they built by their inquisition and the boots of their desert men. We have lived a long period under the humiliation of Arab nationalism, and it pains us to say that we had to wait for the Israeli conquest in order to become aware of human relationships with citizens.

And if any further proof is needed of Jordan's attitude towards the Palestinians, we need only recall Yassir Arafat's announcement on the night of April 9, 1971, that "the Palestinian Revolution has lost 20,000 killed and wounded in Jordan."

Pending an overall political solution which cannot be isolated from the overall Middle East problem, Israel is proud of its record in the territories. Before looking at possible solutions for those areas, it is worth examining some aspects of Israel's administration in the last ten years and of the policies which led the New York *Times* to characterize this administration as "surely the most benign occupation in history."

Recently published international financial statistics reveal that the West Bank and Gaza led all their neighbors in economic growth. In terms of per capita gross national product, both territories have grown faster than Israel, Egypt, Jordan, Syria, Iraq and Lebanon. The real growth in the GNP has averaged 18 percent per annum since 1967. Income per capita increased by 80 percent in the West Bank and by 120 percent in Gaza over this period. Private consumption rose by 9 percent per annum in both territories, and the total export of goods and services has risen annually by 24 percent in the West Bank and by 30 percent in the Gaza Strip. The net daily wage has risen annually by 35 percent in the West Bank and by 39 percent in Gaza, while the unemployment rate dropped from some 10 percent in the West Bank and almost 30 percent in the Gaza Strip in 1967 to nearly zero by 1975. There is ten times as much agricultural machinery in both territories now as there was ten years ago.

Significant advances have been made in many other fields. The number of educational institutions and classrooms has grown by 46 percent in a system which provides free education in the West Bank and Gaza. The education budget allotted by Egypt for Gaza and northern Sinai in 1967–1968 was only about $2 million for a population of 400,000. The Jordanian education budget for the

West Bank population of 650,000 was about $7 million. Israel's allocation for education in Gaza and northern Sinai in 1976 was ten times larger than it was a decade earlier, while the education budget for the West Bank was nine times what it was under the Jordanians. The Egyptian health budget for 1967–1968 in Gaza and northern Sinai was only $800,000—a mere $2 per head. This had increased thirtyfold under Israel's administration, while the West Bank health budget has increased twentyfold.

An example of the changes that have taken place can be seen in the following comments which appeared in an article in the West German publication *Die Rheinphalz* on January 5, 1976:

> One cannot help but be impressed by the efforts undertaken by the military administration in the Gaza Strip to "normalize" the situation of the Palestinian refugees. . . . During the entire period of Egyptian rule nothing had been done to improve their economic and social lot. At the time of my first visit to Gaza in 1969, there appeared to be no solution for the misery and despair of the Palestinian refugees rotting in the camps. Yet, much has changed since. The Israeli administration has learned from experience . . . There is virtually no longer any unemployment in the Gaza Strip. Private income per capita has risen from IL [Israeli pounds] 553 to IL 1,158.
>
> . . . Apart from security, the administration of the Gaza region is largely in the hands of the Arab authorities . . . Israel has developed a blueprint to free the refugees from the run-down camps. They can purchase houses of their own on very favorable terms . . . The main aim is to ensure that the new building sites do not themselves turn into refugee camps. To guarantee fairness, the plots of land being sold are chosen by lot. Interest in this new program is so great that the authorities have considerable trouble coping with demand. Israel invested about IL 50 million during 1974, without any political strings attached.

Today Gaza is a prosperous area, and despite attempts to incite the population from the outside there have been no disturbances. The people of Gaza who have suffered the cruelty and oppression of Egyptian occupation for nineteen years are not inclined to be influenced by baseless condemnations of Israel's administration. The issues today in Gaza are of a local nature, of a purely municipal and financial kind such as occur in any society engaged in day-to-day living.

Complete freedom of passage and movement exists between

Israel and the territories on the one hand, and across the Jordan River to and from the West Bank on the other hand. As a result, 75,000 Arab workers cross every day into Israel to work, protected by the Trade Union Organization of Israel. Since June 1967, nearly 5 million people crossed the open bridges of the River Jordan in both directions, including 800,000 Arab tourists arriving from different Arab countries to spend their vacation in the territories and in Israel itself. In addition, thousands of Arabs from all over the Middle East line up at Israel's hospitals for medical treatment. Although no international law requires Israel to do so, Israel authorities have permitted students in Gaza, the West Bank and the Golan Heights to continue their studies at universities in Cairo, Amman, Damascus and elsewhere. Significantly, however, despite the freedom of movement, there is no Arab migration from the territories.

Life in the administered areas is far from the hell on earth that many of the Arab states have attempted to portray. As the West German weekly *Der Spiegel* noted: "The Zionist hell is [an Arab] tourist's paradise." But over and above the material and social advances I have described, Israel has maintained a scrupulous respect for human rights in the territories which goes far beyond its obligations under international law.

Despite the intense provocation under which Israelis live, despite the brutal massacres and acts of terrorism directed against innocent civilians, Israel has not carried out a single death sentence against a terrorist. Those arrested are entitled to their own lawyers and to a fair trial in an open court. By contrast, PLO terrorists accused in 1976 of attacking the Semiramis Hotel in Damascus were hanged in a public square after a token twelve-minute trial in which the judge announced openly that there was not even enough time for a coffee break. Terrorists arrested in Cairo and Amman have met a similar fate on the gallows, and Libya has lately carried out mass executions. No wonder that after the "Black September" of 1970, over a hundred PLO members came voluntarily to Israel rather than risk the mercies of Jordanian justice.

It is also worth noting that Israel is one of the few countries in the Middle East which allows the International Red Cross access to its prisoners on a routine basis. During these weekly visits, prisoners can talk to Red Cross officials without any guards being present. How many Arab countries have opened their prisons to international inspection, and in how many have criminals been sentenced by due process of law as in Israel? On December 14, 1975, Colin Legum wrote in the *Observer* of London:

> Because Israel insists that its own society should be judged by the world's highest standards, it is much more likely to be traduced than other countries where the lot of political prisoners and the rule of law are very much below its own standards.

But perhaps most significant of all is the fact that the administered areas are the only places in the entire Arab world in which Arabs are free to express their opinion, avail themselves of a free press and engage in the free democratic process of election by secret ballot. Of 16,000 administrative officials in the territories, only 500 are Israelis, and all the mayors and municipal councils have been elected by free and secret ballot. Arab editors and journalists with absolute freedom to express any political opinion, including extreme views opposing the State of Israel, write, edit and publish the three Arabic-language newspapers in East Jerusalem.

The PLO, incidentally, vigorously opposed the holding of elections in the West Bank and actively called for disturbances. Radio Cairo and other Arab broadcasts engaged in open incitement in an attempt to sabotage the election process. The local Palestinian Arabs preferred ballots to bullets. They ignored the PLO threats and went to the polling booths in an orderly manner to cast their votes. The PLO was certainly not eager to countenance the rise of a young militant Arab leadership in the West Bank, freely elected into office by its own people and not determined by the muzzle of a terrorist rifle or by the assassin's bullet. This leadership, while its views may diverge from those of the Israeli Administration, has its roots in the population and is engaged in daily dialogue with both the Israeli and the Jordanian governments. It is this dialogue which the PLO incitement was designed to prevent. We hoped that those elected in the West Bank would not allow themselves to be pawns in the hands of the Arab states, nor to be dictated to by the émigré leadership of the PLO, which does not even live among the population it purports to liberate.

Even before the most recent elections, it appeared obvious that candidates hostile to Israel would be returned. Indeed, under Jordanian law, which is applied in the West Bank, the Israeli government had the right to ignore the election results and to appoint its own candidates. This was in fact the practice of the Jordanian occupation authorities. As a matter of principle, Israel respected the election results, appointed all those elected, and has scrupulously refrained from interfering in the municipal affairs of the various towns, regardless of the political opinions of those elected. The West Bank Arabs had to wait for an Israeli administration to enjoy these freedoms.

Having considered the current situation in the administered areas, we must now examine possible solutions as to the ultimate disposition of these territories. One of the proposals advanced has been a Palestinian state in the West Bank and Gaza.

Before we consider Israel's position on such a state, let us consider that of the Arab states. It is often conveniently forgotten that those very states which are now most loudly advocating the idea of a Palestinian Arab state in the administered areas had every opportunity for nineteen years to create such an entity but did not do so. During those nineteen years there were no so-called complications arising from Israeli settlements in the West Bank, since there were no such settlements. Nor were there any difficulties arising from the reunification of Jerusalem, since the city was divided and since Jews had been driven out of the Jewish Quarter of the Old City by the Arab Legion in 1948 and their homes had been expropriated by the Jordanians. The simple truth is that the Arab states had no intention of implementing the formula which they today proclaim would produce the utopia which will bring Middle East peace.

Those well-meaning Western writers who advocate total Israeli withdrawal and the establishment of a Palestinian state should at least have the intellectual honesty to demand from Arab spokesmen a measure of consistency between their statements and their actions and a clarification of their actual intentions. The demand is made, for example, for a West Bank–Gaza Palestinian State to be run by the PLO. At the same time, the PLO has spelled out very clearly what it intends to do with these territories if it controls them. Abu Ayad, second in command to Arafat in the Fatah organization, told the Lebanese newspaper *al-Moharrer,* on March 1, 1976:

> The PLO has an unquestionable right to set up its national authority on part of Palestinian soil, but that does not at all mean we will settle for a partial settlement or recognition of Israel. On the contrary, we want to recover part of Palestine to try to liberate the rest. . . .

And to this day not a single PLO spokesman is on record as declaring that a Palestinian state on territories evacuated by Israel would satisfy them or that the PLO would ever recognize the 1967 lines as peace borders.

What, then, does Egypt mean by a PLO-run West Bank–Gaza state, and why should Israel withdraw to lines which, according to the supposed new rulers of such a state, would constitute a renewed invitation to war?

Since the Soviet Union backs the PLO today, a PLO-controlled Palestinian state would be nothing more than an economically unviable Soviet-sponsored mini-state (as has been conclusively proved by an American professor *) which, given a hostile posture, could by means of suitably sited modern surface-to-air missiles render air travel in Israel's air space impossible. Every single center of population in Israel would be within range of surface-to-surface missiles, of the type being supplied today by the Soviet Union to Arab countries, situated in the West Bank and Gaza.

We must never forget that during the nineteen years in which Arab rule prevailed in the West Bank and Gaza, those two areas were the bases from which countless raids into Israel were mounted, raids which involved indiscriminate loss of life, road ambushes, mines, barbed wire and destruction. The 1967 lines brought Israel war and would do so again if it ever returned to them. This is not the figment of anyone's imagination—it has

---

* Vivian A. Bull, *The West Bank—Is It Viable?* (Lexington, Mass., D. C. Heath and Company, 1975).

been publicly promised Israel by the very leaders to whom it is expected to surrender the West Bank.

Israel is not, however, the only state bordering on the proposed Palestinian state. The other potential neighbor is Jordan. King Hussein, while paying lip service to the PLO in the interests of apparent Arab unity, has not forgotten the bloody battles of 1970 in which the PLO attempted to overthrow the Hashemite regime. Nor has he forgotten recent public statements by PLO leaders such as Arafat and Kaddoumi vowing to depose him and to topple the Jordanian government. Nor indeed are King Hussein, his people and the inhabitants of the West Bank unmindful of the catastrophic civil war which the PLO brought on Lebanon.

The Jordanian government is in fact no more interested in a Soviet-sponsored mini-state on its borders, ruled by an avowedly hostile element to the Hashemite regime, than is Israel. Neither country has any illusion that such a state would be anything but exactly what the official PLO program maintains it will be—a springboard for mounting hostile action against both Israel and Jordan.

If, instead of imposing on the West Bank a terrorist authority which would be overtly hostile to both its neighbors, we attempt rather to derive a solution from the existing reality, we are far more likely to arrive at a reasonable solution. The fact is that although the West Bank is administered by an Israeli military government, Jordanian presence and influence are preponderant. All the inhabitants of the West Bank are citizens of Jordan and hold Jordanian passports. Fifty percent of the Jordanian Parliament is composed of deputies representing the West Bank. People and trade flow freely in both directions across the Jordan River between Jordan and the West Bank. Jordanian currency is legal tender in the West Bank (as is Israeli currency), Jordanian law is applied in the courts, Jordanian curricula are taught in the schools. A Jordanian civil service administers the affairs of the area. The mayors, who are elected in free and secret elections and who are autonomous in municipal matters, take their guidance from Jordan, pay homage to the royal court in Amman and frequently receive subventions from the Jordanian Treasury. A percentage of the Cabinet in Amman is invariably composed of Palestinians from the West Bank. The late Queen Alia of Jordan was a daughter of the West Bank. Palestinians live on both sides of the River Jordan, linked by ties of family, of economy, of language, of culture, of citizenship, of loyalties, of education.

The half-hearted Jordanian statements on behalf of the PLO notwithstanding, Jordan's policy and actions on the ground clearly indicate its firm opposition to a PLO-governed state and its decided preference to participate directly in the negotiations over the West Bank.

Another undeniable reality in the West Bank is the daily dialogue which has been established between Israelis and the major element of the Palestinian Arabs. Despite the very real differences of opinion that exist, this dialogue, which has developed from a decade of social and economic progress under Israeli administration, has brought about a greater degree of mutual understanding than has ever been achieved before. We have witnessed the development of daily grass-roots Arab-Jewish cooperation in all fields of human endeavor: medicine, agriculture, commerce, politics, science and higher education. In stark contrast to the bombs and threats of the PLO, this cooperation, manifested in every town, village and field of the West Bank, has created the foundations from which to advance further towards the solution of the Palestine Arab issue on a basis of growing understanding.

The facts and figures themselves speak for a solution in the context of an Israeli-Jordanian peace agreement. Of 2.8 million Palestinian Arabs, 1.75 million in the East and West Banks are citizens of Jordan, and hold Jordanian passports. Half a million are citizens of Israel and hold Israeli passports. Thus 80 percent of all Palestinian Arabs live in Jordan, Israel and Israeli-administered territories. The area of the present Kingdom of Jordan comprises 80 percent of what was originally Mandatory Palestine. For these basic reasons and because of the close interrelationship between the West and East Banks of the Jordan, Israel's policy has been and continues to be that the solution to the problem must be achieved in the framework of peace negotiations between Israel and Jordan whether at Geneva or elsewhere. Numerous proposals have been put forward at various times, including a Palestinian mini-state in the West Bank and the Gaza Strip, or some form of redivision of the territories between Israel and Jordan. I have already explained why a Palestinian—or, more accurately, a PLO mini-state —is unacceptable. As regards redivision, the fact is that, as Moshe Dayan, the Israeli Foreign Minister, pointed out to the UN General Assembly on October 6, 1977:

> For ten years, between 1967 and 1977, the Government of Israel was committed to territorial concessions in return for genuine peace, and this implied the redivision of the area, but to no avail. Now our view is that redivision is not the answer. Nowhere is it possible to draw a dividing line which will satisfy not only the security, but also the historical, economic and social needs of all sides. Bethlehem, a satellite town of Jerusalem, dependent on Jerusalem for its tourist trade and indeed its very existence, cannot be cut off from the Holy City. Mount Scopus, the site of the Hebrew University, and the Hadassah Hospital, cannot be separated from Israel. The Arabs in Gaza cannot once again be bottled up in an intolerably narrow strip of land, unable to get out without passing an international frontier. The model for the future must be united Jerusalem—where since 1967 Jews and Arabs have proved that they can live together harmoniously to their mutual benefit, where all residents enjoy freedom of movement in all parts of the Holy City, and where freedom of access to the holy places is assured for all. There is no room, and no need, for barbed wire any more.

In short, the solution must be based on coexistence between Israel and the Palestinian Arabs in the territories. This concept arises from the twofold experience of the ten years between 1967 and 1977 when, on the one hand, the Arab states refused to take up Israel's repeated offers of generous territorial concessions in return for genuine peace, and when, on the other hand, Jews and Arabs proved that they could live together very successfully. Coexistence means mutual respect and also, in the present context, the preservation on an equal footing of each other's heritage and national affiliations. Translated into practical terms, this calls for what might be called "functional partition"—an arrangement whereby the Arabs in the territories would remain Jordanian subjects and elect their representatives to the Jordanian Parliament, and the Jews Israeli citizens and elect representatives to the Knesset; the inhabitants of the territory would enjoy local autonomy and home rule, while Israel's defense border would remain at the River Jordan and Israel would be responsible for the security of the whole area. The concept is perhaps an unusual one in an era which accepts the automatic equation of political rights with geographical boundaries. But the very concept of the "nation-state" as we know it today is a comparatively recent one in human history and there are signs that Western Europe is already moving beyond it. It should be recalled that Italy and Germany themselves were not nations until the latter part of the nineteenth century. The conflict in the Middle East is a complex one, and it requires imaginative solutions if we are to break out of the impasse that has already resulted in several wars and thousands of deaths. The notion of a "functional partition" of political sovereignty in which Jews would be citizens of a Jewish state and Arabs of an Arab state, while preserving the geographical unity and integrity of the region, may be an unusual idea, but there is no reason that it cannot be a workable one. In any case, it is one of the possibilities that merits serious discussion in any negotiations between Israel and its neighbors.

This solution, which has been proposed by Israel in the recent Sadat-Begin talks, is *sui generis*, purposely avoiding as it does the thorny and intricate issue of sovereignty * and concentrating on the issue of human beings, Arabs and Jews, living side by side. Central to this vision of the future is coexistence—the concept of Jews and Arabs living side by side and proving to the world not only that wars between them are futile but that solutions based on a Solomonic approach to partition are unnecessary.

Because we have so far considered Jewish-Arab coexistence in the West Bank only in general terms, it is worth looking at one specific case study. Hebron, one of the oldest cities in the world, and a holy city for the Jewish people, has in recent years become a focus of attention, as the United Nations, the Islamic Conference and various other bodies have issued condemnations of Israel's policies here. Since Arab propaganda has consistently denied the Jewish connection to Hebron, and since that town represents a particularly powerful example of the continuity of Jewish history in the land of Israel, it is worth recounting briefly the story of Hebron from Biblical times to the present.

---

* For Israel's case on sovereignty in the West Bank and Gaza, see Chapter 7.

Hebron has been the site of almost continuous Jewish settlement since about 2000 B.C.E. The Bible tells how the Hebron Patriarch Abraham, the founding father of the Jewish people and religion, settled in Hebron.* When Abraham's wife, Sarah, died "in Kiryat Arba—that is Hebron," † Abraham bought a burial place for 400 shekels of silver from Ephron the Hittite, and "buried Sarah his wife in the cave of the field of Machpela before Mamre—that is Hebron." ‡ This contract, it must be emphasized, was transacted four thousand years ago.

Later, Genesis 49:29–31 relates how the Patriarch Jacob, also known as Israel, asked to be buried with his fathers in the Cave of Machpela. "There they buried Abraham and Sarah his wife; there they buried Isaac and Rebecca his wife; and there I buried Leah," Jacob recalls. The Cave of Machpela, the Tomb of the Patriarchs, thus became the most ancient shrine and Holy Place of the Jewish people and is revered by Jews until this very day.

Hebron maintained its importance throughout the following centuries. Here David reigned as King of Judah for seven and one half years, and here six of his sons were born.

Jews moved from the city with the First (Babylonian) Exile in the sixth century B.C.E., but they returned within half a century. Five hundred years later Herod the Great, the Jewish king and rebuilder of Jerusalem, reshaped the Tomb of the Patriarchs and gave it its present form. Not long after, during the Jewish wars against Rome, the Roman commander Cerealius burned down Hebron as an important Jewish center. Nonetheless, Jews continued to live there, even during the Byzantine period, when the Church of St. Abraham was erected over the Cave of Machpela. In the sixth century C.E., the church was divided into two parts— one for Jews, the other for Christians.

The Arabs conquered Hebron in 638 C.E., and in memory of the Hebrew Patriarch Abraham, renamed the town Khalil al-Rahman ("the companion of [God] the Merciful") or simply Al-Khalil. The Arabs allowed the Jews to be supervisors of the Cave of Machpela, although part of it was now used as a mosque—the Mosque of Ibrahim. With the Crusader conquest in 1100 C.E., the

---

* Gen. 13:18 and 18:1.
† *Ibid.*, 23:2.
‡ *Ibid.*, 23:19.

Mosque of Ibrahim once more became the Church of St. Abraham, and both Moslems and Jews were expelled. However, Jewish pilgrims continued to visit Hebron and the site of the Cave of Machpela, even though they were not allowed to enter the Tomb proper.

During the Mameluke rule, the small Jewish community, which lived in a closed-off ghettolike section of Hebron, once again gained access to the Cave of Machpela. They prayed there daily, and many of them also sought to be buried in the vicinity of the Tomb.

The Mameluke Sultan Baybars again prohibited the Jews and Christians from praying within the area in the year 1267; however, Jews were permitted to ascend five, later seven, steps on the side of the Eastern Wall and to insert petitions into a hole opposite the fourth step. This awkward limitation was strictly enforced until the twentieth century; nonetheless, the local Jewish community remained, and Jewish pilgrims to the Holy Land did not consider their pilgrimage complete without a visit to Hebron.

Under the Ottomans, the Jewish community in Hebron continued to develop, despite occasional persecution and plunder. In 1659 it established a yeshiva (theological college) named Hesed Le-Avraham that later became an important center of scholarship and a primary factor in the spiritual prominence of the local Jewish community. In the nineteenth century the community developed significantly, and several Jewish public institutions, such as schools, alms houses and a hospital, were set up.

In August 1929, at the end of the first decade of the British Mandate, the Arab population dealt a tragic blow to the Jewish community of Hebron. Incited by their religious leaders, Arab mobs launched a well-planned assault with the obvious goals of eliminating the Jewish community. They did not spare women, children or the elderly—sixty-seven were massacred and sixty were wounded. They destroyed the community, razed synagogues and burned Torah scrolls. The centuries-old Jewish presence in Hebron came to a virtual halt at the hands of Arab rioters.

My own great-grandmother, an old lady of eighty, was one of those cut down by an Arab dagger in 1929. And I can recall as a child being threatened by a sword when I tried to put my foot on the eighth step of the tombs.

After the war of 1948, Transjordan occupied the West Bank and later annexed it within the Hashemite Kingdom of Jordan. During the years 1948 to 1967 no Jews lived in Hebron, and none were allowed to visit the town or its Holy Places.

As a result of the Jordanian aggression on June 5, 1967, Israel found itself in control of Judea and Samaria (the "West Bank"), including the town of Hebron. Returning to Hebron for the first time in over twenty years, Israelis found the old Jewish Quarter totally destroyed; the Avraham Avinu Synagogue turned into a public latrine and a municipal warehouse; and the ancient Jewish cemetery of Hebron almost obliterated.

But immediately after the war, the Israeli government decided that the Holy Places throughout the territories should be open to all worshipers of all faiths. The government proclaimed, on June 28, 1967, the Protection of Holy Places Law, which guaranteed to members of all religions free access to their respective Holy Places. Thus, for the first time in exactly seven hundred years, the Tomb of the Patriarchs was opened to members of all faiths and in particular to the followers of the three major monotheistic religions—Judaism, Christianity and Islam.

At the same time, nothing has been done to minimize in any way the responsibility exercised by the Moslem Waqf over the Cave of Machpela. The personnel of the Waqf Bureau hold the keys to the Cave and are responsible for the daily opening and closing of the Cave, as well as for its maintenance. The orderly conduct of Moslem prayers has in no way been interfered with, and no division of the Cave and no physical partition has been erected in this holy shrine.

As the Cave of Machpela is holy to both Judaism and Islam, arrangements have been made which enable both Moslems and Jews to worship and pray in an orderly manner based on mutual respect. The Isaac and Rebekah Hall, the largest and most important hall to all religions, which contains the iman's pulpit, or mimbar, is reserved exclusively for Moslem prayers twenty-four hours a day, every day of the week, while Jewish services take place in the Hall of Abraham and Sarah. The present arrangements, which have been made with the greatest consideration for Moslem religious sentiments and without infringing on Arab privileges, have been working to the satsifaction of all sides since 1967.

A Jewish community has also been permitted to re-establish it-self—not in the town of Hebron itself, but nearby. The Israeli government decided that the optimal way to organize life in the Hebron area was to allow the Arab inhabitants to develop their city as they wished, in keeping with their own way of life, while a Jewish township bearing the ancient name of the "City of the Patriarchs"—Kiryat Arba—was set up outside the municipal boundaries of Hebron. The Jewish town has not supplanted Arab Hebron, but the two coexist side by side, with each growing and developing in its own way.

The daily reality is that Jews and Moslems worship side by side under the same roof in the Tomb of the Patriarchs while the two settlements coexist peacefully. Religious fanaticism has caused too many tragic events in the past to allow irresponsible incitement from outside to foment hatred between Arab and Jew. The sad experience has been that for over fifty-five years, violence, terrorism and endless indoctrination of hate against Jews and Israel —through the radio and press and in the schools and the mosques —have been cardinal principles of policy in many Arab states. It is fortunate that both Jewish and Moslem leaders in the territories and in Israel itself have made every effort to maintain the mutual respect, coexistence and freedom of worship which have been the hallmarks of Israel's policy in Hebron for more than a decade.

# 7

# Jewish Settlements in the Territories

WE HAVE recently witnessed an attempt to focus attention on a side issue which is not central to the real problems in the Middle East and irrelevant for any future peace agreement. Jewish settlements in the administered areas, which have not wrongfully dispossessed a single Arab, which have not cost a single life, and which were never an issue in the Middle East conflict, have now become the focal point for world-wide alarm and condemnation. It has been declared that Jewish settlements beyond the 1967 borders are "illegal," that they have brought about "demographic changes" in the territories and that they constitute an "obstacle to peace" in the area. In October 1977 the General Assembly of the United Nations passed a resolution to this effect. It is necessary therefore to examine each of the allegations in turn in order to expose the insidious intentions behind the current preoccupation with this issue.

First, it should be recalled that seven Arab armies, including the Transjordanian Legion, invaded Palestine on May 15, 1948, with the avowed purpose of destroying the State of Israel at its birth. As was stated by a Soviet delegate in the Security Council at the time:

. . . an armed struggle is taking place in Palestine as a result of the unlawful invasion by a number of states of the territory of Palestine, which does not form part of the territory of any of the states whose armed forces have invaded it.*

Because of the aggressive character of their invasion of Palestine, the invading states could not acquire rights or sovereignty over the territories which they occupied. U.S. Representative Warren Austin termed the Jordanian invasion of Judea and Samaria "the highest type of the international violation of the law."

The rights of the invading states in the territories of the former Palestine Mandate occupied by them were, therefore, at the most the rights of an occupant without any authority to annex the occupied territory. Jordan's unilateral "annexation" of Judea and Samaria in 1950 had, therefore, no basis or validity in international law. The Jordanian "annexation" never received international sanction: only Britain, which at the time was the real power behind Abdullah's Jordan, and Pakistan granted recognition to this Jordanian measure, and even Britain excluded East Jerusalem from its recognition. The member states of the Arab League went so far as to threaten Jordan with expulsion from their ranks because of that "annexation."

In 1967 Israel was again the victim of aggression as Arab leaders openly vowed to annihilate Israel. Egypt blockaded the Straits of Tiran and moved its armies into Sinai while Jordan ignored Israel's advice to keep out of the war and launched a military attack on Israel, shelling towns and villages, including the Holy City of Jerusalem.

When the Israel Defense Forces entered Judea and Samaria in June 1967—in the course of repelling the renewed Jordanian aggression—they ousted from these territories not the armies of the "legitimate sovereign," but illegal invaders who enjoyed, at the most, the rights of an occupant. However, the rights of an occupant are self-terminating upon the conclusion of the occupation, and no rights remain in the hands of the former occupant thereafter.

Since Jordan never was a "legitimate sovereign" in Judea and

* Vassili Tarasenko, Ukrainian Socialist Soviet Republic, Security Council, May 27, 1948.

Samaria, the provisions of the Fourth Geneva Convention—including those of its Article 49, which were intended to protect the rights of the "legitimate sovereign"—do not apply in respect of Jordan. Therefore, Israel is not affected by those provisions, and need not consider itself to be restricted by them. In other words, Israel cannot be considered an "occupying power," within the meaning of the Convention, in any part of the former Palestine Mandate, including Judea and Samaria.

A similar conclusion can be inferred from a reading of Professor Stephen H. Schwebel's article, published in 1970 in the *American Journal of International Law*, where he wrote:

> Having regard to the consideration that . . . Israel [acted] defensively in 1948 and 1967 . . . and her Arab neighbours . . . [acted] aggressively in 1948 and 1967 . . . Israel has better title in the territory that was Palestine, including the whole of Jerusalem, than do Jordan and Egypt.

Professor Schwebel pointed out in the same article that it is a principle of international law that although a country's right to a territory cannot be based on conquest, other applicable principles are that "no legal right shall spring from a wrong," and that members of the United Nations shall not employ "the threat or use of force against the territorial integrity or political independence of any state." In his article Professor Schwebel concluded that Jordan and Egypt annexed territory in 1948 through "aggressive conquest," which was unlawful, but that Israel's conquests in 1967 were "defensive" ones.

Professor Schwebel, in his 1970 article, also emphasized three points about "defensive conquests." First, a state may lawfully seize and occupy foreign territory if "necessary to its self-defense." Second, a state may require, before it withdraws from territory occupied in a defensive conquest, that satisfactory security arrangements be established to safeguard its security. Third, the state that holds territory through lawful defensive conquest has, vis-à-vis the prior occupant that acquired the territory through unlawful offensive conquest, better title to the land.

The state of the law has been correctly summarized by Elihu Lauterpacht, a distinguished authority on international law, as follows:

Territorial change cannot properly take place as a result of the *unlawful* use of force. But to omit the word "unlawful" is to change the substantive content of the rule and to turn an important safeguard of legal principle into an aggressor's charter. For if force can never be used to effect lawful territorial change, then, if territory has once changed hands as a result of the unlawful use of force, the illegitimacy of the position thus established is sterilized by the prohibition upon the use of force to restore the lawful sovereign. This cannot be regarded as reasonable or correct.*

A measure of the rather superficial manner in which the entire problem has been approached can be gauged from the fact that most statements lump together all the territories, although their international legal status is entirely different one from the other. The fallacy in this argument has been pointed out by Alfred L. Atherton, Jr., Assistant Secretary of State for the Near East and South Asia, in testimony before the House International Relations Subcommittees on International Organization and on Europe and the Middle East. There he drew a clear distinction between the legal status of Sinai and the Golan on the one hand (Egypt has never made a sovereign claim to the Gaza Strip), and that of the West Bank:

> In the West Bank and Gaza, however, the situation is different. Both of these territories were part of the British Mandate of Palestine. While the legitimate existence of a sovereign Israel in part of Palestine is recognized, the question of sovereignty in the part of Palestine remaining outside of Israel under the 1949 armistice agreements has not been finally resolved.

In sum, Professor Schwebel, now with the U.S. State Department, stated that from an international legal point of view, "Israel has better title in the territory that was Palestine, including the whole of Jerusalem than do Jordan and Egypt," while the Assistant Secretary of State for the Near East and South Asia, whose government had, incidentally, previously suggested that such settlement was illegal, admitted under congressional examination that the question of sovereignty in the West Bank and Gaza has not been finally resolved.

* Lecture by Lauterpacht to the Anglo-Israel Association, "Jerusalem and the Holy Places," published by the association as a pamphlet (London, October 1968), p. 52.

The legal case against Israeli settlements has generally been based on the provisions of the Fourth Geneva Convention. A reading of that document, however, makes it quite clear that it is not applicable to the territories. The Fourth Geneva Convention, where it might be applied (to my knowledge it has never formally been applied anywhere in the world) is intended for short-term military occupation and is not relevant to the *sui generis* situation in this area. Moreover, even were the laws of belligerent occupancy applicable, these rules, including the 1907 Hague Regulations, contain no restriction on the freedom of persons to take up residence in the areas involved.

It has been claimed, however, that Article 49 of the Fourth Geneva Convention is pertinent here. From the overall reading of Article 49 it is evident that its purpose is to protect the local population from deportation and displacement. Paragraph 6 must be read in the light of the general purpose of the article. It thus becomes apparent that the movement of population into the territory under control is prohibited only to the extent that it involved the displacement of the local population.

This conclusion finds expression in the leading treatise on the subject:

> The occupying power must not deport or transfer parts of its own civilian population into the territory occupied by him—a prohibition intended to cover cases of the occupant bringing in its nationals for the purpose of displacing the population of the occupied territory.*

Article 49 must be understood against the background of World War II. It was aimed in part against such horrors as the barbarous extermination camps in occupied Europe to which Jews and others were taken by the Nazis and in part against the displacement of the local population with a view to making room for the German invaders.

Bearing in mind both the provisions of the article and its legislative history, it is clear that the situation envisaged by Article 49 does not apply to the Jewish settlements in question. No Arab in-

---

* Lassa Oppenheim, *International Law*, ed. by H. Lauterpacht. Vol. II, *Disputes, War and Neutrality*, 7th ed. (New York: McKay, 1952), p. 452.

habitants have been displaced by these peaceful villages and town-ships. According to international law, therefore, the Israeli settle-ments are not "illegal," because Israel has better title legally to this area of the West Bank and Gaza than any other country. Furthermore, many of the settlements under discussion were es-tablished within the framework of the security requirements of Israel as seen by its government.

It is conveniently forgotten that the Arab states maintain that a state of war exists with Israel. Nevertheless, when Israel takes steps to ensure its security, they are deplored. As long as its neigh-bors maintain that a state of war exists, it is the duty of the Israeli government—a duty which is clearly recognized in international law—to do what it sees fit to protect its inhabitants. Israel cer-tainly cannot be expected to pretend that time stands still and to ignore its security requirements while the world waits until this or that Arab leader deigns to open negotiations instead of send-ing his delegate to the UN to engage in name-calling and abuse.

In this connection it should be noted that other political and juridical questions also exist. For example, recognized political borders between Israel and its Arab neighbors have never existed. Since the wars of 1967 and 1973, special agreements are in force until the achievement of a "just and lasting peace" as required by Security Council resolutions 242 and 338, a peace intended, *inter alia,* to establish secure and recognized borders.

There is, however, still a further aspect to the question of the settlements which has been totally overlooked. For centuries Jews have owned land in Judea, Samaria and Gaza, and have of course lived there. They lived on these lands during the period of the Ottoman Empire and the British Mandate. They were driven out by Jordanian and Egyptian aggression, which was not recognized by the Arab international community, let alone by the general international community. If one subscribes to the notion that for a Jew to settle on land which he owns, wherever it may be, has no legal validity for the simple reason that he is a Jew, then one is in fact subscribing to the hateful Nazi Nuremberg Laws—many of which apply today in the racist legal codes of the Arab countries. Let us consider, for example, the Jordanian citizenship law No. 6 of February 4, 1954, whereby Jordanian nationality is granted to residents of Judea and Samaria, which had been illegally annexed to Jordan. Paragraph 3 of this law states: "Any man will be a Jordanian subject . . . (3) if he is not Jewish." In addition, a comparatively recent law notes that sale of land to a Jew is punishable by death.

Now it has been suggested that a Jew, by virtue of being a Jew, and for no other reason, cannot settle on land which he and his family own and have owned for tens and perhaps hundreds of years. There are settlements on Jewish-owned land in the Hebron Hills, in the Gaza Strip, in the Jordan Valley, by the Dead Sea.

What the UN resolution on the settlements demands is that I be forbidden to settle on land of a village in the Hebron Hills, Masuoth Yitzchak, which bears my late father's name and which is Jewish-owned, for one reason and one reason only: because I happen to be a member of the Jewish people. This is the vicious anti-Semitic Nazi philosophy behind the Jordanian citizenship laws and behind the UN resolution on the settlements. It is particularly disturbing that European countries which arose out of the ashes of post-Nazi Germany have supported a prohibition which amounts to an extension of the Nuremberg Laws.

It has been claimed that the settlements are being established at the expense of expropriated Arab lands. This is untrue. The overwhelming majority of settlements have been set up on government and public land that was barren, rock-strewn hillsides and deserts for centuries. In the very few instances where private land was involved, it was acquired for public purposes in accordance with Jordanian law, which applies in Judea and Samaria, and against full compensation. Similar laws providing for acquisition of land for public purposes exist in Israel and in most other countries.

In all cases of such land acquisition, any owner who feels aggrieved, or feels that the compensation is insufficient, has right of access to the Israeli Supreme Court, sitting as the high court of justice. This Court can and does issue writs against the government or the military authorities whenever it feels that any person, including residents of the territories, has a legitimate grievance. In a number of instances the Court has found against the authorities and redressed the plaintiffs.

Perhaps the most preposterous assertion of all in the United

Nations resolution is that the Jewish settlements constitute "demographic changes." This new international slogan, which attempts to mask Arab racist anti-Jewish policy, has unfortunately been adopted by gullible spokesmen of many countries whose philosophy is far removed from such racism and racist philosophy.

What it means is that it is wrong for Jews to live among and with Arabs, because they are Jews. If 50,000 Arabs have returned to the territories since 1967 under the family reunion scheme and the total population of the territories has increased by 17.4 percent in the last ten years, that is not considered a "demographic change." If the Arab population of Israel has grown from 150,000 in 1949 to 550,000 today, that is not considered a "demographic change." But if a total of approximately 6,000 Jews settle in Judea, Samaria, Sinai, Gaza and Golan, in an area populated by 1¼ million Arabs, this is termed a "demographic change." When approximately 2,500 Jews settled in an area populated by 750,000 Arabs in Judea and Samaria, and not one life was lost thereby or one person dispossessed, the United Nations saw fit to ignore all the tragedies besetting this world in order to express its concern about what it calls "demographic changes." Over 500,000 Arabs live in Israel in a predominantly Jewish population side by side with their Jewish neighbors. But it is apparently considered wrong for a few thousand Jews to live in a predominantly Arab population.

The racist philosophy behind these claims is the same that calls for the exclusion of all non-Arab elements from the Middle East: the Christians from Lebanon, the Assyrians and the Kurds from Iraq, the Jews from the Arab world, the Jews from Israel, the Christians from southern Sudan, the Copts from Egypt, and so on. This philosophy was summed up by Yassir Arafat in his organization's Nazi covenant that calls for the destruction of a nation: "There will be no presence in the region other then the Arab presence." The prohibition on Israeli settlement amounts to an endorsement of the Nazi racist philosophy of creating an area that is *Judenrein*—"free of Jews." It is sad to see nations which suffered from the Nazi yoke and oppression now supporting the resurrection of this hated anti-Semitic thesis which brought a holocaust and tragedy to the world.

Israel, on the contrary, believes that the fruitful coexistence between Jews and 500,000 Arabs in Israel and 1¼ million Arabs in the territories has created a bridge to the Arab world. By living together with this Arab population, Israel has established a daily dialogue with a major element of the Palestinian Arabs. It has brought about a greater degree of mutual understanding than has ever been achieved before, and has developed daily grass-roots Arab-Jewish cooperation in all fields of human endeavor, medicine, agriculture, commerce, politics and science.

Thus, Israel has created the foundations from which to advance further towards the solution of the Palestine Arab problem on a basis of growing understanding.

Israel believes that the only effective way of bridging the gap between Jew and Arab in the Middle East is by the peoples maintaining a continuous dialogue and learning to live side by side. Only then can a bridge to peace be established. It will certainly not be built by a slavish pandering to the basic racist and anti-Semitic philosophy which calls for the establishment in this age of Jew-free areas from which individuals are to be excluded solely because they are Jews.

Finally, it has been alleged that the establishment of settlements is an obstacle to peace. This allegation is a cynical falsification of history.

For nineteen years, from 1948 to 1967, Israel was not establishing settlements in Judea, Samaria, Gaza, Sinai and Golan, because Israel was not in those places. There was no such "obstacle" from 1948 to 1967, yet the Arabs refused even to talk about peace. Not only was Israel not in the territories, Jordan and Egypt were there. Israel was not establishing settlements and bringing agricultural progress to these areas. Nor, indeed, did Egypt and Jordan take advantage of their presence to establish farms and settlements. They let those territories languish in disease and poverty (30 percent unemployment, indescribable conditions in impoverished refugee camps, etc.). They were in control of the West Bank and Gaza, but they did not permit the establishment of a Palestinian state because then, as now, they did not want one. Jordan saw itself rightly to be the Palestinian state, which it is. The Arabs, who were in control of the West Bank and Gaza and could have established a PLO-controlled Palestinian state, formed the PLO in 1964 not over the issue of the settlements in Judea and

Samaria or Gaza. That is—and never was—central. The issue was and is Jewish settlement in Israel. The issue is not Kaddum or Etzion or Regavim or Yamit or Ramat Magshimim. The issue is Tel Aviv or Haifa, as the representative of the PLO has said in the United Nations itself. The issue has been and is every settlement Israel has ever established wherever it may be—in the Galilee, in the Negev, in the Gilboa, in the Sharon, in Judea, in Samaria and in the coastal plain.

That this is not a political issue was made crystal-clear by Israel's Foreign Minister Moshe Dayan in the United Nations General Assembly: "The settlements will not decide the final borders between Israel and its neighbors. The borders will be decided upon in negotiations between Israel and its neighbors. The settlements are by no means an obstacle to peace, because if they were, we should have had peace years ago."

There is no connection between the progress towards a Middle East peace agreement and the establishment of settlements. The settlement issue is simply a device to cover up for the Arab states' stubborn refusal to negotiate with Israel, whose destruction many of them seek. The recent course of events in the Middle East proves that the settlements have in no way hindered progress towards agreements. The disengagement agreements with Egypt and Syria were reached without the settlements being mentioned at all.

The negotiations relating to the reconvening of the Geneva Peace Conference were not related to the settlements. They concerned such questions as that of Palestinian representation, the number of delegations, etc. These problems would have to be discussed even if there were not a single Jewish settlement in the Israeli-administered areas. As observed by Professor Fred Gottheil of the University of Illinois, at the House of Representatives hearings, on September 12, 1977: "Jewish settlements are an issue because the existence of the State of Israel is an issue."

In these territories, Jewish history began four thousand years ago and has continued uninterrupted.

Long before most of the nations of the world even dreamed of statehood, a great Jewish civilization was flourishing in the cities and villages of Judea and Samaria. The judges of Israel dispensed justice in Jerusalem on the basis of one of the most advanced and enlightened codes of law in history. Hebron is the burial place of the Jewish Patriarchs to this day and it was there that King David ruled until he moved his capital to Jerusalem.

The Kingdom of Israel was centered upon the hills of Judea and Samaria. The Biblical name of Samaria is Shomron, and it was the capital of the ancient Kingdom of Israel.

For Jews, the Bible is not just something one teaches at Sunday School. It is, rather, a record of the living experience of a people which has continued in an unbroken chain of history of greatness, of tragedy, of unparalleled human contribution, of struggle for existence against overwhelming odds, and always of triumph and advance.

The fact is that the settlements are a side issue, as President Sadat himself admitted on ABC television in an interview on August 4, 1977. When asked about the settlements, he stated: "Well, in my opinion, this is a side issue." They are certainly not an obstacle to peace. The obstacle to peace is the Arab refusal to recognize the Jewish people's right to sovereignty in its ancient homeland. The obstacle to peace is an implacable Arab refusal to recognize Israel, to negotiate with Israel, to make peace with Israel. The obstacle to peace is the refusal of the Arab countries to sit down at the negotiating table with Israel.*

The obstacle to peace lies in the failure of world leadership and opinion to insist that both sides sit down and negotiate face to face. The obstacle to peace lies in the encouragement given to Arab intransigence because of reasons of expediency. The obstacle to peace is a basic Arab attitude and until that attitude is changed, no real advance towards peace can be made. These are the obstacles to peace and any attempt to point a finger at Israel's actions and to characterize them as obstacles to peace is untrue and baseless and is nothing but a grave misinterpretation of events in the Middle East.

The Arab states must learn that they will not be able to change the legal status, the geographical nature and the demographic composition of the territories by pushing through yet another anti-Israel resolution at the United Nations. They will only be able

---

* This statement has been vindicated by developments following President Sadat's visit to Jerusalem.

to obtain changes by fulfilling Resolution 242 and negotiating secure and recognized boundaries with Israel.

As the late UN Secretary-General Dag Hammarskjöld once said: "You can condemn a state or you can negotiate with it but you cannot do both." By that criterion, the condemnation of Israel on the settlements in the General Assembly constitutes a retrograde step which only further poisons the atmosphere and prejudices the prospects for peace.

# 8

# Inside the Arab World: The Confrontation States

THE major issue facing the world in the Middle East today is not the Israel-Arab issue, but the Arab world itself—torn, disunited, working at cross-purposes, conspiring one against the other, unstable and prey every day and in each country to the personal ambitions of some aspiring colonel. This is an issue created by the impact of the twentieth century, coupled with vast sums of oil money, on a medieval society. The seeeds of international tragedy arising out of military conflict and unbridled international terror backed by unlimited wealth exist in the Arab world today without reference to any outside element. The Arab world —not the Israeli-Arab conflict—poses serious problems to the freedom and security of our world.

Only recently, Egyptian and Libyan troops were locked in battle. Egyptian planes bombed airfields and military and civilian installations far and wide inside Libya; the conflict has not yet been resolved. Today, forces of Somalia, a member of the Arab League, backed by other members of the Arab League like Saudi Arabia, Egypt and Sudan, is openly committing an act of aggression against Ethiopia, an independent black country in the horn of Africa. They have reportedly occupied almost one third of

Ethiopia in a military invasion while thousands of Ethiopians are dying on the battlefields. Every month hundreds die in the struggle between Algeria on the one hand, and Morocco and Mauritania on the other. All members of the Arab League, they continue a sporadic war that is rarely even noticed in the media today. For years a bloody struggle took place in the hills and sands of Dhofar, Oman, with one side being backed by Communist-dominated South Yemen and the other side by Saudi Arabia, Jordan and Iran. Only recently the Deputy Foreign Minister of Oman described before the UN General Assembly how half a million refugees had been created as a result of this Communist aggression. All these conflicts had nothing to do with the Arab-Israeli conflict.

We have also witnessed Arabs slaughtering Arabs by the tens of thousands in Lebanon. Arab armies have been poised against each other on the Iraqi-Syrian border, on the Iraqi-Kuwaiti border. For five years in the early sixties, Arabs waged a bloody war against one another in Yemen. And in 1970 Arabs struggled in bloody conflict in the streets of Amman in a PLO endeavor to destroy the Hashemite Kingdom of Jordan. Arabs killed Arabs in a Libyan-sponsored revolution attempt to overthrow the government of Sudan, and Tunisia expelled Libyan agents accused of having been sent on an assassination mission to that country. These conflicts, totally unrelated to the Arab-Israeli conflict, reveal the inherent instability of the Arab world which must of necessity affect the prospects of peace in the world today.

But in addition to destroying one another, the Arab states are incapable of tolerating the presence of any other element in their area. If one contemplates the somber and grim fate of the Kurds of Iraq, one wonders why the United Nations does not debate the inalienable rights of millions of Kurds to their own country in Iraq. Half a million black Christians were slaughtered in southern Sudan, but the issue was again not worthy of consideration in the UN. The existence of hundreds of thousands of Christians in Lebanon was threatened by an Arab Moslem onslaught, but the world remained silent. Given the chance, the Arabs would doubtless do to the Jewish population in Israel what they have succeeded in doing to the Jewish population in all the Arab countries to date, and what they have done to the Kurds, to the

Christians, to the blacks—particularly since we see today a concerted move by the PLO and their allies to realize Yassir Arafat's avowed aim, as he put it in a speech in Libya in 1975, that "there will be no presence in the region other than the Arab presence."

In other words, when we analyze the Arab attitude to the Israeli problem we must see it in the context of the Arab attitude to the minorities living in the Arab world. And we must equate their protestations of good will and statements of peace with the facts and with their record. The world has been somewhat gullible and has tended to treat the Arabs with a certain benign forgiveness. Nations have shown too great a tendency to react to the inflammatory public statements of the Arabs with the facile explanation that they don't really mean what they say and that their public statements bear no relation to the mild, moderate statements made privately by Arab statesmen.

The most ominous recent development in the Arab world has been the unfolding of an elaborate Syrian design with far-reaching implications. Syria, ruled by a series of military dictatorships for years, has long been an intransigent extreme element in the Middle East. The comparative stability which Syria has enjoyed over the past few years results from the recent cessation of the revolutions which had been taking place since the establishment of the Syrian state on an average of approximately one a year. The present dictator, Hafez al-Assad, has been in power for some seven years and represents a branch of the Ba'ath party that espouses an indeterminate form of Arab socialism. His regime is a cruel and harsh one. We have learned from bitter experience that Syria's behavior towards its prisoners is medieval and brutal in the extreme. Its Jewish community lives virtually imprisoned as hostages. Syria has been Israel's most hostile and implacable enemy over the years, and to this day has not explicitly acknowledged UN Security Council Resolution 242.*

Israel is not, however, the only country to find Syria an unpleasant neighbor. Its relations with Turkey have been uneasy, and its relations with the opposing Ba'ath faction regime in Iraq

---

* Syria's hostile reaction to President Sadat's initiative at the end of 1977 was very much in character.

have been unfriendly, to say the least. Syria's two armored divisions were at one point poised on the Iraqi border, while Syrian tampering with the flow of water to Iraq has from time to time led to increased tension.

It is in Lebanon that Syria's objectives have finally been revealed. The war in Lebanon emphasized for all to see the complete and utter impotence of the Arab world with its Arab League and its summit conferences and its so-called peacekeeping forces. Lebanon has been and is today the arena in which the various inter-Arab ambitions, hatreds and rivalries find expression in the most brutal manner. It is impossible to appreciate the developments in Lebanon without understanding the key point in the whole issue, namely Syria's basic approach to Lebanon: Syria has always regarded Lebanon as part of Greater Syria. No diplomatic relations have ever existed between Syria and Lebanon, and the two countries have not exchanged ambassadors. This is a natural corollary of Syria's claim over Lebanon, for it is argued that a state does not maintain diplomatic relations with part of itself.

The Syrians would have been only too happy to swallow up Lebanon. Militarily they could have done so with comparative ease had they devoted the necessary forces to this purpose. However, a number of deterrents prevented them from doing this— the complex inter-Arab relationships, the reaction to Syria's moves in the Arab world, and the attitude of the major powers and of Israel. Accordingly, Syria chose a second course—namely, to turn Lebanon into a vassal state, or at least to include it absolutely in its area of influence. Syria will not and cannot afford to make concessions in this regard, for Lebanon is vital strategic territory in Syria's struggle against Israel.

Control of Lebanon is also a major element in the Syrian effort to achieve hegemony in the Arab world. Syria has never forgone its plans to create a bloc of countries of the Mashrak (the East) as opposed to the countries of the Maghreb (the West) of North Africa that includes Egypt. Only a powerful bloc of the Mashrak, controlled and led by Syria, can serve as a counterbalance to the leadership of Egypt and to the Cairo-Riyadh axis which Damascus regards with great disfavor. Lebanon is therefore a vital link in this eastern-bloc plan, and if it cannot be taken over militarily, it will remain outwardly Lebanese but under Syrian patronage to a degree that in effect means a loss of independence.

The Syrians believe that this can be achieved by maintaining a delicate and fragile political stalemate between Moslems and Christians. The resultant confrontation between them tends to ensure the result of a weak Lebanon dependent entirely on Syria. The events in the first phase of the Lebanese war coincided with Syria's interests. The Christian Maronites were the dominant political and economic power in Lebanon, and a diminution of their strength with a consequent increase in that of the Moslems was desirable to the Syrians.

From the outset the Syrians therefore supported the Moslem establishment, though not the radical left wing, whose interests are diametrically opposed to those of Syria, so that both the Shiite and the Sunni Moslems in Lebanon enjoyed Syrian support.

On February 14, 1976, it appeared that the Syrians had achieved their goal. The Christian Maronites and the Moslems signed a new political agreement that established an amended balance of power reducing the strength of the Christians while adding to the strength of the Moslem establishment. A Maronite President with reduced authority, a Moslem Sunni Prime Minister with increased authority, and an equal division of seats in Parliament were agreed to by the parties. Had this agreement been honored, the Lebanese war would have come to a conclusion and the resultant weak creation would have enabled Syria to turn Lebanon into a vassal state.

However, a complex alliance composed of the radical left-wing Moslems led by the late Kemal Jumblat (an eccentric Druze millionaire socialist leader), several Communist groups, groupings of the pro-Iraq Ba'ath party, and others sought to exploit the unstable situation to advance their interests further at the expense of the Christians.

The Syrians reversed their attitude, effecting a change of 180 degrees. They began to support the Maronites against the left wing in order to prevent the latter from taking control of Lebanon against Syria's interests. This was the reason why, in June 1976, large Syrian forces, estimated at some 20,000 troops and 400 tanks, entered Lebanon in support of the Christians. The basic purpose was to prevent either side in the conflict from creating a politically stable and strong Lebanon, and to maintain the status quo of a weak, polarized Lebanon, dependent on Syria. In an interview with a Saudi Arabian newspaper, *Ukaze*, given at the beginning of 1977, President Sadat was very clear and unequivocal about the cynical Syrian moves, pointing out that the Syrians were supplying arms to the Christians to kill Moslems and to the Moslems to kill Christians.

There is an interesting observation to be made here, namely that in the Arab world ideological considerations invariably take second place to vital national interests as each Arab country sees them. All the accepted divisions in the Western world of right and left, radical and conservative, are not really applicable in the Arab world.

The situation in Syria and in Lebanon must be understood in relation to the PLO, which, though a major element in Lebanon, had to fight for its very existence in that country. After King Hussein drove the PLO members out of Jordan in 1970–1971, they established their base of operations in Lebanon and from there developed terrorist operations against Israel. Since they were either banned or tightly controlled in Jordan, Syria and Egypt, Lebanon became the only confrontation country in which the PLO was free to operate as a state within a state.

During the first phase of the Lebanese conflict, the PLO straddled the fence and followed the progress of the war. However, when Syria began to support the Maronites, the PLO realized that should Syria either take control of Lebanon or turn it into a vassal state, the PLO would lose the only area in which it had a degree of freedom of action. The PLO decided then to side with the radical-left Moslems in their battle against Syria.

The confrontation tended to break down the PLO into its various components, and in fact led to a process of fragmentation. All the various constituent elements of the PLO reflected the policies of their backers, and these groupings became nothing but instruments in the hands of different Arab states. The Syrian-controlled al-Saiqa was seriously affected, and Ahmed Jibril's organization, the General Command, went over to the Syrians. The Fatah organization remained the strongest Palestinian group of all in numbers of fighters, fighting ability and internal coherence. They succeeded in causing casualties to the Syrian armor and commandos and to al-Saiqa, and George Habash's PFLP. In general, the PLO became a more extreme organization.

When Syria completed its takeover of Lebanon—an issue on which Syria would entertain no compromise—the PLO lost the limited freedom of action which it previously enjoyed in Syria and the comparatively unlimited freedom of action which it had in Lebanon. Weakened both politically and militarily, the PLO then began strengthening its political image abroad in the hope that its standing in the Middle East would thus be enhanced.

Syria's relationship with Jordan has varied in degrees of hostility over the years. When Syrian agents killed the Prime Minister of Jordan in Amman in 1960, the British and American ambassadors had great difficulty talking King Hussein out of invading Syria with his army. The Syrian air force attempted to shoot down King Hussein while he was piloting his plane over Syrian territory, and several attempts on the King's life were mounted from Syria. King Hussein himself has written in bitter terms in his autobiography of Syrian attempts on his life.

In September 1970, when King Hussein's forces were locked in a life-and-death struggle with the PLO forces in the streets of Amman and elsewhere, and when Jordan was convulsed by civil war, the Syrian army stabbed the King in the back by invading northern Jordan. At that time they maintained, falsely, that the invading armored forces were Palestinian. Jordan was saved then by very clear and unequivocal indications that neither the United States nor Israel would view with equanimity a Syrian invasion of Jordan. An Israeli mobilization, American troop dispositions in Europe and elsewhere, and the movement of the U.S. Sixth Fleet to the Levant coast impressed the Russians sufficiently to advise the Syrians to withdraw. Jordan—in a move that Arabs have consistently criticized—subsequently outlawed the PLO. After the PLO was driven out of Jordan in July 1971, the Syrians, as the main sponsors of the PLO in the area, broadcast nightly vitriolic diatribes against the King for not carrying out his Arab duty and allowing the PLO to operate from Jordanian territory against Israel. The King was adamant and Syrian hostility did not subside.

Then, in an incredible volte-face, there developed in 1976 a rapprochement between the Syrians and the Jordanians. Suddenly the years of hostility and hatred evaporated. Mutual visits between the Jordanian leadership and that of Syria took place, and joint planning committees were established. The most remarkable aspect of the new situation was that the Syrian government tacitly acquiesced in the total exclusion of the PLO, which is today largely an instrument of Syrian policy, from Jordan, and did not find the Jordanian hostility towards the PLO irreconcilable with public manifestations of friendship between Jordan and Syria.

An analysis of what went on over the years between these countries must arouse one's suspicions, for it is inconceivable that basic political and philosophic differences could be discarded so lightly. The Syrians house, arm and back elements of the PLO whose avowed purpose is to destroy the Hashemite Kingdom in Jordan, in addition to the State of Israel. PLO leaders have time and again asserted that Jordan is Palestine. There is no doubt that the fundamental hostility and lack of trust between them still remains, for the regimes are basically irreconcilable. Jordan is a conservative, Western-oriented monarchy, while Syria is ruled by an extremely radical regime militarily equipped by the Soviet Union, and trained by a force of three to four thousand Soviet military advisers, not to mention the North Korean pilots, the North Vietnamese units and the Cuban advisers stationed from time to time in Syria.

What is quite evident is that Syria has decided to use Jordan as an instrument in pursuit of its policy while for a time the Jordanians appeared to be falling into a trap set by the Syrians. Syrian policy has been served by mending its fences with Jordan and removing any possible distractions along the border. Having ensured its flanks, Syria could then move into Lebanon in the first step of its overall plan to create a Greater Syria. This plan, which in effect envisages a confederation composed of Jordan, Syria and Lebanon, is a Syrian move to counterbalance Egyptian influence in the Middle East. It is conceivably either a move designed to create a coherent group in the East capable of waging war against Israel without Egypt—a revolutionary concept in the Arab world—or to create a group strong enough politically to take the necessary steps toward political accommodation with Israel.

Jordan required the alliance with Syria because a union with a radical Arab regime legitimized the Jordanian regime, which had to some degree been suspect in the eyes of the Arab world. There is also no doubt that this accommodation between Syria and Jordan was achieved at the expense of the PLO. The Jordanian attitude to the PLO is unequivocal, for it is a matter of life and death to King Hussein.

It is interesting to observe the divergence in basic attitudes receiving expression in the relations between the two countries. The Syrians for a time pressed for an all-out federation or confederation, proposing a military union and even a political union which would abolish separate embassies. Hussein for his part succeeded in walking a tightrope with his usual skill, maintaining good relations with Syria while at the same time deferring to his army's suspicion about Syrian intentions and its refusal to lose its Jordanian identity.* Most of the practical proposals put forward by Syria for more than a formal union or all-out confederation were, however, firmly declined by the Jordanians; they are only too aware of the danger inherent in the Syrian connection and are thus trying to get the best of both worlds while keeping the Syrians at arm's length.

But Jordan has another objective as well.

While the Syrians are developing their master plan in Lebanon, the Jordanians are using this new situation to reassume their position of responsibility in the West Bank, the Rabat Summit Conference decision of 1974 notwithstanding. (This decision, which was made over King Hussein's opposition, declared that the PLO represents the Palestinian people, including those in the West Bank.) However, the King played his cards extremely carefully, paying lip service to the Rabat decision but never for a moment relinquishing his hold on the West Bank. He has therefore continued to pay the civil service—a fortunate body of people which, for political reasons, receives double salaries, one from Israel and one from Jordan. He did not disband Parliament, 50 percent of whose members represent the West Bank, but merely suspended it and postponed elections so that it could be activated at any time. Hussein's relations with the West Bank mayors remain close

* Hussein's caution was exhibited again when Jordan chose to remain on the fence when invited by President Sadat to the Cairo Conference in December 1977.

despite the radical stance publicly adopted by them. The mayors have been well received in Amman and have willingly accepted development loans from Jordan as well as Israel. Thus, we are witness to the increasing influence of King Hussein in the West Bank, and to a gradual erosion of the Rabat decisions.*

Despite the obvious Jordanian gains, I believe that Jordan is playing with fire and that King Hussein will learn that he has made a serious error in assuming that he can outwit the Syrians at their own game. He and all others involved in the area will sadly find themselves playing the Syrian game.

The unfolding of the Syrian plan is a most disturbing development in the area, and unless it is arrested the Syrians, supported as they are by the Soviet Union, may cause a deterioration in the Middle East serious enough to lead to dangerous developments in the West. For the moment, despite its extreme policy, Syria cannot ignore the attitude of Saudi Arabia, which is uncompromisingly opposed to Soviet expansion and a source of financial support for many Arab countries, including Syria. It therefore treads a cautious path. The role of the Soviet Union in fomenting strife and dissension in the Middle East was emphasized by President Sadat when he pointed out bitterly that the Soviet Union is guilty of attacking Egypt via Syria, of countering Syria via Egypt, of pressing on Iraq through Syria and on Syria through Iraq, of intriguing against Egypt through Libya and against Libya through Egypt; in other words, of engaging in wholesale intrigue indiscriminately to further its aims in the Middle East. This whole development should give rise to much anxiety and apprehension in the West, let alone in the Middle East. For as the Syrian plot of expansion and annexation moves forward, a major change is taking place which could have serious consequences for the entire area. It is again a realization of the sinister role which the Soviet Union played in the Middle East—so vividly described by President Sadat —that the joint U.S.-Soviet declaration issued on October 1, 1977, was received with such alarm and concern not only by Israel but also by Egypt.

---

* The Israeli-presented proposals to President Sadat for a settlement in the West Bank districts of Judea and Samaria, and for Gaza, envisage an important role for Jordan.

# 9

# Israel and the Task of Economic Cooperation

IT IS IMPORTANT in the case of a small developing country, as Israel is, that we consider not only what the other countries can do for us, but also what we can do for ourselves and how we can, in our own way, contribute to the welfare of each other. In this connection, Israel welcomed the remarks made at the 7th Session of the UN General Assembly by the head of the Chinese delegation, Mr. Li Chiang. He said:

> Mutual assistance and economic cooperation among developing countries are especially important. We are developing countries, and we understand best each other's difficulties and needs, so we should support and help each other. Such cooperation is based on genuine equality and has broad prospects.*

Despite the very difficult challenges which have faced Israel and which still confront us today, we have, over the years, tried to improve our lot and to maintain economic growth. Unfortunately, excessive military expenditures, occasioned by our specific problem, do not always enable us to take full advantage of the bene-

* UN Document, A/PV 2329, September 2, 1975, p. 31.

fits of our economic progress. In achieving this progress we have, as have many other developing nations, enjoyed considerable aid from friendly countries.

Furthermore, Israel not only has fully utilized this aid, but has considered it to be its duty as a member of the community of nations to ensure that the benefits it has received are passed on to other countries in forms that can be readily translated to fit their own peculiar requirements.

In this context, the Israeli government's policy has been to institute programs of cooperation and technical aid with other emerging and developing countries. Indeed, it is a source of pride to note that Israel, without the gift of natural resources or native sources of energy, is currently cooperating in one technical form or another with some fifty countries around the world.

What distinguishes Israel's ability to provide experience and assistance in economic and social development from that of most industrialized countries is precisely the fact that Israel is itself a young developing country. As President Jomo Kenyatta of Kenya has said, Israelis "have shown what a small country can do for itself through hard work and faith in its destiny. The good example of Israel has been a useful lesson which other developing countries are trying to follow." *

It has been an inescapable fact of Israel's own economic situation and its status as a developing country that it has not been able to afford to lend or grant huge sums of money for capital projects. Instead, two salient features have distinguished the Israeli international cooperation program: the almost total focus on technical assistance and the emphasis on cooperation.

Israel's technical aid program began in Ghana soon after that country won its independence in 1967, and later spread from Africa to Asia and Latin America. The program's reputation was made by advisers who helped plan agricultural and regional development and who introduced new techniques in medicine, education, labor and trade union organization.

---

* Leopold Laufer, "Israel and the Third World," *Political Science Quarterly*, Vol. LXXXVII, No. 4 (December 1972). Much of the data in this section is based on Laufer's article and on Shimeon Amir, *Israel's Development Cooperation with Africa, Asia and Latin America* (London: Praeger, 1974).

Projects have ranged from instruction in livestock rearing and the setting up of veterinary services in Africa to leadership training programs for youth movements in the Caribbean. Israelis helped to set up Ghana's Black Star merchant marine and a system of water supply for the Accra district. They started an engineering faculty at Addis Ababa University and instructed Ethiopians in port maintenance, traffic engineering and tourism development. Israelis provided ophthalmic services to Liberia, planned the construction of an oil refinery in Sierra Leone, and were involved in a water resources project in the Malagasy Republic.

Israel's outlay for the programs goes almost entirely on the nuts and bolts of technical assistance—training experts, and for some support items such as seeds and tools. But Israel's relatively small monetary investment is compensated for by a consistently high standard of achievement. The requirement that local partners make a relatively heavy investment in Israeli-supported projects often generates an exceptional sense of local involvement and concern for the success of a project.

At the same time, the personal involvement of the Israeli experts seems to reflect a widely held belief that the program is an important investment of precious national resources. This may help explain the dedication with which many Israeli technical cooperation workers perform their assignments. For example, recently an Israeli farm manager in an African country journeyed to the distant capital one night to warn his ambassador that a sudden attack by pests threatened to decimate his crop within forty-eight hours. Unable to locate the necessary pesticide in the country, the ambassador telephoned Jerusalem, and a few hours later two planes were on their way, loaded with pesticide and accompanied by a plant entomologist. The crop was saved and the bonds of cooperation fortified.

But dedication, involvement and ingenuity alone do not explain the apparent attractiveness to the newly developing countries of Israeli efforts. What seems at least equally important is Israel's success in creating in a comparatively brief period of time a modern economy, a fairly well integrated society and a social system in which cooperative and socialist principles of organization and distribution play an important role.

For example, socialist-oriented Tanzania, although usually critical of Israel in international forums since the 1967 war, nevertheless asked Israel to provide a special training course in agricultural cooperation in connection with the Tanzanian drive to establish new forms of cooperative agricultural settlements—the *ujamaa* (socialist) village scheme. Israel was the only free world country to which Tanzania looked for instruction in this area; the other countries reportedly approached were the Soviet Union, Bulgaria and Yugoslavia. Similarly, in Ghana during the reign of Kwame Nkrumah, only four out of the more than one hundred state farms were entrusted to foreign advisers—two to Israeli and two to Soviet experts.

Interest in the Israeli-supported program of activities with developing countries evidently centers on Israel's agricultural and cooperative achievements. More than 40 percent of the trainees coming to Israel receive instruction in agricultural or cooperative practices, and one third of the expert assignments have been in those specialties.

At the same time as Israel's own base of science- and technology-oriented industries and institutions has continued to grow, so has her capacity to assist other nations in this area. The impetus has come from Israel's various technical and scientific institutions, spearheaded by the Weizmann Institute for Science in Rehovot, since the early 1960s.

Because Israel has been perhaps the only newborn state to have inherited the scientific revolution in full, Abba Eban, formerly Foreign Minister, saw Israel as a possible meeting place for scientists of the old world and statesmen of the new. He regarded Israel's initiatives in linking scientific progress to problems of development as "an exhortation to new states to link their future to the scientific age . . . [and] an effort to galvanize the scientific conscience into a deeper preoccupation with the problems of new struggling societies." *

In addition to the impact of this program outside Israel, it has also had a powerful effect within Israeli society. It has focused greater attention on and sensitivity to the needs of the Third World in such areas as agricultural research, arid-zone ecology, ground-water research, and the development of sister relationships

* *Ibid.*

with academic and scientific institutions in developing countries. The relatively small but important UN Development Program in Israel has furthered this idea by supporting science-related projects such as desalination and the use of brackish water, which could potentially prove useful to many low-income, resource-poor countries of the world.

Most pervasive among the characteristics of Israel's cooperation program is the emphasis on nation building and personal participation in development. This pedagogic approach flows from Israel's own labor-oriented social philosophy and institutions, especially its mass youth movements and nation-building programs. Accordingly, foreign trainees in Israel are usually exposed to manual labor and to life on a cooperative settlement, while Israeli exports abroad often succeed as much by their personal example, leadership qualities and sense of commitment as by their technical experience.

Unfortunately, this program of technical assistance to Africa has been reduced since 1973 *through no intention* on Israel's part. As a result of intense pressure from the Arab states, especially Libya, most African countries broke diplomatic relations with Israel at that time.

Although Israel maintains assistance programs in several African countries despite the absence of diplomatic relations, other governments decided to terminate the economic links as well. It is an interesting fact that 10 percent of the thousand students from abroad attending courses at educational institutions in Israel are from African countries which have broken diplomatic relations with Israel.

Many of these developing countries have in recent years experienced frustration and disillusionment with this Arab pressure. As *The Echo* of Ghana put it:

> In 1974 the Arabs were able to get member states of the OAU [Organization of African Unity] to break diplomatic relations with Israel. And what did we get in return for our support? Higher and higher oil prices. As if that was not enough, the Arabs, some of whom do not know how much they have in the banks of the Western World, sought to placate the over 40 independent African States with the paltry sum of two hundred million dollars (US) to alleviate

the harsh oil prices. What is $200 million to 40 states when the sum is not even enough to meet Ghana's crude-oil bill? *

Aside from the severe hardships suffered by most developing countries as a result of the fourfold increase in oil prices since 1973, there have been other problems associated with the Afro-Arab link. Arab economic assistance strongly favors the Islamic countries, and Libya's Qaddafi has been actively attempting to convert African leaders to Islam. Furthermore, actual disbursements have often lagged far behind pledges. For example, the Saudis have only itemized how 15 percent of the $1 billion they pledged at the recent Afro-Arab summit would be spent.

In an article in the Autumn 1976 edition of the prestigious *Middle East Journal,* two Arab scientists, Ragaei El Malakh and Mihssen Khadim, had the following to say about Arab aid to the Third World:

> The dramatic increases of oil prices in 1973 resulted in huge transfers of income and wealth from the rest of the world to the oil-exporting nations. While this process posed many serious difficulties for the industrial world, its impact on the numerous poor and populous less developed countries was devastating. These nations must contend not only with the problems arising from high energy costs, but also with insufficient export receipts and rampant world inflation.
>
> The Arab oil exporters responded to the plight of these developing countries with a plenitude of promises and commitments involving substantial transfers of capital in the form of loans, grants and investments. These promises and commitments were largely made on a bilateral basis following official visits by heads of state, thus generating much news and publicity. However, disbursements lagged far behind, creating confusion and uncertainty as to the actual level of aid.

According to the authors, the paid-up capital of the various Arab development funds, which should have reached $8.742 million, amounted to only between one third and one half of that sum in actual fact. Of the total, only 3 percent was specifically earmarked for non-Arab African countries. Whereas published disbursements, mostly to Arab and other Moslem countries,

---

* Ray Kakraba-Quarshie, in *The Echo,* Ghana (June 6, 1976).

amounted to $1.504 million, no figures were available for loans from the funds which were earmarked for African countries.

It is no wonder, therefore, that at the 1977 Arab-African summit meeting in Cairo, the African leaders insisted on substantial Arab aid. After much pressure, promises were exacted for large sums, about $1.4 billion. However, the promised funds are to be provided for an unspecified period, and their disbursement will be completely in Arab hands, thereby putting the African nations at the mercy of the Arab states and exposing them to political pressures of the crudest kind.

These promises may seem impressive, but looking at the record, one wonders how much the African countries will actually receive of the huge sums promised.

Finally, there have in recent months been some open expressions of regret as several countries have seen the effects of sending the Israeli experts home. Lacking experienced labor, some African governments tried to import workers from Bangladesh, Pakistan, Czechoslovakia and Egypt. Now, in Zambia, members of Parliament are demanding that the Minister of Agricultural Development bring back the Israelis to raise agricultural output. The representative from the Bhati district, Valentine Cafoya, said the Israelis worked wonders "helping our ignorant villagers transform their plains into farms and flower gardens." But when the Israelis left, the land returned to wilderness. Villagers are cutting valuable timber and pillaging the natural resources in order to survive.

Cafoya particularly questioned the value of Egyptian workers. "Egypt is not a land of food growers," he said. "How can they teach us farming when they import most of their own fresh food?" And John Mwanaktawey, former Finance Minister, complained that the foreign workers sit in offices, whereas the Israelis got out in the fields and showed the villagers how to farm.* More recently, on March 16, 1977, the *Times* of London carried an article on the subject under the heading "Africans Miss Israel's Expertise Despite Arab Promises of Aid."

Despite the obvious setback in Israel's relations with Africa since 1973, there are still seven African countries which quietly

* *Times of Zambia* (May 6, 1976).

welcome Israeli experts, while some others—despite the lack of diplomatic relations—are eager to send their students to Israel to participate in projects financed partially by Israel and partially by other government and intergovernmental agencies.

At the height of its good relations with Africa in the 1960s, Israel was represented in most black African states and had 1,800 technical advisers working simultaneously throughout the continent. Today only about a hundred are left, mostly accredited with international organizations. Some large Israeli concerns, such as the Histadrut labor syndicate's building firm, Solel Boneh, and its industrial complex, Koor, still operate private contracts in some African states.

Israel would welcome the restoration of educational and economic links with Africa, an association which for many years proved so productive and constructive for both sides. Meanwhile, Israel today has about 110 experts engaged in projects in twenty Latin American countries and about seventy experts in Asia, in addition to those in Africa, and continues to welcome hundreds of students from abroad to its educational institutions to learn the skills necessary to assist in developmental tasks in their own land.

So far we have discussed Israel's program of cooperation with other developing nations in terms of what has already been done and what now exists, its achievements and its setbacks. But the value of such a discussion would be limited unless we also looked into the future. In terms of Israel's past experience and achievements, what can the country contribute to its own region—the Middle East?

Let us begin by making some rather dramatic assumptions. Let us look ahead to the year 2000 and suppose that the Middle East conflict has been resolved and that Israel and its Arab neighbors are living together in peace. Let us further imagine that there has evolved a Middle East Common Market, based on principles similar to those of the European Common Market and in association with it. The Middle East Common Market, with its headquarters possibly in Beirut, would comprise a regional water and irrigation authority, a desert development authority, an oil authority, a tourist development authority, and so on. There would be free and rapid communication between Middle East centers by air and land. On an international highway Cairo would be a mere three hours from Jerusalem and just nine hours from Baghdad.

As education and development budgets exceed defense spending, the populations of the Middle East may expect improved medical services, a longer life span and a rising standard of living. The less that is spent for military purposes, the more will be available for constructive investment, which will in turn contribute to the rising standard of living.

Projections have been made for Egypt's economy under this scenario. Assuming a population of 65 million by the year 2000, and assuming that the conflict has long been resolved, Egypt's GNP could be $16 billion, or $250 per capita. If the state of war lasts until the year 2000, the GNP would probably not rise beyond $11 billion, or $170 per capita.

There are likely to be other changes in priorities also. Since all oil-producing countries in the Middle East are also desert countries, a large part of their income may be dedicated to desert development, a field in which Israel has significant expertise. Major technologies of irrigation, water desalination and desert agriculture would be developed in common, and rising agricultural yields could be expected.

Tourism would be a major Middle Eastern industry and educational exchanges would take place between universities in Damascus, Jerusalem, Cairo and other centers. Eradication of disease would be a major priority. Diseases such as eye trachoma in Egypt, which affects a large portion of the population, could be virtually eliminated. Infant mortality, currently over 20 percent in some Middle Eastern countries, could be lowered to below 1 percent, and tuberculosis could be liquidated.

Utopian? Perhaps, but any Middle Easterner who is sincere about peace has not only a right but a duty to look beyond the boundaries of the present conflict and into a more constructive future. And in this process Israel must look not only to what it can derive from peaceful coexistence with its neighbors, but to what it can contribute to the well-being of the entire region. In this connection it is perhaps relevant to mention a few examples of important advances which might play a significant role in the economic cooperation that is envisaged.

As a result of the development of a revolutionary irrigation technique and the raising of hardy, salt-resistant plant varieties, scientists at the Israeli Research and Development Authority have broken the barrier of desert farming. They now offer hope for those arid areas which constitute so large a part of the Middle East, and indeed, almost half of the earth's surface.

There are already several communities in the Negev Desert settled around fields of fruits and vegetables made possible by the use of brackish water. Israel has also improved its artificial rain-making techniques, and rainfall in the country is believed to have increased by 20 percent through employment of this technology.

But aside from increasing the supply and volume of water, the greatest advance of Israeli scientists has been in the conservation and application of water. The drip or trickle irrigation method, which is an Israeli innovation and is being widely applied in Israel, saves up to 50 percent of the water required and can also be combined with fertilizer dissolved in the water. Minute amounts of water, together with certain quantities of soluble fertilizers and chemicals, are applied directly to the soil surface close to the plant. This method has been successfully applied not only on normal land but also in the Arava Valley in the arid Negev, with saline water, which is unusable in other irrigation systems. Furthermore, the method has been tried successfully on steep hills which have never been used for agricultural purposes. In addition to its agricultural importance, brackish water is now also being used in experiments to irrigate parks and recreation areas in the desert.

Israeli researchers at the Weizmann Institute of Science have recently announced the development of a high-yield disease-resisting variety of wheat. At present Israel grows only 55 percent of its wheat requirements. When this new development is fully exploited, Israel may reach almost complete self-sufficiency in wheat production.

Research and development in the use of solar energy has been, and is, a major field of endeavor in Israel. Those who have visited Israel are probably familiar with the universal use of solar heaters, a technique which has been exported. Israel is also concentrating on several projects with respect to solar-energy utilization for agricultural and industrial purposes. These efforts are of course spurred on by the need to develop local sources for energy requirements. Our research is adapted to the peculiar requirements of the area and is linked to the very extensive development in Israel of the use of water resources, including the process of desalination of sea water. This research and development, which includes the highest degree of water control achieved by any country in the world, is directed towards turning arid deserts into green, fruitful, food-bearing soil. Significant steps are being taken in these fields.

As an act of good will without reference to political differences dividing countries in the area, the government of Israel is prepared to place at the disposal of its neighbors the benefits of its research and development in these vital fields in the form of a regional project so that the lot of man in the Middle East may be improved. Accordingly, Israel is prepared to convert the existing research center on arid zones in the Negev Desert and the various ancillary institutions of research and development in the fields of agriculture and water from a national center into a regional center which will be open to all countries in the Middle East desiring to participate and cooperate. To this end, Israel has offered the Arid Zones Research Center as her contribution to the United Nations University.

Secondly, the government of Israel continues to welcome trainees from all interested countries in all areas of development, technical and cultural, medical and other, in which Israel has achieved a certain expertise. This is a continuation of a policy which the government of Israel has pursued from the outset.

Finally, Israel has announced that it is prepared unilaterally and without reference to the political problems dividing the area, to allow the free passage of goods to its immediate neighbors, to and from the ports of Israel. This, to repeat, is an offer without strings attached and without prejudice to the ultimate solution of the political problems which beset the area.

If some would criticize these proposals as "impractical," it is important to consider what has already taken place between Israel and its neighbors. Through the "open bridges" policy on the River Jordan, an extensive flow of trade and tourist traffic is already a fact. Tens of thousands of Arab tourists from all over the

Middle East cross the River Jordan every year to visit relatives, to pray at the Holy Places in Jerusalem and to visit tourist as well as development attractions.

Extensive agricultural cooperation between Israelis and Arab farmers in the West Bank has resulted in greatly increased productivity. A study published just this year by the Carnegie Endowment for International Peace states:

> There can be no doubt that the growth rate of the West Bank and the Gaza Strip has been high. Judgments may differ about the precise figures that should be used to describe the growth performance, but in absolute terms, and compared to previous experience here and with other economies, the growth has been impressive . . .
> The Bank of Israel estimates growth of the gross national product (i.e., product including the incomes earned by Palestinians working in the Israeli economy) to have averaged 18% per annum, and per capita product to have grown at 15% per annum from 1968 to 1973.*

The benefits of this economic cooperation have not been limited to the West Bank. Israel's Ministry of Agriculture operates an extension service which trains experts and advisers in farming techniques. The turnover of extension service officers in the West Bank is known to be high for the simple reason that they are often lured by larger wages to neighboring countries as far away as the Gulf emirates. The higher wages they receive are due, at least partially, to their Israeli training. In addition, the extension service broadcasts in Arabic, and it is known that Jordanian farmers across the river listen in and learn. Whenever there is a field day devoted to a specific agricultural problem, the extension service faces a demand for large quantities of written material in Arabic, some of which finds its way to neighboring countries.

But the greatest advance in cooperation has undoubtedly been in the field of medicine. Soon after gaining independence in 1948, many Arabs from neighboring countries quietly appeared in Israeli hospitals seeking medical attention—for eye care and gynecological treatment in particular. Since eye disease was a serious

---

* Brian van Arkadie, *Benefits and Burdens: A Report on the West Bank and Gaza Strip Economies Since 1967* (New York, Carnegie Endowment for International Peace, 1977).

problem in the region, Israel quickly became known throughout the Middle East for its medical expertise. Within a decade Israel had virtually eliminated eye disease within its borders and continued to draw patients from neighboring countries. Today hundreds of patients from all over the Middle East receive treatment at Jerusalem's Hadassah Hospital for a wide range of illnesses.

Even beyond the Middle East, medical know-how has become a vital Israeli export. Indeed, the term "world health" means precious little if not the mutual responsibility of nations to share resources to help the sick who might otherwise not be treated. Since 1958, Israel has had no fewer than 551 medical programs operating in 25 countries, serving within the framework of the World Health Organization.

One of the most successful innovations in medical cooperation within our own region has been a weekly radio program on Dar el-Izaa el-Israiliyya, Israel's Arabic broadcasting station. The program, called *Doctor Behind the Microphone*, usually features specialists from the Hadassah Hospital answering questions to letters from throughout the Middle East. Whenever possible, Arabic-speaking doctors appear; otherwise, the specialist's reply is translated from Hebrew. In many cases the service does not stop with the broadcast of medical information. It is often the first step in arranging a visit to an Israeli medical facility, a process which is not difficult if the prospective patient has relatives in Israel or in the administered areas.

The examples given above have not made headlines in an international press which inevitably prefers to focus on tension and conflict. And in truth, it must be confessed that this economic and medical cooperation is no more than a drop in the bucket compared to what could be achieved if real peace existed. The opening of the "good fence" with Lebanon, where Lebanese citizens received medical attention, food supplies and basic commodities from Israel at a time when a brutal civil war was ravaging their country, is another small example of the cooperation which could exist between Israel and its neighbors. As Chairman Mao Tse-tung once wrote: "An advance of a thousand miles begins with one step." That step has been taken, if we only knew where to go from there.

On May 11, 1976, in Brussels, Israel entered into an agreement for the establishment of a free trade area with the European Economic Community. On that historic occasion Yigal Allon, Israel's Foreign Minister at the time, expressed his prayer that "this agreement will not only create a free trade area for industrial goods, and facilitate the export of our agricultural products. It will also have great political importance.

"Europe is paving the way to a new kind of cooperation which, we believe, may provide a model for regional cooperation in our area. It may seem utopian today, but we are sure that the day will come when the states of the Middle East will live in peace, will trade freely with each other and exchange their knowledge and technology for the mutual advantage of all their populations. In the Middle East, as elsewhere, economic integration could well be an important element of peaceful coexistence. The government of Israel believes that the best interests of our area will be served by the creation in the Middle East of regional economic integration."

A word of caution: the developments I have spoken about and projected for the future are all feasible—but they are not inevitable. If all thinking citizens of the Middle East were to sit down and wait for the developments to occur, then nothing would happen. In the words of a popular Israeli song: "We cannot wait for the day to come; we must bring the day."

Those countries whose central effort remains tied to power and destruction, rather than the amelioration of the human condition, will find themselves increasingly lagging behind. Instead of belonging to the vanguard of human venture, they will belong to the desperate rear guard, clinging to the past. Their world, thirty years hence, will not be a much better world, and the human condition in their countries will remain miserable.

There is only one rational alternative: to rise above the conflicts of daily life, to put aside the divisions and differences which beset our world, and to unite to find solutions for the common man, woman and child who are all too frequently ignored in the heat of political debates and in the rarefied atmosphere of international conferences.

We must stir the conscience of man and reawaken his desire

to help his fellows, in the spirit of the ancient Prophets of Israel who gave the world the concept of the fatherhood of God and the brotherhood of man. We, the peoples of the Middle East, the area which gave birth to the great ideals of mankind, can surely apply those ideals to our own future.

# III

# Israel
# on the
# International
# Scene

# 10

# Israel and the United Nations

ONE of the cornerstones of Judaism is justice. It was God's foremost commandment to man that he should do justice and deal justly with his fellow-men. *Tzedek tzedek tirdof*—"Ye shall pursue justice"—is one of the most insistent exhortations in the Bible. According to the Talmud, the conscientious judge who does justice is God's partner in the creation of the world, for justice is the foundation and bulwark of the universe. Doing justice, it was written, is tantamount to bringing truth, love and peace into the world. On this basis, the Jewish people have given to the world one of the most enlightened codes of law in history, a legal system which, above all else, recognizes the special reciprocal tie between law and morality.

The fundamental principle of procedural justice is equality.

"What is justice in the process of law" asks Maimonides, and replies "It is the equalisation of both parties for all purposes; not that one should be allowed to speak as he pleases and the other cut short; not that one be treated with courtesy and the other with irritation . . . not that one should stand and the other be seated, or that one should sit above and the other below, but both should stand or sit next to each other . . . you may not hear one party in the absence of the other: not only may you not make a decision without having heard 'the other party' first, but you must hear both parties in the presence and hearing of each other." *

Incidentally, this latter injunction is an innovation peculiar to Jewish law. Thus our sages, echoing the Bible, the Prophets and the Psalmists, never tire of accentuating the paramount importance of the right administration of justice, which they regard as one of the three pillars supporting the entire edifice of civilized society. *Al shlosha de'varim ha'olam kayam: al ha'din, al ha'emet v'al ha'shalom*—"The world exists on three principles: justice, truth and peace."

How tragic it is, therefore, to contemplate the systematic destruction of this pillar of justice in world society, threatening as this process does the inexorable collapse of civilized society. Daily, principles which we consider to be self-understood and sacred to our way of life are being betrayed and trampled underfoot in derision and disdain at the United Nations. Nothing could better illustrate this process than a meeting of the Security Council convened in March 1976 to consider a complaint brought against Israel by Pakistan and Libya. A group of Jews had attempted to pray on the Temple Mount in defiance of a Government of Israel Order and in contravention, incidentally, of rabbinical law. (An Israeli Supreme Court decision had upheld the government's order forbidding Jewish prayer on that site.) They were arrested by the Moslem police on the Temple Mount and arraigned before an Israeli magistrate for having caused public disorder under the Criminal Code Ordinance. The magistrate held that it was not a case of public disorder under the ordinance. The government appealed the decision in an effort to protect Moslem interests, and that case was *sub judice* in the courts of Israel at the time of the Security Council meeting. Despite these facts, a flagrant attempt was made at the United Nations to incite Moslem religious hatred against the Jewish people for political reasons.

Even leaving aside the motivations of the accusers, one assumes that under the principles of natural justice the party which is charged will be given a fair hearing in an atmosphere of impartiality. The Security Council would thus be expected to hear the ac-

* Maimonides, *Hilkhot Sonhedrin*, Cap 21 (a) (b) (c).

cusations, listen to Israel's reply, deliberate and then decide. In actual fact, the idea of an impartial hearing was replaced by the notion that United Nations organs are both prosecutor and judge. The charge was framed and judgment was formulated before I had the opportunity of presenting Israel's case. Even before I spoke, a draft resolution prejudging the issue was being discussed by Security Council members who were well aware that the entire allegation was a lie. To prepare a judgment before both sides have been heard is a travesty of the basic principles of justice, which Israel judges were dispensing in Jerusalem when most of the states in the United Nations today were but primitive societies. Indeed, it is precisely those who have totally abandoned the principles given by the Jewish people to the world in their national and international practice who now would sit in judgment on Israel. *Oy lo lador she shofet et shoftav*—"Damned is the generation that sits in judgment of its judges," said our sages. Damned is a world that must sit in judgment of those who would seek to pass judgment.

Such procedures have become commonplace in what is truly an Alice in Wonderland situation: "Let the jury consider their verdict," the King said. . . . "No, no," said the Queen of Hearts, "sentence first, verdict afterwards." Had Lewis Carroll lived today, he would not have been obliged to create a wonderland to house the incongruous. He need not have done more than let Alice loose in the UN Building. She would only have had to wear a Star of David in order to hear the imperious "Off with her head" at every turn. This process is even more alarming when those who consider the principles of natural law to be sacred in their own societies nevertheless allow expediency to subvert morality in their international relations and acquiesce in a process which negates all that they uphold. Had the Security Council on that occasion acted as an impartial judiciary, it would undoubtedly have condemned those who had proffered a false charge for a flagrant act of racial and religious incitement calculated to inflame passions and disturb the peace. Instead we were witness once again to the casual violation of the norms of natural law, a process which is rapidly destroying the original concept of the United Nations.

The Talmud maintained that *Kol dayan sheayno dan din emet, emet la'amito, gorem la'schina shetistalek mi-Yisrael*—"A judge who judges not truly makes the Divine Presence depart from Israel."

In contemplating what is happening in the United Nations, with its bias, one-sidedness and injustice, we may today say that the Divine Presence is departing from the world as it sinks back into the Middle Ages. This process is all the more fearsome because of the twin advance of barbaric immorality and modern technology.

There is barely an organ or forum of the United Nations that has not succumbed to this dangerous and abhorrent process. The Economic Commission for Western Asia excludes Israel but seats the PLO, in direct contravention of its own charter, which permits only membership by states. The Human Rights Commission meets in Geneva to condemn Israel for "war crimes" but refuses to discuss the mass slaughter of civilians in Uganda, while those voting to condemn Israel themselves daily commit the most heinous crimes against their own citizens. In the Security Council, charged with maintaining international peace and security, Libya —the primary sponsor and financer of international terrorism— presides solemnly over meetings. The PLO takes credit for a dastardly bomb explosion in Jerusalem and then cites General Assembly Resolution 3236 as the legitimization of its activities,* to which the UN responds by inviting the representative of that criminal organization to sit at the Security Council table.

These events are now a daily occurrence in the United Nations. Every time that a United Nations body has voted to establish a commission of inquiry to examine some allegation against Israel, the resolution appointing the body has condemned Israel in advance, has prejudged the issue, has set out the allegations preferred against Israel as proven facts and has then proceeded blithely to appoint a committee to examine the facts and verify the conditions. Invariably the composition of the committee itself is openly biased. The so-called Committee for the Exercise of the Inalienable Rights of the Palestinian People, for example, includes

* Resolution 3236 (XXIX) of November 22, 1974, in effect reiterates the PLO program for the destruction of Israel. Yassir Arafat said of Resolution 3236: "This resolution comprises the liquidation of Zionist existence" (quoted in the Lebanese newspaper *al-Balagh*, January 5, 1975).

nineteen countries which have no diplomatic relations with Israel, and only four that do (Rumania, Malta, Cyprus and Turkey). The fact that the entire Western world refused to participate in its deliberations, and that not one country which maintains diplomatic relations with Israel agreed to appear before it, did not deter this committee. It prepared a report, with the active assistance of the PLO, which called in effect for the dismemberment of Israel. When the Security Council did not accept the report, it was brought before the General Assembly, which accepted it.

Until comparatively recently, it was possible to claim that at least the specialized agencies, such as WHO, ILO, FAO and UNESCO,* vindicated the existence of the United Nations even if the General Assembly did not. However, the extremist Arab states could not rest easy until they had subordinated every institution to their narrow aims, and we have witnessed the diversion of the specialized agencies from their original purposes of health, education and labor, and their conversion into political arenas by the introduction of irrelevant anti-Israel resolutions. The absurdity of this process was demonstrated in 1976 at the UN Conference on Water Resources, an area in which Israel is one of the most advanced countries in the world. Once again the Arab states turned the conference into a political forum by introducing the inevitable resolutions condemning Israel, despite the fact that Israel is currently assisting many countries on several continents in the very field which the conference was supposed to be discussing.

But perhaps the classic example of the disappearance of natural law as a basis for the deliberations of the UN occurred in 1976 in Geneva at the World Health Organization. Having condemned Israel in advance on the state of health administration in the administered territories, WHO then proceeded to appoint a committee of inquiry of three delegates, two of whom represented governments that maintain no diplomatic relations with Israel. This fact notwithstanding, Israel agreed to the visit of the delegates of these countries to Israel and the administered territories to make their inquiries. After their visit, the members of the

---

* World Health Organization, International Labor Organization, the Food and Agriculture Organization, and United Nations Educational, Scientific and Cultural Organization.

committee were left without any alternative but to note that "medical care in the Arab territories occupied by Israel has shown slow but steady improvement in the nine years since the 1967 war."

WHO then constituted itself as a kangaroo court when by a 65–18 vote with 14 abstentions, it refused to consider the committee's report. India put forward the motion to reject the report on behalf of the Arab nations and a group of other nations. Furthermore, even before the Indian motion was voted upon, discussion of the committee's findings was blocked by a majority vote. Indeed, in solidarity with the proponents of this abhorrent vote, Rumania, Indonesia and Senegal disowned the position of the experts they themselves had appointed by voting against the receivability of their report.

One's mind boggles at the degree of cynicism reflected in this decision. After all, we are talking about one of the most highly advanced countries in the world in medicine, despite its size. We are talking about a country which has done more proportionally than any other country in the world to help underdeveloped countries within the framework of WHO. We are talking about a country to which thousands from all over the Middle East, Arab and non-Arab, leaders and common people, come every month to receive medical assistance, which is given freely without any consideration of the political situation in the area. We are talking about the administered territories, in which the population enjoys health services today, thanks to Israel, that are superior to any available in any Arab country in the world today. All this while the countries which comprise the automatic majority at the UN vote to condemn a standard of health administration in Israel and the administered territories which is a remote utopia in their far-off dreams as far as their home countries are concerned. But of course they will condemn, because the resolution appointing the committee of inquiry has already condemned.

The same happened at UNESCO. A distinguished Belgian professor was instructed to examine the archaeological excavations in Jerusalem to see if the digs were damaging ancient Holy Places. He returned with a report which did not substantiate the allegations. Accordingly, the Security Council voted by a majority not to hear his report and then proceeded to condemn Israel for transgressions which were proved by its own commissioned report to be false.

This perversion of justice was taken to its absurdist extremes during the session of the 31st General Assembly in 1976, when the Special Political Committee debated about the territories. The issue at stake was stark in its simplicity. Syria requested to show a film to the committee. Israel requested to do likewise. Predictably, the Arab group along with its customary supporters rose and objected to the screening of Israel's film—for fear that it would reveal just a glimpse of the true situation in the territories which Israel administers. These objections sparked off what can only be described as a surrealistic performance: two days of serious deliberations were devoted to the problem of whether the committee should see one or two films. In between, an adjournment was moved to allow time for consultations, and, no doubt, reference to governments for guidance on how their delegations should proceed. Finally, a decision was adopted by 66 votes to 23 with 16 abstentions, preventing Israel from showing its film, but, of course, allowing Syria to do so.

In flagrant violation of Article 2(1) of the UN Charter, which stipulates that the United Nations "is based on the principle of sovereign equality of all its members," Arab political warfare is now apparently aimed at preventing Israel from even expressing its views and, correspondingly, from stopping other member states from hearing the facts and exercising their fundamental right to judge matters for themselves.

The tyranny of the automatic majority not only manifests itself in debates but has come to permeate the very structure of the United Nations itself. One of the most disturbing developments has been the enrollment of incompetent public servants as a result of political and regional pressures exercised on the Secretary-General. As a result, certain countries are now significantly over-represented in the Secretariat, which is supposed to recruit its staff according to a "desirable range" quota for each country. Thus, while Algeria's quota, for example, ranges from 3 to 7 persons, it has in fact 14 staff members in the UN, one of them even as an Under-Secretary-General. Egypt, to take another example, is represented by 25 staff members, also with an Under-

Secretary-General, while its quota range is between 3 and 8, or less than that of Israel. Iraq, with a quota range of 4 to 9 has 16 high-ranking members on the Secretariat staff. Syria has 14 members in the Secretariat, while its range is 2 to 7. Lebanon, a country which seemingly would be in dire need of its good people at home, has 20 staff members at the United Nations, while its range is 3 to 8. Compared with this, needless to say, Israel with a quota range of 6 to 11, has only 7 employees on the staff of the United Nations—all of them in low grades.

In other words, if you add to this sinister development in UN staffing what is happening in the staff recruitment from Communist and so-called nonaligned countries (i.e., not allied with any other nations), you will discover that the Western countries, with the United States in the lead, are financing the creation of an international civil service, the majority of which is hostile in its outlook and philosophy to the principles which animate Western democracy—the principles of the freedom of man, and of man's equality before the law.

In this connection it is of interest to note to what extent these overrepresented countries contribute to the budget of the United Nations. According to the 1978–1979 scale of assessments, Algeria will pay 0.10 percent of the United Nations budget. Egypt and Iraq will each pay just 0.08 percent. Syria is not ashamed to contribute 0.02 percent to the budget, while 13 of its nationals are employed at high-ranking levels. Saudi Arabia, with a surplus of $17 billion per annum in its national budget, will contribute 0.23 percent, the same amount as Israel, which has a deficit of $3½ billion.

The United States, incidentally, pays 25 percent of the general budget of the United Nations, while all the Arab members of OPEC (Organization of Petroleum Exporting Countries) together pay slightly over 1 percent. Israel, in comparison, with 7 staff members, pays 0.23 percent of the budget, or one quarter of the sum paid by the Arab oil exporters. If political and regional pressures are to continue to dictate the composition of this body, how can we expect efficiency, competence, devotion and dedication in the United Nations?

The writing is already on the wall, and the warning signs are unmistakable. The capabilities and the international character of the world organization are being downgraded and replaced by narrow national and political vested interests far removed from the lofty concepts which animated the founders of the United Nations. The practical effects of this development in day-to-day life in the UN are not far to follow. A senior official in the UN Secretariat was horrified recently to hear from a very senior Arab official that his dream is to witness the disappearance of Israel. A senior Algerian official threatened a Jewish employee with dismissal for failing to applaud Idi Amin when he called in the General Assembly for the extinction of Israel. The Algerian was reprimanded by a European superior who overheard the exchange. A recent candidate for employment described to me how in her interview she was regaled with a long anti-Israel tirade in order to draw her out and discover if she had pro-Israel sympathies or not.

The lack of equilibrium between Israel and the Arab states in the United Nations has been reflected not only in votes and political pressures but in the very composition of the decision-making bodies. The bloc system permeates every facet of life within the organization, ensuring representation to members of the African group, to the Latins, Arabs, Europeans, East Europeans, and so on. But since Israel belongs to no bloc or grouping of nations, it is impossible for it to be proposed for nomination to any UN body, committee or council. As a result, Israel has failed to get elected even once to any of the three major councils: the Security Council, the Economic and Social Council, and the Trusteeship Council. Israel accordingly raised in the General Assembly a proposal whereby appointments to UN bodies should be on an impartial alphabetical rotational basis and not on a partial bloc system. But to no avail.

The unjust situation will undoubtedly continue as long as the present voting system goes on pretending as it does to be a form of democracy. The vast majority of those playing the democratic game at the UN represent tyrannies, dictatorships and one-party systems with no experience of democracy at home. Furthermore, few countries vote as their conscience dictates for they are all frequently bound against their better instincts by the bloc to which they belong. This system encourages "deals" between blocs which bear no relation whatsoever to the merits of the issue under discussion. A voting system like that of a Parliament is good when those voting have a responsibility to more than the party to which they belong, and when the majority has a responsibility to the minority. Thus, for instance, a member of Parliament has a responsibility when he votes not only to Parliament but to his country, a responsibility which frequently is much more powerful than that to his party. In the United Nations this dual responsibility does not exist, for few countries really care what happens to the United Nations as long as they pursue their selfish interests.

If the United Nations, as many propose, abandons the voting system and turns towards a system based on consultations and attempts to reach consensus, a practice often used in the Security Council, then perhaps an important advance can be made. Without the one-upmanship and competition inherent in the voting process, delegates may well direct themselves to the specific problems and not to proving that their bloc is stronger than the other. Be that as it may, and whatever the solution may be, the United Nations system requires an overhauling before it degenerates into an instrument of the extreme despotisms. If the free and independent-thinking countries in the world do not arrest this process, the United Nations will surely fade from the world as did the League of Nations, yet another lost opportunity of history.

Many decent people, aware of the hypocritical charade that unfolds daily at the United Nations, tend nowadays to raise their hands in a gesture of hopelessness. But it is not enough to do so, for, as we discovered during the Yom Kippur War, it is an error and a weakness to underestimate our adversaries. For too long we in Israel have tended to shrug off the United Nations as a hostile body instead of analyzing it, understanding it and attempting to find even a partial solution to dealing with it. The time has come to ask how and why this distressing perversion of a noble ideal took place.

Not a few observers, jolted by theater-of-the-absurd scenes at the United Nations, tend to put the blame on the profound metamorphosis which the UN had undergone in recent years. It is popularly believed that the United Nations, which in the olden days was composed of serious and dignified statesmen, has now been taken over by a group of irresponsible second-raters who have brought this august organization to the brink. But this is not so. Admittedly, the United Nations of 1975 has very little in common with the United Nations envisaged in 1945. The 51 founding members are now a distinct minority in the total of 149 states. In 1945 Europeans and Americans set the tone. Today the Afro-Asians prevail. Mini-states can today outvote rich and populous countries. One hundred million Arabs have 22 votes; the 200 million people of the United States have one vote. The vote of the Maldive Islands is equivalent to that of India. But these incongruities do not in themselves explain what has happened for they ignore the time span of the process of deterioration. As a brief chronology will illustrate, Israel has never fared well at the United Nations except for an initial and brief period of grace extending from 1947 to 1952.*

The United Nations came into being following a world war which decimated the populations of many countries, and a holocaust in which the Jewish people were singled out for destruction. Created initially as an anti-Nazi alliance, the organization was conceived of a desire to create a better society for all mankind, based upon the lofty principles of universal peace and the brotherhood of man. The words of Isaiah to this day grace the marble wall facing the United Nations, an acknowledgment that the founding principles of the world organization were those which the Jewish Prophets gave to the world. It was in this atmosphere of hope and promise that the General Assembly, on November 29, 1947, passed the Partition Resolution dividing the Land of Israel into a Jewish state and an Arab state

But here already begins the first major misconception, as expressed by those who contend that the Jewish state was "created" by the United Nations. The fact is that Israel was created nearly four thousand years ago and was expounding the great moral values of the Bible millennia before the United Nations existed. All the modern history which brought about the State of Israel has little or no validity without the religious and historic basis which has guided the Jewish people through the centuries.

All the United Nations did in 1947 was to reaffirm the debt of the world, and of history, to the Jewish people. Within the con-

* Elements of the historical analysis which follows were first presented by Professor Yaram Dinstein in an address to the Israel–UN Association in 1974.

text of modern Zionist history, the Partition Resolution became merely one important link in the chain of events that brought the State of Israel into being. Even then, Israel acquired its sovereignty not from a technical motion in Flushing Meadow, but from an ordeal in battle in Palestine. The scales of statehood were tipped finally by the sword, and Israel emerged as a sovereign state from the throes of its war of independence. Still, had it not been for the UN Partition Resolution, the scenario which ended in statehood would not have unfolded in quite the same way. In 1947, Jews everywhere were hanging on the lips of the General Assembly and had an almost preternatural faith in the UN as a *deus ex machina*. These emotions of deference and devotion did not last long, but were gradually replaced by disenchantment, disapproval, distrust and finally defiance.

The disenchantment started as early as 1948, when it became clear that the United Nations collective security system was not functioning, and that it was left to the newly emergent state of Israel to defend itself as best it could against the combined onslaught of Arab armies. Disapproval commenced in the 1950s. While Israel was subjected to constant attacks by Arab marauders, the UN showed remarkable indifference to the bloodshed and concerned itself exclusively with Israeli reprisal actions. Distrust came with the withdrawal of the United Nations Emergency Force on the eve of the Six-Day War in 1967, at the end of a decade of relative tranquillity and at the very moment when the services of the force were most needed. Israel learned that it had been lulled into a sense of false security by the presence of the force. Defiance followed the Six-Day War, when a spate of undisguised anti-Israel resolutions came pouring from the United Nations. Such resolutions have practically become the cutting edge of the sword of Arab propaganda, and since 1967, Israel has viewed the organization with mounting hostility.

In 1974 the world organization sank to its lowest depths yet. But those who witnessed the bizarre spectacle of Arafat sermonizing to the General Assembly were so taken aback that they largely failed to realize that this outrage was the culmination of a long process. They hardly expected therefore to see the United Nations, a year later, sink lower yet in the resolution equating Zionism with racism.

We live in an era of irresponsibility, an era when Western society, which used to pride itself on its forthright approach to
ethical issues, has grown accustomed to negotiating seriously with
assassins and bowing hastily to the demands of blackmailers.
Nevertheless, when Yassir Arafat—Mr. Terrorism in person—was
received with adulation by the General Assembly of the United Nations in 1974, the ripples of public astonishment threatened for a
while to grow into a tidal wave. After all, there are gradations in
humiliation. To submit meekly to the ultimatum of a blackguard
is one thing, but to treat Arafat with the veneration due a right-
eous man can only be regarded with revulsion. Nowhere was this
revulsion stronger than in Israel. The adoration of Arafat was a
collective slap in the face to the state which he has vowed to
wipe off the map. In a long love-hate relationship between Israel
and the UN—typically characterized by feelings of aversion and
fixation, admiration and hostility—this was perhaps the most
striking perversion since 1947. Indeed, in many respects, the 1974
session of the General Assembly was the reverse of the historic
1947 session.

But new depths were reached the following year with the
resolution equating Zionism with racism. Few resolutions have
created so much discord in the United Nations and have contributed in such a degree to turning the General Assembly into an
object of derision, into an organization which is not to be taken
seriously. This is the Arab contribution to the world organization,
and regretfully, the damage will not be undone. One can but view
these proceedings as a tragedy in which the United Nations is in-
exorably dragged down against its will to the basest levels of
human dissension, intransigent hate and unbridled vituperation.
Indeed, the Zionism resolution represented the first major international anti-Semitic attack on Jewry since the days of Hitler.
It was a head-on attack on Zionism, Judaism, on our religion,
on our faith, on our beliefs. It was the first time that the United
Nations had discussed ideals, a belief, a philosophy, a faith, and
it is no accident in the light of the virulent anti-Semitic attacks
which are apparent everywhere today that the first attack of this
nature was directed against the Jewish people.

Even before the Zionism resolution, serious moves were afoot
to oust or suspend Israel from the United Nations. These moves

were designed to sabotage the process of negotiation and peace and to move the Middle East back into a state of war. They would ultimately have destroyed the United Nations, as they had already undermined UNESCO (the UN Educational, Scientific and Cultural Organization) and ILO (the International Labor Organization). Had Israel been suspended from the General Assembly, then in the final analysis there would be no General Assembly. These consequences were recognized by the African countries meeting in 1975 in Kampala at that time and by the nonaligned nations meeting in Lima that year, many of whom rejected the Arab attempt to dictate to them. The United States, Western Europe and most of Latin America acted forthrightly to abort that vicious move. If Israel had been ousted from the UN, it would have had no choice but to suspend all UN activities in Israel, including the peacekeeping forces—UNEF in Sinai, UNDOF in the Golan, and UNTSO, as well as UNRWA and the UN headquarters in Jerusalem, to mention but a few.* In other words, an entire structure designed to create a basis for negotiation and peace would have collapsed with the resultant serious consequences.

It would be a mistake even now to underestimate the strength of the dangerous lunatic fringe in the international community which attempted the move to suspend Israel. In the final analysis, the world organization today must still decide whether its moral basis will be that of the middle Ages as represented by Muammar Qaddafi or Idi Amin, who continue to urge our dismissal. The issue is not Israel. The issue is the United Nations.

If the last four years at the United Nations prove anything, it is that our enemies do not distinguish in any way between Israel and the Jewish people. Despite their labored attempts to attack only Zionism, they daily engage in the vilest anti-Semitic attacks. It is no exaggeration to say that the resolution on Zionism converted the United Nations into the main center of anti-Semitism in the world today. Because of the sense of relief at the failure of the extremists to suspend Israel from the United Nations, the Jewish people must not lose sight of the very serious nature of the resolutions which are still being passed continuously at the United

---

* UNEF = United Nations Emergency Force. UNDOF = United Nations Disengagement Observer Force. UNTSO = United Nations Truce Supervision Organization. UNRWA = United Nations Relief and Works Agency.

Nations. These resolutions, which were drafted by the PLO and the Arab states, recall from the shadows of the past the racist vituperations of *Der Stürmer* in Nazi Germany. The violent anti-Semitic tone which has been injected into these resolutions is gradually joining the automatic slogans of vilification and hate which have become part of the international political vocabulary in the Soviet and so-called nonaligned world. On some days, at least ten resolutions decry Israel, revealing to what an intense and dangerous degree the condemnation of Israel has become an idiom of international life. The tragedy is that many of the countries adhering to these resolutions do not really agree with them; their representatives say so privately, but do nothing about it.

If we look back over this long process of deterioration in the UN, we will see that its major cause has been Great Power rivalry. At the outset, in 1947, Israel was the beneficiary of a rare overlap of interests between the United States and the USSR. Three or four years after its independence the situation changed radically. The USSR reached the conclusion that a political investment in the Arab countries would pay handsome strategic dividends, and it went all out in supporting the Arabs against Israel in every UN body in addition to the Security Council. It was nothing new for the Soviet Union to treat a small country with hostility, but the problem for Israel was compounded by its inability to counterbalance Moscow's ill will with the active assistance of the Western bloc. The Soviets established a full-fledged partnership with the Arabs, while Western support for Israel was always based on the principle of limited liability. Unlike the Arabs, Israel could not rely as a matter of course on the exercise of a vote or a veto in its favor. In the fifties, Western countries, primarily the United States, could, but would not support Israel to the hilt. In the seventies the United States perhaps would have liked to but all too often could not extend meaningful help to Israel. This was due not so much to actual Afro-Asian power as to the American loss of interest which occurred over the years in the United Nations. Frequently the Afro-Asians and the Soviets simply filled a vacuum deliberately left by the United States.

The American policy of disengagement and its abdication of leadership in the late sixties and early seventies not only had a very unfortunate impact on the UN but was bad for Israel as well.

The United States may have lost interest in the United Nations, but the UN had not lost interest in Israel. In the past the UN has devoted more time and energy, meetings and discussions to the Middle East than to any other conflict area in the world, and there is every reason to believe that this interest will not flag in the foreseeable future. For a Great Power, the United Nations at its worst is not much more than a nuisance. But for a small and embattled country such as Israel, it can become a major headache. UN mediators and conciliation committees, troops and observers —not to mention refugee agencies and special missions—have traditionally played important political roles in the Middle East, for better or worse. In all likelihood Israel will continue to feel the UN presence in the Middle East for some time to come. Israel has no choice but to regard the world organization as an important arena.

It is encouraging, therefore, to note an apparent major re-evaluation of the U.S. position at the United Nations, a change which has been marked recently by a renewed assertion of its leadership role. This policy change appears to date from the un-equivocal American stands on Puerto Rico and on the possible suspension of Israel in 1975. It was reflected in Ambassador Daniel P. Moynihan's forthright reaction to the antics of Idi Amin in the General Assembly and in the magnificent stand of the United States on the Zionism issue. Ambassador Moynihan's successors, William Scranton and Andrew Young, have both maintained this leadership role—a policy that has already yielded important results as far as Israel is concerned—but it is too early to predict whether the steady decline of the United Nations has been arrested.

Finally, we must look at the tragic way the United Nations has dealt with the whole problem of the Middle East. Its international implications are terrifying and sinister, for the very purpose of the world organization should have been to encourage negotiations, and to strive for consensus and compromise—the only way the problem of the Middle East could be resolved. Instead, the United Nations, by allowing itself to be dominated by a group of in-transigent extremists whose declared purpose is to fight against any move towards peace, has encouraged dissent instead of accord, intransigence instead of compromise, fanaticism instead of accommodation, and conflict instead of peace.

The Israelis have learned that it is unrealistic for a small nation to place its hopes in the United Nations to solve a major conflict. At best the world organization is nothing more than a conscience tranquilizer for perplexed statesmen and world leaders when facing seemingly insoluble problems. The United Nations, in our experience, achieves results when the two world superpowers agree on any specific issue, although their common conclusion is not necessarily a good one, as we learned to our sorrow after the 1956 Sinai campaign. When they disagree, as is usually the case, the UN is impotent and the resolution of international problems remains a bilateral issue rather than a multilateral one. Frequently the parties to a bilateral dispute will, for face-saving reasons, clothe the issue in a multilateral cloak. This is not only true of the United Nations, for we have seen the same happening in Africa despite the Organization of African Unity, and in Lebanon despite the Arab League. The fragility and the ineffectiveness of these multilateral political organizations are partially compensated for by the relative success of economic associations and unions such as the European Economic Community, indicating perhaps that regional economic bonds are a more reliable guarantor of stability than their political counterparts.

The one conclusion that emerges from an evaluation of the scene at the UN today is that neither a common origin, common color, common religion nor a common political philosophy guarantees peaceful relations. The confrontations in debates at the UN reflect the bitter cruelty of the struggle of Arab against Arab, the inherent hatred between, on the one hand, the Chinese-led and, on the other hand, the Soviet-Cuban Marxist blocs, and the unrelenting hostility between the various African groupings, to quote but a few examples. In short, while I would have wished to re-echo here the words of Isaiah about world peace, I must say that my period of multilateral experience at the United Nations has somewhat disenchanted me. This is not to say that the UN can never play a positive role, for once a bilateral process of negotiation has solved a particular dispute or achieved a consensus, there could be room for such international participation.

The peacekeeping forces in Sinai and the Golan Heights, UNEF and UNDOF, are two such examples, following, as they did, bilateral agreements between Israel and Egypt and between Israel and Syria. In the present circumstances, however, the function of such activities must necessarily be limited to implementation and not to negotiation.

It is no exaggeration to say that the Communists and Arabs are gradually turning the United Nations into a weapon which will be a danger to democracy everywhere. Ironically, the United Nations is still being financed largely by the free world while it is being increasingly run by the most extreme despotisms, whose primary aim is to use the organization as an instrument against the free world. It is time that the civilized world awoke to the fact that it is gradually becoming an integral part of a dangerous and abhorrent process which is destroying the original concept of the United Nations. I know that there are enlightened free countries which are dismayed and ashamed by what is going on, but until they have the moral courage to stand up and speak out, they are as guilty as those who participate in the crime.

# 11

# Racism,
# Human Rights and
# Double Standards

THE basic tenets of Judaism are irreconcilable with any form of racism and racial discrimination. The Jews are themselves a multiracial people of all colors and backgrounds, whose religion can be freely adopted by all, regardless of race, color and sex. Indeed, the Jewish people's opposition to racism is enshrined in the Bible, which teaches that "God created man in his own image," * a dictum that applies to all people of all races. The Book of Exodus unambiguously rejects a system whose legal code does not apply equally to all citizens: "One law shall be to him that is homeborn, and unto the stranger that sojourneth among you." † And the Book of Leviticus states clearly that freedom is indivisible: "And ye shall . . . proclaim liberty throughout all the land unto all the inhabitants thereof," ‡ a proclamation engraved on the Liberty Bell of the United States.

But the traditional Jewish support for the struggle against racism stems not merely from a deep-rooted abhorrence of the very notion of discrimination based on race, color or creed, but also from

* Gen. 1:27.
† Exod. 12:49.
‡ Lev. 25:10.

the fact that for centuries the Jewish people have been the classic victims of racial discrimination. Our ancient history began with slavery and the yearning for freedom. During the Middle Ages, Jews lived for hundreds of years in ghettos, subject to an unending succession of pogroms, expulsions and suffering from the most ruthless persecution and oppression. Only a generation ago we lost one third of our people, including a million children, murdered by the most brutal racist regime in human history—the Jewishness of our dead constituted their only crime.

It is therefore not mere sympathy and compassion for the modern-day victims of racism which motivates us, but rather a complete identification and solidarity born of our own painful historic experience. Jewish communities throughout the world have transformed the determination to end racial discrimination into action. In the United Kingdom, for example, the Board of Deputies of British Jews, organized in 1760, has assumed a leading role in fighting racism in that country. Since the 1930s the board, which is the official organization and voice of 400,000 British Jews, has been lobbying actively and consistently for legislation to outlaw racial discrimination and to prevent incitement to racial hatred. When the British government passed the Race Relations acts of 1965 and 1968, the Board of Deputies wrote to the Home Secretary welcoming "legislation which would have the effect of preventing discrimination against members of any group irrespective of race, creed or colour" and expressed in its annual report the hope that now "all minority groups will be free from the calumnies put out by fascist and racialist groups."

In the United States, Jews and Jewish organizations were in the forefront of the struggle for civil rights. Jews marched, organized, demonstrated and raised funds, and in Mississippi, young Jewish activists died alongside their black brothers in the fight for justice. In the words of Vernon Jordan, director of the National Urban League, the Jewish community "stood with us in the darkest days of oppression and marched by our side in the brightest days of the common struggle." * The Reverend Martin Luther King, Jr., wrote that "Jews have identified with Negroes voluntarily in

---

* Speech to the Annual Meeting of the Atlanta Chapter of the American Jewish Committee, Atlanta, Georgia, June 2, 1974.

the freedom movement, motivated by their religious and cultural commitment to justice . . ." \* Dr. King, Nobel Peace Prize-winner and one of the greatest symbols of the fight against racism in this century, knew full well that racism is indivisible and he vigorously denounced anti-Semitism, warning some months before his death:

> When people criticize Zionists, they mean Jews . . .
> It is not just that anti-Semitism is immoral, though that alone is enough. It is used to divide Negro and Jew, who have effectively collaborated in the struggle for justice. It injures Negroes because it upholds the doctrine of racism which they have the greatest stake in destroying.

Indeed, it has been forgotten that it was an anti-Semitic assault that led the United Nations itself to become involved in combating racism. In the wake of a world-wide swastika epidemic in 1959, the UN-affiliated Jewish nongovernmental organizations brought the question of racial discrimination to the United Nations for the first time, an initiative that was vigorously supported by the newly emerging African nations which were then entering the world organization. But the direct link between the Jewish experience of racial persecution and the determination of Jews to end racial discrimination had been manifested in the United Nations years before, during its very first session. After the adoption of Resolution 96 (I) in 1946 declaring genocide a crime under international law, Raphael Lemkin, a Jewish lawyer whose family was wiped out in Poland during the war, was instrumental in writing the Convention on the Prevention and Punishment of the Crime of Genocide, adopted by the United Nations on December 9, 1948. Since that time, Jewish organizations in more than forty countries had campaigned actively for ratification by those countries of that convention which outlaws the most extreme and brutal form of racism known to man—the attempt to liquidate an entire race or ethnic group.

For a clear expression of Jewish attitudes on the question of racial discrimination, we need only look to the founder of the Zionist movement, Theodor Herzl, writing in his book *Altneuland*, as early as 1902:

---

\* Letter to Morris B. Abram, September 28, 1967.

There is still one problem of racial misfortune unsolved. The depths of that problem only a Jew can comprehend. I refer to the problem of the Blacks. Just call to mind all those terrible episodes of the slave trade, of human beings who merely because they were black were stolen like cattle, taken prisoners, captured and sold. Their children grew up in strange lands, the objects of contempt and hostility because their complexions were different. I am not ashamed to say, though I may expose myself to ridicule in saying so, that once I have witnessed the redemption of Israel, my people, I wish to assist in the redemption of the Black People.*

Israel has been faithful to Herzl's words.

As a democracy, and with regard for its diverse ethnic, religious and linguistic groupings, the State of Israel has from its very inception been guided by the principles of freedom, justice and peace, and has done its utmost to ensure equality of social and political rights for all its inhabitants. Given the sea of hostility which surrounds us, it is surely no mean achievement for Israel to have consistently upheld the rights, both personal and national, of its Arab citizens, so that they are represented in every walk of Israeli life, ranging from our Parliament and government to our Defense Forces. The same is true in the territories administered by Israel since 1967, the only place in the whole Arab world, incidentally, where the Arab inhabitants have been able to conduct free elections. In a word, the modern State of Israel embodies traditional Jewish attitudes towards racism, for it has created a free and multiracial society.

It follows that the policies of apartheid as practiced in South Africa are as abhorrent to Israel and the Jewish people as any other form of racism. Despite this, and despite our own history of struggle against racial discrimination, we have recently witnessed a most insidious attempt to draw parallels between Israel and South Africa. This cynical exercise in international hypocrisy, which singles out Israel for having relations with South Africa and which attempts to imply some sort of equation between Zionism and apartheid, has seriously detracted from the campaign against

---

* Reprinted in English as *Old-New Land* (New York: Bloch Publishing Company and The Herzl Press, 1960), p. 170.

apartheid. Oblivious to the objectives of the African nations, the extremist Arab states have continued their political warfare against Israel in every available international forum, thereby promoting divisiveness and mutual recrimination where there should have been a universal consensus against apartheid.

The notion that Zionism and apartheid are in any way similar is an outrageous lie. In 1948, the same year that the term apartheid was first used, Israel issued its Declaration of Independence, which stated unambiguously:

> The State of Israel . . . will foster the development of the country for the benefit of all its inhabitants; it will be based on freedom, justice and peace as envisaged by the prophets of Israel; it will ensure complete equality of social and political rights to all its inhabitants irrespective of religion, race or sex; it will guarantee freedom of religion, conscience, language, education and culture. . . .

The Declaration contained a special guarantee to the Arab inhabitants of the State of Israel of "full and equal citizenship and due representation in all its provisional and permanent institutions."

In accordance with these principles, the Israeli government is based on majority rule and is elected by a citizenry with full political rights, including the right to vote and elect the government of its choice by secret popular ballot, the right to organize political parties and the right to express freely its political opinions. Israel's Arab citizens participate fully, actively and without restrictions in this political process and they are represented in the Knesset and in all branches of the Administration. Arab citizens are free to organize politically and even to belong to political groupings which vigorously oppose the State of Israel, a recent example of this freedom in practice being the election of a Communist mayor in Nazareth. Israel's domestic legislation applies equally to all citizens without exception and without restriction, with the one proviso that Arabs are not conscripted into the Israel Defense Forces (though they may volunteer), on the grounds that until peace is achieved, it would be patently unreasonable to place an Arab citizen of Israel in a situation where he may have to take up arms against his Arab brothers. Israel's labor laws apply equally to all citizens. Arab workers belong to the Histadrut trade union federation, as do Jewish workers, and they receive the same wages and work benefits. Transportation, public services, universities and recreational facilities are fully integrated, and Arabs not only from Israel and the administered areas but from all over the Middle East are admitted to the Hadassah and other top hospitals for treatment which is recognized as equivalent to the best in the world.

Moslem law has equivalent legal status in Israel with Christian and Jewish law in personal matters relating to marriage, divorce, inheritance, and so on. There is total freedom of worship and conscience, and governmental interference in matters of personal choice such as marriage, friendship and place of residence is totally abhorrent to our way of life. In the words of the chief United Nations representative for the Congress of Racial Equality, Edward H. Brown, Jr., the false equation of Zionism with racism is "simply an Arab ploy to take the focus off of the real enemies of humanity. Zionism," he concluded, "is a healthy form of nationalism."

But perhaps even more hypocritical than the spurious arguments about Zionism is the condemnation of Israel for having relations with South Africa. On this issue, the only difference between Israel and those who attack it is that while Israel openly acknowledges the existence of such relations, they deny their own. The fact is that most of the world maintains links with South Africa, but only Israel is singled out for doing so. According to the monthly newspaper of the United Nations Associations: "The list of nations which currently trade with South Africa is as long as, and in many cases, identical to the roll-call of states which have proclaimed their hostility to the Apartheid regime."

According to international statistics, Israel's trade with South Africa constitutes a mere two fifths of 1 percent of South Africa's $14½ billion foreign trade—infinitely smaller than the share of many Arab and some African countries. The question of who carries on the remaining 99⅗ percent of South Africa's trade is a question rarely asked. Investment figures illustrate the absurdity even more blatantly. Of the $19 billion foreign investment in

South Africa, Europe's share came to $13 billion. In addition, Africa invested $572 million and Asia $400 million.* Israel's total investment in South Africa is in the thousands of dollars and comes to about one tenth of 1 percent of the investment in South Africa of Asia alone.

While the present exercise in selectivity and double standard continues, Israel cannot remain silent. Most black African countries have done business with South Africa, and many have received considerable aid from South Africa. Mauritius receives 50,000 South African tourists each year, Mozambique sends workers to South African mines while its economy is entirely dependent on services from Pretoria, and South African government ministers visited some sixteen African countries in 1975–1976. According to the July 1977 "Direction of Trade" report of the International Monetary Fund, the African countries account for 8 percent of South Africa's trade, or over $1 billion.

International statistics also indicate a 13 percent increase in trade between the Communist bloc and South Africa, while the Soviet Union's huge diamond output is marketed through the South African concern of De Beers. In addition, the Soviet bloc supplies large quantities of arms to South Africa. On November 4, 1977, after commenting on South Africa's own arms industry, CBS News pointed out:

> There is also another means of supply: the Communist Bloc. These pamphlets [said the CBS correspondent in Johannesburg, holding up Soviet arms catalogues] are samples of up to 50 percent of imports for private sale now come from Czechoslovakia and the Soviet Union. South African arms dealers point to this trend as the ultimate irony—they claim they are forced to buy Soviet supplies because the West has decided to cut off weapons as a means of pushing for change and allegedly avoiding Communist intervention in Southern Africa.

A few days later the Washington *Post* (November 8), in a dispatch from Johannesburg, confirmed the Soviet involvement in arms trading: "It is estimated that the bloc supplies up to half of South Africa's private weapons, such as Soviet-made Baikal

* New York *Times* (November 6, 1977).

shotguns and Czech Brno automatic rifles. They are displayed in arms shops next to American-made Colt pistols."

But it is the Arab states who are most vulnerable to the dictum that "those who live in glass houses should not throw stones." While they all profess sincere support for black Africa and condemn Israel for its ties to Pretoria, the Arab states themselves carry on a flourishing and ever-increasing trade with South Africa. They have announced an oil boycott against the Republic but in fact continue the flow of oil surreptitiously. The Lebanese newspaper *al-Hadaf* wrote, on April 24, 1976: "[The Arabs] met with maximum success in their attempts to conceal the fact that South Africa is receiving Arab oil, reciprocating African support for the Arabs . . . [with] the flow of oil to Black Africa's major . . . enemy." Also in 1976, the United Nations published a document entitled "World Energy Supplies: 1950–1974" which reveals that oil supplies from Iraq, Qatar and Kuwait totaled 10 percent of South Africa's oil imports in 1974. These figures are of course merely those that have escaped the information blackout imposed by the Arab governments as reported by *al-Hadaf*. South Africa's Prime Minister, John Vorster, himself stated openly that his relations with Israel would not "harm South Africa's relations with its Arab oil suppliers." *

But Arab relations with South Africa are not limited to oil supplies. The list is too long to burden the reader with here, and a few easily verifiable examples will suffice. The royal family of Kuwait controls considerable investments in South Africa through its holdings in the Lonrho (London and Rhodesia) Corporation, holdings which cost more than £40 million sterling and amount to nearly 23 percent of the corporation's stock.† Arabs have offered to underwrite the very Bantustans which they consistently condemn at the United Nations. According to the *Sunday Express* of South Africa (June 15, 1975), "Arab financial interests have offered loans of more than R100 million [rands] to homeland governments in South Africa." Egypt appears to have steadily strengthened its relations with South Africa, including negotiations

* New York *Times* (April 11, 1976).
† *Africa*, No. 56 (April 1976), p. 98; *The Times*, London (November 2, 1976).

with a South African tour operation TFC to take tourists to Egypt, secret trips to Cairo by South African government officials and educational links between the two governments.*

President Julius Nyerere of Tanzania himself was constrained to complain about the hundreds of millions of dollars' worth of trade between the Arab states and South Africa in which they exchange oil for gold. Reporting on the soaring price of gold bullion, the New York *Times* (November 4, 1977) remarked: "Today the hungriest market for gold is the oil-rich Middle East, which last year absorbed almost 16 million ounces, or one-third the total mine output." The *Metal Bulletin* (on June 14, 1977) was even more specific, naming Saudi Arabia, the Gulf, Iraq, Egypt, Syria, Jordan and Yemen as among the Middle Eastern countries which "provided the main thrust for gold demand. . . . Direct shipments to these countries amounted to 500 tons of gold, one-third of the global supply."

As a result of this relationship, many leading Africans have begun to re-evaluate their attitudes towards the Middle East. On September 2, 1977, the Kenya *Daily Nation* cited reports "that Arabs are buying South African gold like hotcakes, thus helping to sustain that country's abominable policy of apartheid. . . . Arabs who sought and continue to woo our support have become business partners in building the South African economy." The newspaper went on to comment: "Research has revealed that Black Africa gained much more from Israel before the Yom Kippur War in terms of trade, technical assistance and training of personnel than they have gained from Arabs' petrodollars." The promise of financial aid to offset the African nations' rising oil bills "turned out to be a big bubble that fizzled away," said the Kenyan newspaper.

In the *Daily Times* of Nigeria (July 27, 1977) a correspondent reported that "Arab oil still finds its way to South Africa. Arms and armament meant for some Arab countries still find their way to South Africa." And in the *Sunday Times* of Nigeria on April 10, 1977, under the headline WE SHOULD RE-OPEN DIPLOMATIC TIES WITH ISRAEL, a correspondent wrote: "It is disgusting to

---

* *Observer*, London; *Sunday Times*, South Africa; *al-Gumhuriyya*, Cairo (August 26, 1976).

see that we are prepared to go to any length with the Arabs even when they supply oil to South Africa. Or do we pretend not to know that the Arabs still sell oil to the apartheid administration in Pretoria?"

We have witnessed the same hypocrisy in relations to arms supplies. A brief glance at the latest issue of *The Military Balance* reveals that South Africa's large armed forces are equipped with modern weapons including sophisticated tanks, artillery, aircraft, destroyers and submarines. Israel's alleged sale of patrol boats to South Africa is minuscule by comparison with the hardware flowing from the Republic's major Western arms suppliers.* Yet none of these countries has been singled out for a special resolution of condemnation as the United Nations has done in relation to Israel. Indeed, Israel's critics appear already to have forgotten Jordan's sale of British-made fighter aircraft and missile systems to South Africa in 1974. They have also ignored the fact that when the Security Council declared a mandatory arms embargo against South Africa in the fall of 1977, Israel announced that it would act in accordance with that resolution.

But it would, in any case, be utterly absurd to imply that relations with a state imply acquiescence in its political, social or economic policies. If it did, every nation in the world would find itself in an awkward, embarrassing and untenable situation. Leaders of the United States confer regularly with their counterparts in the Soviet Union and China and carry on an expanding trade, while East and West Germany have met to consult on their future relations without any implication that they agree with each other's systems of government. On the contrary, these leaders have demonstrated that dialogue and persuasion can lead to progress and change, an attitude which appears infinitely more mature than the continued obstinate refusal of Arab representatives to meet with their Israeli counterparts.

The specious singling out of Israel for its relations with South Africa therefore serves no one and no purpose but the fruitless campaign of political warfare to which the Arab states are addicted. To quote Bayard Rustin, a veteran black civil rights leader in the United States:

* *The Military Balance* 1977–1978, published by the International Institute for Strategic Studies (London, 1977), p. 44.

As one who has very serious reservations about detente because of the repressive nature of the Soviet Government, I do not interpret American trade with the USSR as approval of the persecution of Jews, intellectuals, artists and scientists. Nor do I think that trade relations with South Africa represents Israeli or the black African nations' approval of apartheid.*

Israel is singled out for special treatment not because of its inconsequential trade with South Africa, but because the Arab states will use each and every opportunity at their disposal to attack Israel. As the publication *West Africa* bluntly stated on March 12, 1973: "The Arabs identify with the Black Africans only because of their votes in the United Nations and other conferences."

In a very real sense this attitude is a new exercise in neocolonialism, since the Arab states impose their will in matters irrelevant to the African world while making promises which do not materialize and issuing veiled threats in violation of national sovereignty. Many African leaders and writers have expressed concern both at the use of petrodollars and economic pressure to exercise political influence and at the continuing increase in oil prices which is crippling much of Africa economically.

Every time an international conference raises a matter of vital importance to the Africans, the Arab representatives convert the discussion into a barren debate on the Middle East. Driven by their old rivalries and hatreds, they have ignored the interests of the African world in order to advance their goal for the destruction of a sovereign state, regardless of whether such action prejudices moves against racism and racial discrimination. It is hardly surprising that they do so, since many of them have written into their constitutions principles and laws based on racism and racial discrimination, laws which, when applied, discriminate against Jews, against women and against blacks, among others. In their inevitable exercise in hypocrisy, these Arab states therefore see in the struggle of the black people merely an opportunity to pursue their own narrow and destructive aims. Fortunately, more and more Africans are viewing this as an infringement on their own independence and are demanding the right to discuss their own issues without interference. And while the Arab states accuse

* Letter to Rabbi Arthur Hertzberg, October 18, 1976.

others of what they themselves are flagrantly guilty, many African leaders recall also the long-term economic, technical, agricultural and social aid which Israel has given to newly emerging African countries, aid which continues to be made available despite the absence of formal relations.

It is time for the world community to decide what should be its basic approach to the question of apartheid. If the aim is to compile a compendium of trade transactions with South Africa, then let us abandon selective accusations and open the books for all to see. Israel has nothing to hide, and it would certainly be appropriate to receive a full account of all trade, investment, tourism, gold purchases, oil supplies, governmental visits and other relations, overt and covert, by all United Nations members with South Africa before passing judgment on any one.

Just as the African states support the struggle of their brothers for freedom in South Africa, so do we in Israel support those of our own brothers who suffer from racism and the deprivation of human rights. We will never relinquish this major obligation on the international scene. We shall never tire in our quest to assist our fellow Jew—wherever he may be—who is still subject to persecution and oppression. This commitment is born out of the conviction that we *are* our brothers' keepers and therefore cannot remain silent while the heinous phenomenon of anti-Semitism is still the order of the day in some countries. The Jewish nation is small in number—mainly because more than any other people on this globe, we have been the object of continuous persecution and repeated pogroms. We in Israel are therefore determined to do our share and raise our voice in protest against the continued discrimination and persecution of Jewish communities.

Jewish communities in two countries concern us in particular. The first is in Syria. About 4,500 in number, these Jews are virtual hostages of the Syrian government. They live in utter misery in the ghettos of Damascus, Aleppo and Qamishli, subject to a long list of discriminatory restrictions which totally ignore the elementary concepts of the rights and freedoms of man. There is a prohibition on the movement of Jews beyond four kilometers from their place of residence, and a special police permit is required for travel from one city to another. All these restrictions were allegedly in-

tended for the protection of the Jews from the anti-Zionist population, a situation that reveals the hypocrisy of the propaganda which
maintains that excellent relations prevail between Moslem and
Jewish citizens.

Unfortunately, these restrictions comprise far from an exhaustive list of anti-Jewish discrimination. While there are fluctuations
in the intensity and strictness with which those repressive regulations are enforced, one fact remains constant: Syria is a prison
for its Jews. No member of the Jewish community is allowed to
leave, not even on such grounds as family reunion. It is no wonder,
then, that many Jews, primarily the younger members of the community, are willing to risk their lives in attempts to escape from
these Syrian ghettos and reach freedom.

The plight of the Jewish community of Syria is not a matter
which could be considered as an internal affair of that state. What
is involved here is a violation of international covenants and agreements. Syria is a signatory to the Universal Declaration of Human
Rights and has ratified the International Covenant on Civil and
Political Rights as well as the International Convention for the
Elimination of All Forms of Racial Discrimination. Syria is guilty
of blatant violation of all three of them. The international community must not close its eyes to the fate of this captive Jewish
minority, nor should it keep silent. Syria is the only country in
the world that does not allow its Jews to emigrate. There is only
one salvation for the Jews of Syria—they must be permitted to depart for lands where they can live in peace, dignity and security.

In a larger sense, the plight of Syrian Jews today simply reflects
the treatment which Jews have experienced at the hands of many
other Arab states. Hundreds of thousands of Jews were driven out
of the Arab countries; their property was expropriated. Innocent
Jews were publicly hanged in the main square in Baghdad. Jordan's
citizenship law number 6 of February 4, 1954, states in paragraph
3, subparagraph 3: "Any man will be a Jordanian subject . . . if
he is not Jewish." Saudi Arabia refuses entry even to American
citizens—if they happen to be Jewish. Racist policies such as these
expose the hypocrisy of the Arab states when they rail against
racism in international conferences.

For many years Israel has been raising the question of the plight
of yet another oppressed Jewish community—the Jewish minority

in the Soviet Union—whose members are not accorded even the most elemental rights existing for other minorities in that country. Jewish religion and culture are suppressed, synagogues have been closed and Hebrew books are confiscated. A planned symposium on Jewish culture in 1976 was suppressed and its organizers placed under arrest. Dozens of Jewish prisoners of conscience still languish in deplorable conditions in Soviet prison camps. Not a single Jewish school exists in the entire USSR, in open breach not only of the Soviet constitution, but of the UNESCO Convention against Discrimination in Education, adopted on December 14, 1960, and ratified by the USSR on August 1, 1962, whereof article 5 (c) recognizes "the right of members of national minorities to carry on educational activities, including the maintenance of schools and, depending on the educational policy of each state, the use or the teaching of their own language."

Millions of copies of anti-Semitic books, pamphlets and magazine articles circulate under official auspices in the USSR, and the Soviet media frequently engage in overt anti-Jewish incitement. A recent television film, *Traders in Souls,* was a vicious debasement of Israel and the Jewish people. This film went so far as to screen the names and addresses of Jewish activists, thus exposing them to verbal and physical abuse. Another movie, *Secret and Open Things,* was described by Washington *Post* columnist George F. Will as "one of the most important exercises in anti-Semitism since the death of Joseph Goebbels."

A recent wave of such anti-Semitic incitement accompanied the fabrication of malicious libel against those active in the cause of immigration to Israel. As this book goes to press, one activist, Anatoly Scharansky, stands falsely accused of treason, his only crime being his desire to live in freedom in Israel. These ominous developments are reminiscent of the darkest period in the history of Jews in the Soviet Union, twenty-five years ago under Stalin.

It is particularly distressing that this deterioration in the situation of Soviet Jews has taken place since the Helsinki Conference on Security and Cooperation in Europe in August 1975. At this conference the Soviet Union signed an agreement in which it undertook to be forthcoming in dealing with the problem of the reunification of families. It was widely hoped that the Soviet Union would live up to the spirit of this historic agreement and enable the Jews who aspired to be reunited with their brethren in their ancient homeland to do so without hindrance. Unfortunately, the campaign of harassment of applicants for emigration has not only continued unabated, but actually intensified since Helsinki. Applicants are often dismissed from work or demoted; their families have been threatened; their telephone service is often cut off, and their mail is intercepted and frequently confiscated in violation of the Universal Postal Convention, to which the Soviet Union is a signatory. Yet despite the harassment, tens of thousands of Soviet Jews continue to apply to leave that country and join their families in Israel.

The Soviet Union's denial of fundamental human rights to its Jewish citizens, particularly the right to emigrate, violates not only the Helsinki accord, but also the Universal Declaration of Human Rights and the Soviet Union's own laws and constitution.

Article 13(2) of the Universal Declaration of Human Rights states: "Everyone has the right to leave any country, including his own, and to return to his country." And article 19: "Everyone has the right to freedom of thought, conscience and religion . . . and freedom, either alone or in community with others and in public or private, to manifest his religion or belief in teaching, practice, worship and observance." Similarly, Article 124 of the USSR constitution asserts "freedom of conscience" and recognizes "freedom of religious worship . . . for all citizens." Israel will not rest until the Jews in the Soviet Union achieve their human and national rights—to live according to their faith, culture, language and national consciousness, and to be reunited with their brothers in Israel or anywhere else they may wish.

Sometimes, as I listen to the tirade of accusations against Israel at the United Nations, I cannot help but look at the vast Assembly of nations gathered there and compute in my mind the sum total of misery that most of them represent. As I contemplate the disease, the malnutrition, the poverty, the lack of freedom, the detentions without trial, the mass death sentences, the brutal suppression of minorities, the torture of dissidents and the denial of basic human rights that affect hundreds of millions of citizens, I know that in such a world we, the Jewish people, can have no illusions. These nations regularly practice every crime they attribute to Israel, and violate every human and natural law in the conduct of their own affairs.

The United Nations itself has taken these norms of hypocrisy and selectiveness to their cynical extreme in the deliberations of its Human Rights Commission. The London *Sunday Times* has published an alarming and horrifying study of the work of the commission which stated:

> The record of the Commission's 29 years shows that it has been more concerned to cover up than to expose human rights violations. It is neither farce nor tragedy, in the proper senses of these two overworked words. But it is, perhaps, the most poignant and disgraceful of false international pretences that the governments of the world have yet had the temerity to devise. To millions of people its name offers a glimmer of hope for justice—that hope is founded on, quite literally, nothing. The Commission is an almost total lie. It plays a vital part in what Sean McBride, U.N. Commissioner for Namibia and 1974 Nobel Peace Prize Winner, has described as "the conspiracy of governments" to deprive the people of their rights.
>
> . . . Since 1970 [the commission] has received over 100,000 complaints from individuals and organizations about alleged violations of human rights throughout the world. Not one has been followed through. . . .*

This record is less surprising when it is considered, according to the Washington *Post*, that three fourths of the thirty-two states represented on the Human Rights Commission are themselves guilty of gross violations of human rights.†

Indeed, in dealing with human rights questions, the United Nations stands in flagrant violation of its own founding Charter, which proclaims unambiguously the principle of universality. In articles 55 and 56 of the Charter of the United Nations, "all members pledge themselves to take joint and separate action" to promote "UNIVERSAL respect for, and observance of, human rights and fundamental freedoms for all without distinction as to race, sex, language or religion." It is no accident that the document in which these freedoms are defined is called the "Universal Declaration of Human Rights" and that every one of the thirty

---

* *Sunday Times* Weekly Review (March 14, 1976).
† Washington *Post* (April 19, 1977).

articles which make up this declaration begins with an affirmation of the principles of universality. But universality in principle has become selectiveness in practice. At its 1977 session the Human Rights Commission spent an entire week condemning Israel but refused to take any action on a British and American initiative to investigate the massacres occurring at that very time in Uganda. The time has come to expose this double standard and examine seriously the credentials of Israel's accusers.

Uganda, a full-fledged member of the Human Rights Commission, was joined by Cuba, India, Upper Volta and Yugoslavia in sponsoring the resolution condemning Israel. The victims of the murderous and bloodthirsty bully who rules Uganda already include several government ministers, the Chief Justice, the Anglican Archbishop Janani Luwum, and an old Jewish lady of seventy-five, Dora Bloch, who was brutally slain on Idi Amin's orders after Israel's rescue of hostages at Entebbe. But cruelest of all are the continuing massacres of Ugandan Christians including a genocidal campaign against two entire Christian tribes, the Langi and the Acholi. The International Commission of Jurists and Amnesty International both estimate Amin's victims at more than 100,000. Yet when this tyrant rose before the General Assembly to call for the elimination of Israel, nearly all the nations of the world greeted him with acclamation.

To catalogue the crimes against humanity which are daily perpetrated by the despots and dictators who condemn us would require volumes. But since these countries have set themselves up to pass judgment on one of the freest and most advanced societies in the world today, a brief survey is in order. There is a saying in Arabic to the effect that no one knows your secrets except your God and your neighbors. And so we hear Algeria accuse Morocco and Mauritania of flagrantly abusing the rights of the inhabitants of the former Spanish Sahara. In 1975 Libya expelled 5,000 Tunisian workers and plotted to kill the Tunisian Premier. The Egyptian newspaper *al-Gumhuriyya* recently characterized Syria as "one big prison," and almost every Arab state deplored the terrifying conditions under Egyptian rule which existed in Gaza prior to 1967. As for Egypt itself, a distinguished Egyptian newspaper editor, Mustapha Amir, in his book *My First Year in Prison*, has described the stark horror of Egyptian prisons and the torture applied there under Nasser. These states have for thirty years kept the Palestinian refugees in camps as political pawns in subhuman conditions. As they lecture Israel on human rights, Israel has absorbed, housed and educated over 600,000 Jewish refugees driven out of their homes in Arab lands. As for our non-Arab accusers, neither Cuba, with its thousands of political prisoners, nor Pakistan, with its rigged elections, nor Yugoslavia, which sends lawyers to prison for defending their clients, nor any other one-party system or military dictatorship is in a position to preach to Israel about respect for human rights.

There are gradations on the scale of credentials to intervene in human rights discussions, and I believe that Iraq is at the bottom. Every time Iraqi representatives eagerly revive the Zionism-racism formula, I reflect on the ancient Jewish community of 160,000 forced to leave Iraq after thousands of years, and on the continued brutal suppression of the Kurdish people. When they talk of human rights I remember the innocent Jews hanging on the public gallows in Baghdad, among them, incidentally, the cousin of a member of my delegation to the United Nations whose young pregnant wife was forced to watch the execution.

Then there was the execution of Alexander Aaronsen, a male nurse, a Dutch Jew, who devoted his life to helping the sick and the injured in the developing countries of Africa and Asia, including in the Albert Schweitzer Hospital in Gabon. While on a mission of mercy to the Kurds in northern Iraq, he was seized by Iraqi soldiers on March 24, 1975. We now know that Aaronsen was executed in December of the same year after a secret trial—a customary occurrence in Iraq. Jan Beekman, a member of the Dutch Parliament who visited Iraq in January 1976, was told by high Iraqi officials, including the Under-Secretary for Foreign Affairs, that Aaronsen was still alive then. The chargé d'affaires of Iraq at The Hague informed Aaronsen's mother by a simple telephone call two months later that her son was dead. This was the reaction of the Dutch Foreign Ministry: "We are dismayed, horrified and deeply outraged, especially by the incredible way the Iraqi authorities have acted. They have fooled us systematically for a year. We are simply perplexed."

But this barbaric act of brutality against a single individual was merely a reflection of the repression of an entire people, the Kurds. Israel has in fact been the only country to stand up in any international forum for the rights of the Kurdish people in their long and bitter struggle for self-determination.

The failure of the UN is most evident in its repression of the issue of human rights. The dimensions of this repression can be gauged from evidence recently presented to the United Nations by the International League for Human Rights. The League accused Iraq of engaging in a "systematic attempt to destroy the political, economic, cultural and linguistic identity of the Kurdish ethnic group" and described "executions, instances of torture, mass detentions, and the deportation of tens of thousands of Kurdish people."

The International League for Human Rights presented evidence of:

> . . . Iraq's forcible deportation of 300,000 Kurds from their homes in the northern mountains to the southern deserts; the confiscation of Kurdish lands without compensation and the settlement of Arab citizens in those areas; the incarceration of 30,000 former members of the Kurdish fighting force in concentration camps where they have been beaten and tortured, in contravention of the Iraqi Amnesty Law of 1975; the execution of 227 Kurds and imprisonment of over 200 others for political reasons. The Iraqi Government further has prohibited the use of Kurdish in schools, has shut down Kurdish newspapers, has forbidden Kurdish ownership of land in oil-rich areas and has authorized the payment of 500 dinars ($1,500) to any Arab who takes a Kurdish spouse (in an attempt to break up Kurdish families).

From the evidence, the League concluded that

> the Government of Iraq has, for well over 15 years, pursued a consistent policy of discrimination against its non-Arab Kurdish population in violation of Article 5 of the Racial Discrimination Convention, which sets forth the civil and political rights of ethnic and racial groups. Evidence demonstrates that the Iraqi Government has repeatedly shown itself unwilling to accept its approximately 2.5 million Kurds as Iraqi citizens in equal standing with Iraq's Arab citizens. It has, in practice, refused to respect the rights due to the Kurds as a distinct non-Arab ethnic group which has lived in

Iraq for over 2,000 years. On the contrary, the Iraqi Government has attempted, and continues to attempt, to destroy the integrity and identity of the Kurdish community.*

Other respected human rights organizations have corroborated this evidence. On October 28, 1976, Amnesty International sent a letter to President Ahmad Hassan al-Bakr, expressing concern over the arrest, torture and execution of Kurds in Iraq, despite proclaimed government amnesties. That letter included a list of more than two hundred Kurds reported to have been executed in Iraq since the general amnesty of March 1975, and expressed concern at the reported detention of several thousand Kurds in camps in the south of the country. Amnesty stated it had received first-hand accounts of their torture and ill treatment during interrogation. And in February 1977 the Syrian government reported that the Iraqi regime had massacred 244 of its alleged opponents.† In the words of the Amnesty International report, 1975–1976, "Iraq remains one of the most serious violators of human rights in the Middle East." It is difficult to believe that this brutal racist regime has the effrontery to accuse Israel of human rights violations. Such, however, are the norms of international hypocrisy today.

Obsessed and preoccupied with its condemnations of Israel, the United Nations bears silent witness to crimes against humanity and refuses to call its own members to account for the very crimes of which they accuse Israel. But the sad truth is that these ominous developments could not have occurred without the passive acquiescence of the West. On the occasion of the "war crimes" resolution against Israel, only one country in the world —the United States—had the moral courage to vote against it. All the Western countries, who knew the allegations to be untrue, abstained. This attitude of cowardly and craven capitulation to expediency can spell disaster for what is left of the democratic and free world. As Dante put it: "The hottest fires in hell are reserved for those who in times of moral crisis are neutral."

---

* Letter and evidence sent by the International League for Human Rights to UN Secretary-General Kurt Waldheim, January 14, 1977.
† *The Times*, London (February 21, 1977).

But it is not only Israel that has been the victim of Western cowardice. In December 1975 a resolution was submitted condemning U.S. imperialism because of the American presence in Guam, the Virgin Islands and Samoa. Eighty-nine countries voted to condemn the United States, including many who are happy to receive U.S. aid. Only Israel, Britain, West Germany, Luxembourg and Nicaragua voted with the United States. Apart from these countries, all the allies of the United States in NATO and elsewhere, who are free because of the United States, abstained.* This lack of moral backbone on the part of the Western countries is all too familiar to Israel. It portends great danger and evil for the world. This turning a blind eye to the behavior of dictatorships and despotisms, this ostrichlike attitude to the irresponsible behavior of petty dictators, this alarming tendency to ingratiate oneself with despots which has become the accepted norm in the West today, are one of the dangers which face the free world.

We are witnessing today signs of appeasement reminiscent of those which a generation ago led to the most terrible holocaust in human history, a holocaust in which six million of our people were murdered, including one million children. There were those who, like the Danish resistance fighters, acted to save their Jewish brothers from destruction and whose courage we will never forget. But there were also many, many more, including powerful political and religious leaders, who knew what was happening and who stood by silently while one third of our people were exterminated. While these leaders undoubtedly abhorred the brutality they witnessed, they nevertheless closed their eyes to human suffering, refused in many cases to offer a haven to fleeing refugees, and thus became, in effect, accessories to the crime. We who have emerged from the darkness of the Holocaust are determined not to be guilty of the same sin of omission.

A former U.S. representative to the United Nations, Governor William Scranton, has stated: "In the field of human rights, justice delayed . . . becomes mass murder condoned." † But Israel refuses to be a party to this conspiracy of silence, to the selective morality and hypocrisy with which human rights are treated. That is

---

* In the subsequent two sessions of the General Assembly, the Western countries improved their vote on this issue in favor of the United States.

† Quoted in London *Times* (November 26, 1976).

why Israel welcomed President Carter's statement that "No member of the United Nations can claim that mistreatment of its citizens . . . is solely its own business. Equally, no member can avoid its responsibilities to review and to speak when torture or unwarranted deprivation of freedom occurs in any part of the world."

It is also the reason that Israel will not remain silent when the U.N. Commission on Human Rights ignores crimes against humanity in the name of political expediency. It is no longer enough to pontificate about human rights and individual freedoms. Rather, the time has come to translate President Carter's bold initiative on human rights into action, to open ourselves to criticism and to spell out violations of human rights wherever and whenever they occur.

No case can better illustrate Governor Scranton's warning than the brutal civil war which, for almost two years, ravaged Lebanon. The war waged as the U.N. General Assembly met in New York and, as usual, devoted 50 percent of its time to condemnations of Israel. The United Nations will live in infamy because while a nation in the Middle East was bleeding to death, while Lebanon— a member country of the organization—was being strangled by internecine warfare, the United Nations lent itself once again to becoming an instrument of political warfare against Israel. As a terrifying human tragedy unraveled before our eyes, the world assembly had not one word to say on the subject because it was too busy castigating and vilifying a free and socially advanced country in the Middle East. Indeed, there can be no greater illustration of the cynical wickedness of international life than the spectacle of the United Nations averting its eyes while one of its members bled.

As the civil war raged, the Security Council had time to discuss Namibia, Timor, Sahara, Israel and the Palestinians but never met once to consider whether the bloodshed in Lebanon constituted a danger to the security of the area. When three people were injured in the West Bank, the Security Council was immediately called into session, the meeting having been requested at the very time that the most horrible slaughter was taking place in Lebanon. Almost 50,000 had been killed, 100,000 wounded and over 1 million refugees made homeless. During the space of nearly two years, hundreds of churches and mosques in Lebanon were burned, razed to the ground and shamefully desecrated. The Maronite Patriarch of Lebanon pleaded with the world as Holy Places were defiled, as monasteries and hospitals were shelled and as religious leaders were attacked. Not once did the Security Council convene. Yet on the very day that the PLO carried out a terrifying massacre in the Lebanese village of Achiyeh in which 300 Christians were reportedly murdered, Egypt called for a Security Council meeting on Hebron, where some holy books had allegedly been desecrated. Perhaps we should no longer be surprised. After all, the Security Council was convened to condemn Israel after we saved 105 Jewish hostages from terrorists at Entebbe but remains silent as tens of thousands of Ugandan Christians are slaughtered; just as it remained silent when 500,000 black Christians were being murdered by a racist regime in Sudan; and just as it continues to remain silent when an entire nation, the Kurds, are being extinguished by Iraqi forces.

History will recall that as the world looked on, the only voice raised in the United Nations as the Christian community in Lebanon faced mortal peril was the voice of Israel. For their own internal reasons the Arab states objected to the issue of Lebanon being raised, and as a result, not one body of the United Nations ever addressed itself to the crisis. As Israel pleaded for action to save the Lebanese Christians, the UN accorded official status to the PLO, the organization which in 1970 had tried to destroy Jordan and which five years later was actively engaged in the dismemberment of Lebanon. This hypocrisy, this silence, this craven and disgraceful behavior will remain forever a reproach against the United Nations.

But perhaps the most horrifying case of international silence in recent times occurred in relation to Cambodia, which Jean Lacouture in the March 31, 1977, issue of the *New York Review of Books* called "the most tightly locked up country in the world, where the bloodiest revolution in history is now taking place."

Genocide usually has been carried out against a foreign population or an internal minority. The new masters of Phnom Penh have

invented something original—auto-genocide. After Auschwitz and
the Gulag, we might have thought this century had produced the
ultimate horror, but we are now seeing the suicide of a people in
the name of revolution; worse: in the name of socialism . . .

[The Khmer Rouge] are systematically massacring, isolating and
starving city and village populations whose crime was to have been
born when they were.

Israel is the only country in the world to have drawn attention
to the fate of the more than one million Cambodians killed by
the present regime since it took power in April 1975. Our plea for
the people of Cambodia was met by a deafening silence on the
part of every other nation in the world without exception. We as
a people have experienced this before and I therefore feel constrained to reproduce here a passage from the London *Times*,
dated February 2, 1977, which I read at the UN to the assembled
nations of the world:

Even in a century which has gorged itself on atrocities until it
has become almost too replete to swallow more, the horrors which
accompanied and have followed the fall of Cambodia to the communists are exceptional both in their peculiarly barbaric nature and
in the colossal scale on which they have been carried out. Millions
of Cambodians were expelled from their homes—the capital was
simply emptied, at bayonet point, of its entire population—and
force-marched into the jungles, there to live as they might or die if
they could not; several hundred thousand were obliged to adopt the
latter course. In addition, many thousands were exterminated by the
Khmer Rouge regime—not as "enemies of the people" but in a
campaign of indiscriminate terror clearly designed to crush any spirit
of independence that might trouble the communist uniformity to
come. Those who were caught trying to escape from the country
were slaughtered on the borders; in the case of those who succeeded,
families they left behind, and indeed entire villages, were exterminated.

That report went on to cite eyewitness accounts, too gruesome
to repeat, of atrocities committed by Khmer Rouge soldiers in
Thai villages across the border.

Writing in the New York *Times* on March 21, 1977, Anthony
Lewis carried a grim warning for the United Nations and for every
state represented in it:

To remain silent in the face of barbarism as enormous as Cambodia's would be to compromise our own humanity. It would be to say that hundreds of thousands of Cambodians do not count in the human scale. . . . In today's world, we ignore mass murder anywhere at our own peril.

In the years to come, when the record is examined, Israel will not be accused of hiding behind the smoke screen of high-sounding rhetoric without having at least spelled out explicitly our solidarity with the victims of repression. But in a world where Uganda, Lebanon and Cambodia can happen without a whimper of protest, we ourselves can have no illusions. The spectacle of tyrants condemning tyranny, of racists denouncing racism and of members of the Human Rights Commission daily violating the human rights of their own populations has accustomed us to a world in which double-talk has become the order of the day. Indeed, we know from experience that there is nothing more completely aligned than the so-called nonaligned countries. If a country has the appellation "socialist" in its title, one can be certain that nothing is further removed from the principles of true socialism than the regime of that country. If a country is called a People's Republic, we can be sure that the people of that country has little to do with choosing its government, as for example the People's Democratic Republic of Yemen. If a country affects the title "democratic," then its association with democracy is purely coincidental, as witness the German Democratic Republic.

The question is how long the free world is prepared to countenance this terrifying Orwellian development which must seriously erode the free societies of the earth, plunge the world into the darkness of totalitarianism and bring tragedy on mankind. For in the final analysis, it has always begun with the Jews but it has never ended with them. An ominous and fearsome process is overtaking the world and we are all silent. Those nations, no matter how enlightened, which continue to be involved in this terrifying process of hypocrisy and double standards without speaking out, are themselves becoming part of that process. Our own bitter experience has taught us that we, the Jewish people, cannot be silent participants. Israel has its faults and its problems, and we stand open to criticism on every issue. Indeed, as a nation with a free and critical press, an open society and a vociferous opposition, criticism is an integral part of our very way of life. All that we demand before the world is that when we are judged, the same standards be applied universally, to all nations without exception, including those who sit in judgment on us. Only then will United Nations discussions and resolutions carry any moral weight and only then will international conferences on human rights begin to reflect the principles of justice and natural law which the Jewish people gave to the world.

## 12

*The Scourge of*
*International*
*Terrorism*

*Address delivered to the Security Council of the United Nations, July 9, 1976, on Israel's rescue operation at Entebbe*

Mr. President,

From a purely formal point of view, this meeting arises from a complaint brought against the Israeli government. However, let me make it quite clear that sitting here as the representative of the Israeli government, as I have the honor to do, I am in no way sitting in the dock as the accused party. On the contrary, I stand here as an accuser on behalf of free and decent people in this world. I stand here as an accuser against the forces of evil which have unleashed a wave of piracy and terrorism which threatens the very foundations of human society. I stand here as an accuser of all those evil forces which in their inherent cowardice and abject craven attitude see blameless wayfarers and innocent women and children—yes, even babes in arms—a legitimate target for their evil intentions. I stand here as an accuser of the countries that because of evil design or lack of moral backbone, have collaborated with these bloodthirsty terrorists. I stand here as an accuser of all those in authority throughout the world who for reasons of cynical expediency have collaborated with terrorism. I stand here as an accuser of this world organization, the United Nations, which has been unable, because of the machinations of the Arab delegates and their supporters, to coordinate effective measures in order to combat the evil of world terrorism. I stand here as an accuser of those delegations to this organization which for reasons of political expediency have remained silent on this issue, an issue which is bound to affect each country in this organization. In so doing, they have themselves become accomplices.

Seated in the dock today with the accusing finger of enlightened world opinion directed against them are the terrorist organizations which are plaguing this world, and whose representatives have been seated here by the world body with rights equal to those of member states. In the dock are all those countries who have collaborated with the terrorists and who have aided and abetted them. There stand here accused those countries which have blocked every international move to deal with this plague of terror which besets the world.

In the dock before us stand members of all those countries—they are all-too-numerous—who cry to the high heavens when they are affected by terrorists, who fulminate at this Security Council table when their citizens or diplomats are threatened, and who remain silent when the same happens to citizens of other countries. Some of them don't even have the doubtful grace to remain silent; they have the wicked effrontery to join in condemnation of a country which tries to prevent these acts. In the dock before us are the representatives of all those countries who stood and applauded the entry into the hall of the General Assembly of a gun-toting terrorist who according to the President of Sudan personally gave the order to execute the American and Belgian diplomats bound hand and foot in the basement of the Saudi Arabian embassy in Khartoum on March 1, 1973. Yes, sir, before us stands accused this rotten, corrupt, brutal, cynical bloodthirsty monster of international terrorism and all those who support it in one way or the other, whether by commission or omission. Facing them today are the ordinary decent human beings throughout the world who seek nothing more than to live a life free from terror and from intimidation, free from the threats of hijackers, the indiscriminate bombs of terrorists, and the blackmail of criminals and murderers.

Israel's action at Entebbe in order to release its hostages has given rise to a world-wide wave of support and approval, such as has rarely been seen from every continent, including Africa, from every walk of life, from countries hostile as well as friendly to Israel. The ordinary man and woman in the street has risen behind us and proclaimed "enough" to this specter of terror, has cried out "enough" to this world body of pontificating diplomats, in which on so many occasions moral cowardice and cynical expediency have combined to drag it down to the depths to which it has plunged.

In more ways than one, this organization is in the accused stand today. Mankind will judge it by its behavior on this occasion because never has the issue been clearer, never has the issue been so clear-cut. There will be no excuse in history for this body or for the constituent members of this body if it fails to condemn terrorism. The issue before this body is not what Israel did in Entebbe Airport; the issue before this body is its own future in the eyes of history.

The representative of Uganda has very conveniently avoided the main issue before us. Let us recount the events as they occurred.

On Sunday, June 27, 1976, an Air France airbus flight 139 en route from Tel Aviv to Paris was hijacked by a group of PLO terrorists, with 256 passengers aboard in addition to a crew of 12. The terrorists took advantage of the by now notorious, lax and negligent security measures obtaining at Athens Airport, and brought on board pistols and approximately twenty grenades.

Thus began a methodically planned and carefully executed act of air piracy by the Popular Front for the Liberation of Palestine, one of the several terrorist groups joined together to form the PLO. Thus began another in a long list of PLO crimes against innocent civilians.

Having commandeered the aircraft, the hijackers forced the French pilots to land in what is by now internationally accepted as the first haven for such criminals—namely, Libya. This was, it will be recalled, the first stop in the flight of the OPEC ministers kidnapped in Austria last year. . . . Having mentioned Libya, I think it is appropriate to draw attention to the central role which this country plays in the promotion and encouragement of international terror in the world today.

This is the country which has for years acted as paymaster of international terror movements, Arab and non-Arab, throughout the world.

This is the country which has been condemned by Sudan and Tunis only recently for its acts of terror and for the sinister and dangerous part it has played in planning to assassinate the leaders of these states, to overthrow their governments.

This is the country whose ambassador was expelled but a few days ago by the Egyptian government for its subversive activities.

It is, I submit, a disgrace to this world organization that the representative of this world sponsor of terrorism is seated as a member of the Security Council, the purpose of which is to encourage the maintenance of international peace and security.

I submit, sir, that under the provision of Article 23 of the Charter the Libyan government is disqualified from membership of the Security Council. Furthermore, under Article 27, paragraph 3, Libya as a party to this dispute is disqualified from voting on this issue. The Libyan government's activities are utterly irreconcilable with its membership of this body, and indeed had the principles of the Charter been adhered to in this body, a member representing this world center of terror would not have been sitting in this body.

The Air France plane was refueled in Benghazi. The destination of the hijackers was, in accordance with a previously prepared plan, Entebbe Airport, outside Kampala in Uganda. The airbus landed at Entebbe Airport on Monday, June 28, and the hijackers were met by a reinforcement of terrorists who awaited them at the terminal armed to the teeth with submachine guns and explosives.

President Idi Amin of Uganda arrived at the airport shortly before the hijacked plane landed and embraced the hijackers in a gesture of welcome and a promise of support and assistance. Ugandan soldiers were then positioned with their guns trained not at the hijackers, but at the innocent civilians.

On Tuesday, June 29, 1976, the hijackers spelled out their demands. These included the release of fifty-three terrorists jailed in
Israel, West Germany, France, Switzerland and Kenya by a deadline of 3 P.M. local time, Thursday, June 30. They threatened to
put the innocent passengers to death if their terms were not met.

When the hijackers released forty-seven women, children and
some sick passengers on Wednesday, June 30, it gradually became
apparent that President Amin was in fact cooperating with the
terrorists under a cloak of deception and false pretense. This was
the situation on the evening of July 1, the first deadline set by the
terrorists. It became obvious that the Israeli passengers—men,
women and children—were in serious and grave danger for their
lives. When a further hundred hostages were released, their story,
when they arrived in Paris, revealed an ominous development.
They described to the waiting reporters how Ugandan soldiers
under direct orders from President Amin supervised the separation
of Jewish passengers from non-Jewish passengers.

This was a development of a nature so sinister and so pregnant
with memories of the past that no member of the Jewish people,
whether in Israel or abroad, could fail to recall its horrible significance. The memory of the terrifying selections carried out during the most horrifying holocaust that mankind has ever seen
flashed immediately upon the inward eye of every member of our
people. We recalled the selections carried out by the Nazis in
the concentration camps as members of the Jewish people were
singled out for the gas chambers and extermination.

Following the never-to-be-forgotten experience of the Holocaust in Europe during World War II an oath was taken, whether
consciously or unconsciously, by every member of the Jewish people, wherever he or she might be, that never again would this happen; that never again would circumstances be allowed to develop
in which such a catastrophe could happen; that Auschwitz, Dachau
and Buchenwald belonged to the past and would never again
return.

On this occasion I solemnly reaffirm before this body the oath
which has been taken by our Jewish people, wherever they are. It
will never happen again.

And so, when this ominous, reminiscent selection began, when
the separation of the Jews was undertaken, it became apparent to

the Israeli government that there was no alternative but to conduct a rescue operation to save the lives of its citizens.

The Israeli government's apprehension was heightened by a knowledge of President Amin's attitude to the Jewish people. In September 1972 President Amin sent a cable which was published on September 13, 1972, to the Secretary-General of the United Nations, Dr. Kurt Waldheim, with copies to the Prime Minister of Israel and to the leader of the PLO, Yassir Arafat. In this cable President Amin applauded the murder of the Israeli sportsmen at the Olympic games who, bound hand and foot, were gunned down by the PLO. Moreover, in the same message he displayed the obscene ghoulishness of praising Hitler for his role in destroying over six million Jews.

Distinguished members of the Council will recall that but nine months ago President Amin in the General Assembly of the United Nations called for the extinction of Israel as a state. The combination of the move to separate Israeli and Jewish passengers from other passengers, the official endorsement of Hitler's policies by the President of Uganda, his call for the extinction of Israel, and the horrible fate of hundreds of thousands of his own countrymen who did not find favor in his eyes (in this connection I refer you, sir, to the terrifying recital of the brutalities of what it refers to as the "Dictatorial Fascist Ruler of Uganda," published on July 7 by the Kenyan government)—all these combined together to bring home to the Israeli government the realization that unless action was taken, the hostages were doomed and could expect no mercy in Entebbe.

What further indication of the wicked and maniacal intentions of the hijackers and of their Ugandan allies could here have been than that among the hostages held until the last moment before the deadline were eleven children and thirty-four women, doomed to be shot in cold blood by these bloodthirsty murderers. There, under the watchful guns of Terror International and President Amin, a kindergarten was organized by the hostages in the shadow of impending death. The tragic scene that this evokes in one's mind is devastating. It is so much in character with the style of these bandits. They were there prepared to shoot down a kindergarten of innocent children, just as their colleagues in Somalia but a few months ago—as we were informed by the distinguished

French ambassador here—threatened to cut the throats of thirty French children, aged six to twelve, being held hostage.

At this point, let me quote from the statement of Prime Minister Yitzhak Rabin to the Knesset on July 4:

> The time of expiry of the ultimatum drew increasingly closer. The release of non-Israeli passengers more and more exposed the evil conspiracy against Israeli citizens. The political efforts bore no fruit. The sand in the hourglass was about to run out, leaving no possibility for any independent rescue effort. Under these conditions, the Government of Israel decided unanimously to take the only way left to rescue our people and declared its readiness to release terrorists detained in Israeli prisons. Following the Cabinet's decision we accordingly informed the French Government, through which the negotiations were being conducted with the terrorists. We were prepared to adopt even this alternative—in default of any other—to rescue our people. This was not a tactic to gain time, and had this choice alone been left—we would have stood by our decision, as a last resort.

The hijackers raised their demands. They announced that Israel would be held responsible for all the terrorists whose release they demanded, including those terrorists not held in Israel, and refused to allow the exchange to be made in France or on neutral territory, outside Uganda. Their sinister tone and new demands boded evil for the hostages. The Israeli government was left with no alternative.

On the night of July 3-4, 1976, the Israel Defense Forces mounted a most remarkable operation—which will go down in history—rescued the hostages and escorted them to safety. I wish to reiterate on this occasion that Israel accepts full and sole responsibility for the action; that no other government was at any stage party to the planning or execution of the operation. The operation was planned and executed by Israel, and we are proud of it.

During that rescue operation three of the hostages were killed by the terrorists before they were gunned down by Israeli troops, a senior Israeli officer was shot in the back, and several soldiers and hostages were wounded.

The weight of evidence before us reveals prior knowledge and active connivance on the part of the Ugandan government in this whole episode. Even if the evidence were not available, and I say it is available in abundance, it is sufficient to read the letter addressed by President Amin to you, sir, on July 4, 1976, in order to reveal that he implicates himself in his own statement. It is quite evident from his letter that the Ugandan troops mounted guard not over the terrorists and hijackers, but over the hostages. In the fifth paragraph of his letter he states: "I directed that the plane be guarded properly."

He then goes on to make the most incredible statement: "The Ugandan Armed Forces were not allowed by the hijackers to go near the airport building." This is known to be false. The Ugandan troops were in and around the building.

He then reveals his complicity in relating the story of the release of the 147 hostages on June 30, 1976, and July 1, 1976, by openly admitting his part in separating the Israeli passengers from the other passengers. We learn also from his letter of the sinister part played by the Somali ambassador to Uganda, the representative of a country which has become a prime troublemaker in the area and a threat to its neighbors in Kenya, Ethiopia and the area of Djibouti, and which only a few months ago was involved in the holding hostage of thirty French children, on which occasion the French government, motivated by the same sentiments which motivated the Israeli government, took armed action in exercise of its rights under international law to save the children from Somalia.

It is no coincidence that one of the terrorists at Entebbe Airport was the head of the PLO office in Somalia.

Mr. President,

The entire story is one of collusion from beginning to end on the part of the Ugandan government. Let me spell out only a small proportion of the facts as recounted by members of the Air France crew and the hostages.

*Advance Complicity*
a. The captain of the Air France plane has stated that the German hijacker Wilfred Böse knew in advance that Entebbe was the plane's destination.

b.   When the plane landed at Entebbe, the German woman hijacker declared, "Everything is O.K.; the army is at the airport."

c.   Böse announced to the passengers when they landed that they had arrived at a safe place.

d.   Immediately on arrival, Ugandan soldiers surrounded the plane. They were accompanied by five armed Arab terrorists, who embraced and kissed the hijackers on the plane. After that, the terrorists' reinforcements took part in the guard duties and in the negotiations.

e.   Before landing, the hijackers advised the passengers that buses would come to collect them.

f.   After the passengers had been concentrated in the terminal's large hall, Amin was seen embracing and shaking hands with the hijackers.

g.   As the plane landed, a black Mercedes car drove up. Two terrorists emerged and one of them took over control of the operation thereafter. He boarded the plane, embraced Böse (the German hijacker) and talked with him.

h.   Michel Cojot, a French company executive who acted as liaison between the passengers and the hijackers, reported that when the Airport Director brought supplies for the hostages he said he was prepared with supplies, as he had been waiting for approximately 260 passengers and crew.

## The Detention of the Hijacked Passengers

a.   In the first twenty-four hours, guard duty was done by Ugandan soldiers, and the hijackers were not in sight. When the hijackers returned refreshed, the Ugandan soldiers supplied them with submachine guns to guard the hijacked passengers.

b.   In the following days the Ugandans guarded outside the building while a large force of them was concentrated on the first floor.

c.   Ugandan soldiers escorted the hostages to and guarded them in the toilets.

d.   The terrorists came and went as if they were at home, with two cars driven by Ugandans (one of them in uniform) at their disposal.

f.   The hijackers received logistic aid and were supplied with arms (submachine guns, pistols and explosives) at the airport. They also received a mobile communications set.

g. The terrorist who took control of the operation in Entebbe took hostages aside under Ugandan guards for interrogation.

h. Every time Amin appeared in the area of the terminal and before the passengers, he was closeted with the terrorists in a most friendly atmosphere.

i. At the outset of the negotiations Amin dismissed the French ambassador and prevented him from establishing contact with the terrorists. This contact was conducted by Amin in person.

j. Amin warned the hijacked passengers not to dare to escape.

k. Apparently for reasons of bravado and to frighten the hijacked passengers, two jet aircraft overflew from time to time the terminal in which they were being held. Near the building an armored vehicle armed with a heavy machine gun was parked. Close to it stood two helicopters.

l. A mixed guard of hijackers and the Ugandan army guarded the hostages; contact between them was constant and free. The Ugandan soldiers were on guard both inside the hall, on the second floor of the terminal, and on the plane.

m. The hijackers were unconcerned and very relaxed during the period on the ground. They left the airport building from time to time and acted with an obvious feeling of assurance that the Ugandan army would not attempt to overpower them. Mr. Tony Russell, an official of the Greater London Council and one of the Britons freed from the hijacked Air France airbus, in an interview with the London *Times* on July 5 said that President Amin had been in a position to release all hostages if he had wished. "Once we were moved from the aircraft," he said, "the terrorists were not in a commanding position. . . . I have the feeling that if Amin wanted to free us after we were transferred to the airport building, it could have been done. The terrorists had had no sleep for thirty hours and had no powerful weapons at their disposal."

n. The commander of the hijackers in Entebbe spent all his time in the company of President Amin, who recounted this fact by telephone to Colonel Bar-Lev, who spoke to him from Israel.

o. While the passengers were being held, Radio Uganda broadcast an announcement of the hijackers praising Amin for his stand against Zionism and imperialism.

p. The hijackers [who were killed during the rescue operation] were buried with full military honors together with soldiers of the Ugandan army.

## Collaboration between Idi Amin and the Arab Terrorist Organization

a. Uganda maintains close ties with the PLO, which has a large presence there. The PLO office operating in Kampala under Khaled al-Shaykh organizes propaganda activities in East Africa. The Popular Front under George Habash has an intelligence office in Kampala responsible for the activities of the organization in the whole of Africa. This office is subordinate to Wadia Haddad, the head of the branch for overseas terror strikes of the Popular Front. Hundreds of Palestinians are employed in key posts in the administration and public services in Uganda as substitutes for the Asians who were expelled from that racist state.

b. Uganda and the PLO maintain close cooperation also on the military level. In Uganda there is a center for the military training of Palestinians. Palestinian pilots train in the Ugandan air force on Mig-21 planes. Members of the PLO are to be found among the bodyguards of President Amin.

## Ugandan Radio Reports

The extent of Ugandan collaboration can be gauged from the news broadcasts in English on the Kampala radio after the aircraft landed at Entebbe. Records of these broadcasts are available from monitoring reports supplied by the British Broadcasting Corporation. If the distinguished delegates will take the trouble to read the reports, they will find that these reports reveal a complete identity of purpose with the hijackers and their demands on the part of the Ugandan state radio.

There is no attempt in the broadcasts to hide an atmosphere of euphoric ecstacy over the hijacking, and identification with the hijackers on the part of the Government of Uganda. Thus the enthusiastic broadcast on June 29 opens with:

We now bring you the special announcement you have been waiting for. The following are the demands of the Popular Front for the Liberation of Palestine. [The announcer reads a six-point statement by the PFLP.]

Mr. President,

One does not really require all this evidence in order to prove that Israel was entirely justified by every norm of natural law and international law to take the action which it took. In viewing the facts of the case, one must reach one of two conclusions: either the Ugandan government was directly implicated in holding as hostages innocent passengers—men, women and children—or the Ugandan government does not exercise sovereignty over its territory and was incapable of dealing with a half-dozen terrorists.

And what better evidence do we have to support this contention of ours than the fact that to date the Ugandan government has not released a seventy-five-year-old lady, Mrs. Dora Bloch, who was on her way to attend the wedding of her son in this country when the plane was hijacked. Moreover, the refusal of the Ugandan government to release the Air France plane immediately after the hijackers were eliminated only tends to confirm the fact of complicity. What other reason could there be for the Ugandan government to refuse to return the plane to the French government in violation of the 1970 Hague Convention, to which Uganda is a signatory?

If the Ugandan government is not implicated in this crime, why was a seventy-five-year-old lady, Mrs. Bloch, not released immediately after the hijackers were eliminated? Why was she held in custody under guard in a hospital in Kampala? Why was she not released to the British consul when he called on her on Sunday July 4 after the rescue operation? Why have we suddenly been notified ominously that the Ugandan authorities, four of whose employees reportedly dragged her screaming from the hospital, are unaware of her whereabouts?

Either the Ugandan government exercises national sovereignty, in which case it knows where she is, or it doesn't.

I ask my colleagues, African and others here, who are joined to condemn Israel for exercising its inherent right of self-defense: Do you or do you not condone the horrifying behavior which is reflected in this act of "chivalry" on the part of President Amin against Mrs. Dora Bloch, aged seventy-five?

For once, have the courage of your convictions and speak out, or be damned by your own silence. . . .

Here you have the unbelievably macabre spectacle of a state waging a war against a seventy-five-year-old ailing lady, supported presumably by those who would associate themselves with this despicable and cowardly behavior. If the Ugandan government is not implicated, let it now and forthwith produce Mrs. Bloch.

Does this Council propose to remain silent on the fate of Mrs. Bloch?

The disappearance of this old lady and the by now all-too-familiar picture of the terrifying happenings in Amin's Uganda provide ample justification in themselves for the premonition which prompted the action taken by the Israeli government.

This type of action, which in principle is not unprecedented, is dealt with at considerable length in international law, and there is no doubt whatsoever but that the weight of international law and precedent lies fully in Israel's favor. However, the Israeli action at Entebbe came to remind us that the law we find in statute books is not the only law of mankind. There is also a moral law, and by all that is moral on this earth, Israel had the right to do what it did. Indeed, it had also the duty to do so.

Uganda violated a basic tenet of international law in failing to protect foreign nationals on its territory. Furthermore, it behaved in a manner which constituted a gross violation of the 1970 Hague Convention on the Suppression of Unlawful Seizure of Aircraft. This convention had been ratified both by Israel and by Uganda. Article 6 maintains that:

> 1. Upon being satisfied that the circumstances so warrant, any contracting state in the territory of which the offender or the alleged offender is present shall take him into custody and other measures shall be as provided in the law of that state but may only be continued for such time as is necessary to enable any criminal or extradition proceedings to be instituted.

Article 9 states:

> 1. When any of the acts mentioned in Article 1 (a) has occurred or is about to occur, contracting states shall take all appropriate

measures to restore control of the aircraft to its lawful commander
or to preserve his control of the aircraft.

2. In the cases contemplated by the preceding paragraph, any con-
tracting state in which the aircraft or its passengers or crew are present shall facilitate the continuation of the journey of the passengers
and crew as soon as practicable, and shall without delay return the
aircraft and its cargo to the persons lawfully entitled to possession.

The right of a state to take military action to protect its nationals in mortal danger is recognized by all legal authorities in
international law. In *Self-Defence in International Law,** Professor
D. W. Bowett states at page 87 that "The right of the state to
intervene by the use or threat of force for the protection of its
nationals suffering injuries within the territory of another state is
generally admitted, both in the writings of jurists and in the
practice of states. In the arbitration between Great Britain and
Spain in 1925, one of the series known as the Spanish Moroccan
claims, Judge Huber, as rapporteur of the commission, stated:

However, it cannot be denied that at a certain point the interest
of a state in exercising protection over its nationals and their property can take precedence over territorial sovereignty, despite the absence of any conventional provisions. This right of intervention has
been claimed by all states. Only its limits are disputed. . . . We now
envisage action by the protecting state which involves a prima facie
violation of the independence and territorial inviolability of the
territorial state. In so far as this action takes effect in derogation of
the sovereignty of the territorial state it must necessarily be exceptional in character and limited to those cases in which no other
means of protection are available. It presupposes the inadequacy of
any other means of protection against some injury, actual or imminent, to the persons or property of nationals and, moreover, an injury which results either from the acts of the territorial state and its
authorities or from the acts of individuals or groups of individuals
which the territorial state is unable, or unwilling, to prevent.

In *Law of Nations,* Brierly states:

Whether the landing of detachments of troops to save the lives
of nationals under imminent threat of death or serious injury owing

* Published in England by the Manchester University Press, 1958, and in
the United States by Praeger, 1961.

to the breakdown of law and order may be justifiable is a delicate question. Cases of this form of intervention have been not infrequent in the past and, when not attended by suspicion of being a pretext for political pressure, have generally been regarded as justified by the sheer necessity of instant action to save the lives of innocent nationals whom the local government is unable or unwilling to protect.

He goes on to observe:

Every effort must be made to get the United Nations to act. But, if the United Nations is not in a position to move in time and the need for instant action is manifest, it would be difficult to deny the legitimacy of action in defence of a national which every responsible government would feel bound to take, if it had the means to do so. This is, of course, on the basis that the action was strictly limited to securing the safe removal of the threatened national.*

To support this contention, we have D. P. O'Connell in *International Law* (second edition, page 303): †

Traditional international law has not prohibited states from protecting their nationals whose lives or property are imperilled by political conditions in another state, provided the degree of physical presence employed in their protection is proportional to the situation. When the sixth international conference of American States at Havana attempted to formulate a legal notion of intervention in 1928, the United States pointed out that intervention would need to be clearly defined, for the United States would not stand by and permit the break-down of government to endanger the lives and property of American citizens in revolution ridden countries. Interposition of a temporary character would not, in such circumstances, it was argued, be illegal.

The author continues:

Article 2 (4) of the United Nations Charter should be interpreted as prohibiting acts of force against the territorial integrity and political independence of nations, and not to prohibit a use of force which is limited in intention and effect to the protection of a state's own integrity and its nationals' vital interests, when the machinery

---

* James L. Brierly, *Law of Nations: An Introduction to the International Law of Peace*, 6th ed. (New York: Oxford University Press, 1963), p. 627.
† Published in London by Stevens, 1970.

envisaged by the United Nations Charter is ineffective in the situation.

The act of hijacking can well be regarded as one of piracy. Pirates have been *hostis humani generis*—enemies of the human race—since the early days of international law in the Middle Ages. During the war against the slave trade and piracy, certain norms were established in international law which permitted intervention in case of ships engaging in slave trade between Africa and America and against the centers of piracy in North Africa. The principle of national sovereignty was overruled by the higher principles of man's liberty. Israel's action in Entebbe was very similar to the humanitarian rescue operation which took place in those days. The slave trade then could have claimed that searching the slave ships was a violation of international maritime law. But civilized man defined a higher law, namely that of human freedom, above which no national sovereignty can claim to be.

Had a Jewish state existed in the thirties, we might well have decided with the rise of Nazism to endeavor to undertake an operation to rescue the inmates of the concentration camps. The logic of those who criticize us today would maintain that by so doing, we would have been in flagrant violation of the national sovereignty of the Third Reich. What would have been more important, Hitler's sovereignty or rescuing innocent people from a holocaust?

Mr. President,

May I recall General Assembly Resolution 2645 of 1970, the consensus adopted by this Council in Document S/10705 on June 20, 1972, on the subject of hijacking and the resolution of the Assembly of the Council of Europe in 1970 condemning acts of hijacking, sabotage, taking of hostages and blackmailing of governments by Palestinian organizations utilizing the territory of certain Arab states as a refuge, training ground and base for action.

I draw these resolutions and many other relevant resolutions by the United Nations and other international bodies to your attention to remind you that the problem is not new, but that no practical and effective steps have been taken to combat it.

The problem of combating terror has exercised countries

throughout the world. Thus the Soviet Union on January 3, 1973, published a new law on criminal liability for the hijacking of aircraft. This law was discussed at length by V. Ivanov in *Izvestiya* on January 16, 1973. Indeed, the mounting of Soviet official concern is evident in Soviet scientific and legal literature and also in a series of official actions.

On December 4, 1970, *Pravda* reported favorably on the ICAO [International Civil Aviation Organization] Conference at The Hague to draw up a new convention concerning the prevention of hijacking of aircraft. In November 1970 *Pravda* published an article by O. Khlestov praising the United Nations General Assembly Resolution 2645 (XXV) 1970. There was a further article in *Izvestiya* on January 16, 1971, by O. Khlestov praising The Hague Convention of 1970.

Attention is also drawn to an article by P. Yevseyev and Y. Kolosov entitled "Air Bandits Outlawed," published in *International Affairs* in Moscow on November 8, 1971, in which both the United Nations General Assembly Resolution 2645 and The Hague Convention of 1970 are discussed and supported.

The right of self-defense is enshrined in international law and in the Charter of the United Nations and can be applied on the basis of the classic formulation as was done in the well-known Caroline Case,* permitting such action where there is a "necessity of self-defense, instant, overwhelming, leaving no choice of means and no moment for deliberation." This was exactly the situation which faced the Israeli government.

In equivalent circumstances, other states have acted in a manner similar to Israel. But a few months ago the Council discussed actions taken by France in freeing a busload of thirty children held hostage on the Somalia border. I refer you, sir, to the remarks of the distinguished representative of France to the Security Council on February 18, 1976.

The representative of France was addressing the Security Council on an incident which arose out of the holding of thirty French

---

* During the insurrection in Canada in 1837, British forces crossed into the United States in pursuit of insurgents and sank the steamer *Caroline* on the American side of the Niagara River. In subsequent litigation Her Majesty's Government maintained that the destruction of the *Caroline* was an act of necessary self-defense.

children, aged six to twelve years of age, in a school bus as hostages, by a group of terrorists in Somalia. The representatives of these terrorists in Somalia made demands on the French government and announced that if their demands were not met, the terrorists would cut the throats of the children. The French forces took action against the terrorists on the Somali border, killing them; in the process one of the children was killed by the terrorists, and five others were wounded. As the French soldiers rushed to save the children, fire was directed at them from the Somali frontier post, seriously wounding a French lieutenant. They, naturally enough, returned fire into Somali territory, causing casualties and damage to the Somalis. In this case too, one hostage was missing and the child was found later to be held in Somalia by terrorists. He was, happily, later returned alive.

The debate is all too familiar to the distinguished delegates. Suffice it, however, to say that France unequivocally rejected any accusation of aggression in this regard. France on that occasion rightfully exercised its duties under international law in a situation which is similar in many respects to the situation which we had in Entebbe.

In the *Mayagüez* incident last year, in which the United States acted to rescue merchant seamen and their ship, President Ford was quoted as saying: "The decision to use force was based 100% and entirely on a single consideration, to get the crew and the ship back."

I could continue and present dozens of cases which reveal that international precedent and international law fully justify the Israeli action and show that every country that respects itself would have taken the same action in similar circumstances had it considered such action feasible.

Only this week, the West German Minister of Justice reaffirmed in this connection that international law recognizes, in cases where it is essential to save lives, the rights of a state to act as Israel did. This principle was emphasized by the British government in the case of British merchant seamen prisoners of war being transported on a German ship, the *Altmark*, back to Germany through the territorial waters of Norway in February 1940. The British flotilla led by the destroyer *Cossack* entered the territorial waters of

Norway, then a neutral country which had allowed passage to this German ship. In 1940 the British prisoners were prisoners of war, taken prisoner in accordance with the law of war.

Winston Churchill personally authorized British ships to fire at the Norwegian naval ships in the area should they open fire and thereby endanger the British force. He sent the following order to Captain Vian on the *Cossack* with regard to the Norwegian torpedo boat: "If she fires upon you . . . you should defend yourself using no more force than is necessary and ceasing fire when she desists." In his history of the Second World War, Sir Winston Churchill enunciates the principle which guided him: "What mattered at home and in the Cabinet was whether British prisoners were found on board or not . . . this was a dominant factor."

What mattered to the Israeli government in this instance was the lives of the hostages in danger of their very lives. No consideration, other than this humanitarian consideration, motivated the Israeli government.

Israel's rescue operation was not directed against Uganda. Israeli forces were not attacking Uganda. They were rescuing their nationals from a terrorist band of kidnappers who were being aided and abetted by the Ugandan authorities. The means used were the minimum necessary to fulfill that purpose.

Some parallels could be drawn with the right of an individual to use appropriate means to defend himself if he kills someone who is trying to kill him. He is not liable to be found guilty of murder. Judgment takes into account the context and the purpose of the act. The same applies to the use of force in international affairs.

In pursuance of its policy of aiding developing countries, Israel has over the years helped Uganda, as indeed it has cooperated and continues to cooperate with many fellow developing countries throughout the world including in Africa. But there is a limit to the aid which we were prepared to make available to Uganda.

In 1972 President Amin came to Israel, produced maps describing his proposed plan to invade Tanzania and asked for Israeli air support in the planned action, including the bombing of Dar es Salaam. Israel's reply to this preposterous and wicked proposition was such as to bring about a dramatic change in attitude towards Israel on the part of Field Marshal Amin. His frustration with Israel's posture, coupled with the lavish blandishments proffered to him by the ruler of Libya, combined to produce an extreme violent anti-Semitic–anti-Israel attitude on the part of the ruler of Uganda.

Mr. President,

The move by the Organization of African Unity to bring this complaint to the Security Council must appear to be completely incongruous were one's senses not completely dulled by the utter incongruity of the proceedings of this organization. The deliberations on this occasion will doubtless be no exception.

Let me recall to my African colleagues the text of a resolution of the Council of Ministers of the OAU in 1970:

> The council of Ministers of the Organization of African Unity, meeting in its fourteenth ordinary session in Adis Ababa, Ethiopia, from 27 February to 6 March 1970,
> having heard the declaration made by the Foreign Minister of Ethiopia regarding the repeated sabotage and hijacking of civil aircraft thereby endangering the safety of passengers, conscious of the disastrous consequences resulting from such criminal acts of international air travel,
> 1. condemns all attempts and acts of hijacking and sabotaging of civil aircraft;
> 2. calls upon all States to undertake strict measures to protest civilian air travel from being endangered;
> 3. appeals to all States to apprehend and punish such criminals in order to ensure the safety of international air travel.

How do they reconcile their attitude with the text of a resolution on this very issue which they accepted? Here we are again being selective. Do the member states of the OAU not realize that by condoning acts of piracy and hijacking they are laying themselves open to such acts on their own airlines and in their own countries? Are we to understand that there is to be a selective cataloguing of hijacking, of international murder, of piracy, of brutality and of brigandage according to race, color or continent to which the murderer or transgressor belongs? We, the Jewish people, are only too familiar with this type of selective behavior and with the awful catastrophe and doom which it brings to those who engage in it.

In this context, may I remind you that only last month in a discussion, in reply to remarks made by the distinguished representative of the Soviet Union on the issue of terror, I recalled that the distinguished Soviet Foreign Minister Maxim Litvinov had once said, "Peace is indivisible." I submitted that terrorism, too, is indivisible. You cannot be selective about it. The nations of the world will either join hands to destroy this scourge which affects mankind or they will be destroyed by it.

It is not enough to raise your voice in horror when it affects only you. If terrorism is bad, it is bad for everybody in every case, on every occasion, by whoever it is committed and whoever the victim might be. It must be eliminated.

Mr. President,

Summing up the daring and imaginative operation which we are discussing, my Prime Minister stated in the Knesset on July 4:

> This rescue operation is an achievement of great importance in the struggle against terrorism. It is Israel's contribution to humanity's struggle against international terror, but it should not be viewed as the final chapter. It will give us encouragement as we continue our efforts, but the struggle is not over; new efforts, new methods and unremitting sophistication will be required. Terrorism will find us neither immobilized nor hidebound by routine.

In many ways this is a moment of truth for this organization. If it will seize this opportunity courageously and without flinching to join hands in a war against international terror for the benefit of ordinary men and women throughout this world, then it will be serving the purpose for which it was established. It can yet retrieve perhaps in small measure the prestige and good will which it has dissipated by becoming hostage to despots and extremists.

The murder of eleven Israeli athletes in Munich 1972 moved the Secretary-General to demand of the General Assembly to devise measures for the eradication of the scourge of terrorism off the map of the world. The Arab states and their friends managed to "bury" the subject through their "automatic majority." Today the question of international terrorism is before the Security Council, not the General Assembly.

If the Council fails to seize this opportunity which has been granted it to eliminate the scourge of terrorists, kidnappers, hijackers and blackmailers from our midst, then it will plunge to the lowest depths in the eyes of mankind and will disappear in history as yet another great and tragic lost opportunity in history.

It has fallen to the lot of my small country, embattled as we are, facing the problems which we do, to demonstrate to the world that there is an alternative to surrender to terrorism and to blackmail.

It has fallen to our lot to prove to the world that this scourge of international terror can be dealt with. It is now for the nations of the world, regardless of political differences that may divide them, to unite against this common enemy which recognizes no authority, knows no borders, respects no sovereignty, ignores all basic human decencies and places no limits on human bestiality.

We come with a simple message to the Council. We are proud of what we have done because we have demonstrated to the world that in a small country in Israel's circumstances, with which the distinguished members of this Council are all too familiar, the dignity of man, human life and human freedom constitute the highest values. We are proud not only because we have saved the lives of over one hundred innocent people—men, women and children—but because of the significance of our act for the cause of human freedom.

We call on this body to declare war on international terror, to outlaw it and eradicate it wherever it may be. We call on this body, and above all, we call on the member states and countries of the world to unite in a common effort to place these criminals outside the pale of human society and to place any country with them which cooperates in any way in their nefarious activities.

In calling this body to action, I cannot ignore its limitations which are daily demonstrated by the fact that this body has sat silent through fifteen months of the greatest tragedy besetting the world today in Lebanon while a nation is torn apart, tens of thousands are killed, tens of thousands more are wounded and the cup of human suffering overflows daily.

Let me remind you that when the hijacking took place, this Security Council was debating the report of the so-called Palestine Committee. The Security Council held four meetings on the Palestinian question while an act of terror carried out by Palestinian terrorists was taking place, yet this Council did not see fit to raise the question and plead for the release of the innocent civilians.

If this body fails to take action, we call on all freedom-loving countries in the world to come together outside the framework of this body, establish accepted norms of behavior in relation to terrorists, and declare in no uncertain terms that each and every one of them will have nothing whatsoever to do with any country that violates these norms and encourages terrorism. Once hijackers have no country in which to land their planes because receiving such a plane would mean exclusion from the world community whether in the field of air transportation trade, commerce or international relations, there will be no hijacking.

We are proud to have given the lead in this struggle against international terrorism. This debate, which is an opportunity for the world to take action on this issue, can affect the lives of every man and woman in the world. Those countries which fail to take a clear and unequivocal position on this issue for reasons of expediency or cowardice will stand damned by all the decent people in this world and despised in history.

There is a time in the affairs of man when even governments must make difficult decisions guided not by considerations of expediency, but by considerations of morality. Israel was guided by these considerations in risking much to save its citizens. May we hope that others will be guided by these principles too? . . .

In view of the overwhelming body of evidence corroborated by most of the 268 passengers and crew of the hijacked plane, I am left with no other choice but to call the two statements of the Foreign Minister of Uganda nothing but the most formidable collection of distortions, half-truths, deliberate omissions and outright falsehoods this Council has heard in a long time.

I shall not tire the Council by listing each and every distortion. They are too numerous to count, and it would prove very time-consuming. However, there is one abominable lie which my country cannot pass over in silence, and it is incumbent upon me to show the true faces of the President of Uganda and his Foreign Minister for what they are.

The Foreign Minister of Uganda has stated before this Security Council:

> When she [Mrs. Bloch] got better in the evening of Saturday, 3 July, she was returned by the medical authorities to the old Entebbe airport to join the other hostages. . . .
>
> The Israelis committed a naked act of aggression by invading Entebbe airport where the hostages, including Mrs. Dora Bloch, were being held by the hijackers. . . . The members of the invading force took away all the hostages—dead, injured or otherwise. . . .
>
> The press reports and diplomatic sources according to which one diplomat saw Mrs. Dora Bloch in hospital on Sunday are false. There is no concrete information about it.*

So much for the statement of the Foreign Minister of Uganda before this Council.

I repeat that that is a damnable lie. Mrs. Bloch was visited in the hospital by a British diplomat on Sunday, July 4, after Israel's rescue operation at Entebbe Airport, as was clearly stated to this Council by the representative of the United Kingdom. The diplomat reported that she was being guarded by two men, and when he returned an hour later he was not allowed to see her. That diplomat, we were informed yesterday by the representative of the United Kingdom, is to be expelled from Uganda today.

And we now have the ominous news that the Ugandan government is applying the threat of blackmail to foreign nationals in Uganda in connection with the current proceedings in the Security Council. In other words, for the first time in history a direct attempt is being made by threats of blackmail of the most ominous character to influence the proceedings in this Council.

How can this Council pass over this in silence? How can it ignore a blatant attempt to influence this body? How can the members of this Council ignore this flagrant attempt to interfere with their national sovereignty? This whole sordid affair condemns not only the Ugandan government but all the countries which have spoken out against the Israeli rescue mission during this de-

---

* Security Council Verbatim Record S/PV 1939, p. 112.

bate. They have ignored the basic cause of this issue, namely the hijacking of the plane, and, for reasons of political expediency, they have not even had the good grace to say one word about the fate of an old lady of seventy-five dragged out of the hospital, in all probability to the horrible fate that has been meted out to tens of thousands of Ugandans, a fate the nature of which has been described by the Foreign Minister of Kenya in the letter he addressed to you today, Mr. President.

With all due respect to the Foreign Minister of Mauritius and to other members who have joined him in condemning Israel, the fact that they did not see fit even to mention in passing the fate of Mrs. Bloch and did not see fit to address an appeal to the Ugandan authorities in respect to her whereabouts removes from them the moral right to any standing in this debate. . . .

I cannot hide my amazement at the fact that the representative of Yugoslavia saw fit this time too, as in cases in the past, to intervene in a debate on the side of those condemning Israel, in his anxious desire to demonstrate his loyal alignment with the remarks of the so-called nonaligned countries. If any country in the world should be interested today in a move against terror, if any country in the world should have had a word of condolence to say for the victims of the hijacking and terror, then it should have been Yugoslavia. The Yugoslav delegate, let it be noted, had words of condolence for Uganda. Innocent Israeli hostages were killed too in this operation. Why had Yugoslavia not one word to say for them? It is sad indeed to see the Yugoslav government, on each occasion in this forum, rushing to the head of the line in order to condemn Israel, regardless of the issue, blinded apparently by an extreme anti-Israel attitude and by an espousal of the cause of the new anti-Semitism in the world today. Yugoslavia, like many other countries which spoke at this debate, does not realize that international terrorism—from which it suffers no less than do others—will yet make them eat the words expressed by their representative on this occasion at this Council table.

Frankly, I regret perhaps more than many of the other interventions that of the representative of Tanzania. I regret it because of the personal high regard in which I hold him and because of the very great respect in which I, together with many others in

Israel, regard his great *mu'allim* (teacher), the President of Tanzania, whose guest I have had the honor to be. In his legal arguments he conveniently forgets that the legal authorities which he quotes do justify, in international law, such actions as we are discussing, on the grounds of individual self-defense or collective self-defense, as I believe I pointed out when quoting at great length from authorities on international law in my speech last Friday. He and others quoted Article 2, paragraph 4 of the United Nations Charter, obligating countries to settle their disputes by peaceful means. Let me again quote O'Connell in *International Law*:

Article 2 (4) of the United Nations Charter should be interpreted as prohibiting acts of force against the territorial integrity and political independence of nations, and not to prohibit a use of force which is limited in intention and effect to the protection of a state's own integrity and its nationals' vital interests, when the machinery envisaged by the United Nations Charter is ineffective in the situation.*

One's mind tends to be dulled and one's memory to be hazy as the debate goes on in this Council. Let me remind the Council that we are talking about a decision by the Israeli government to protect its citizens, hostages threatened with their very lives, over a hundred men, women and children held at gun point by terrorists who had hijacked them, who recognize no sovereignty, know no law, and who have proved in the past that there are no limits to their bestiality.

These are the selfsame people who shot diplomats, bound hand and foot; who murdered sportsmen at the Olympic games, bound hand and foot; and who, in the past, have held children hostage and were ready to slaughter them. These people were being aided and abetted by a government headed by a racist murderer who had applauded the slaughter of Israeli sportsmen, bound hand and foot by the same terrorists; who had called for the extinction of Israel in this United Nations; and who had not only praised Hitler for the murder of six million Jews but had proposed build-

* O'Connell, *op. cit.*, p. 303.

ing a monument to Hitler—a move which prompted even the Soviet ambassador in Kampala to suggest to President Amin that he was going too far.

This was the problem that faced the Israeli government: over a hundred men, women and children, hostages with terrorist guns pointed at them and with no doubt whatsoever in anybody's mind as to the intention of these terrorists to carry out their wicked plan and slaughter innocent people as they had done in the past. This is the picture which must be in the mind's eye of representatives as they discuss this problem.

I regret many of the remarks made by the representative of Tanzania because I suspect they do not reflect his true feelings or the true feelings of the Tanzanian government.

I reject out of hand his ridiculous attempt to equate with an attack on Africa this Israeli rescue operation to save its passengers. How can the representative of Tanzania make such a remark?

Would Africa have looked better if Palestinian terrorists, in connivance with President Amin, had slaughtered over a hundred men, women and children?

Would Africa have looked better with the blood of those innocent victims bespattering the soil of Africa?

Who has besmirched Africa? Israel, for exercising its right to save its citizens in accordance with international law? Or that racist regime in Uganda, waging a heroic war against a defenseless old lady of seventy-five years?

Who is threatening Africa? Israel, which has done so much to help so many African countries, including many today, in the fields of agriculture, of technology, of health? Or the country which has dispatched this week thirty fighter-planes as reinforcements to Uganda, namely the Libyan government? Against whom are these planes directed and by whom are they flown? You know as well as I do that they are directed against Kenya and Tanzania, which have been threatened and continue to be threatened openly in statements by the President of Uganda, and that the planes are flown by, among others, PLO pilots.

Who is threatening Africa and the Africans? Israel, whose refusal to be associated in any way with President Amin's proposal to invade and bomb Tanzania in 1972 brought about Uganda's break with Israel, or the head of state who produced in Israel—and in other countries, incidentally—maps describing his plans to invade Tanzania?

Who has treated Africa with contempt if not the President of Uganda, who has labeled the President of Tanzania, a man of international stature and standing, in words which are despicable and disgusting and which I do not wish to repeat because of the high regard which I and my people have for the President of Tanzania.

The representative of Tanzania says he "would have preferred principles to be given priority over expediency." What principles are you talking about? The principles of Uganda, which are reflected in the grim recital of murder, kidnapping and banditry in the document distributed today by the Foreign Minister of Kenya? Have you said one word here against these Ugandan principles? Is it principle or expediency which brought you, the distinguished representative of a very distinguished country, to be a co-sponsor of this resolution with Libya, the paymaster and center of world terrorism and the country which is supplying fighter aircraft to Uganda? You know as well as I do that those planes will not be used by Uganda against Israel.

If you, my dear friend, wish to discuss principles and expediency, by all means let us do so. But let us spell them out too. Let us not be selective about principles and expediency, just as we should not be selective about terror and rescue operations.

Is the representative of the Soviet Union not aware that since 1954 the Soviet Union has blocked every attempt on the part of Israel to bring its case to the Security Council? For twenty-two years we have had no remedy in this Council because of the Soviet veto. We are used to cynicism in this body, but the cynical question of the representative of the Soviet Union—"Why did we not complain to this Council?"—when he knows in advance that without regard to the substance of the claim he would have vetoed it, is, I submit, the height of cynicism.

I note the Soviet representative's concern for the inviolability of African territory, and I sincerely trust that his touching concern will be reflected in Soviet Union policies and actions.

The representative of the Soviet Union talked about aggression and the inviolability of territorial integrity and national sovereignty. On these subjects I defer to him, considering the Soviet Union's very considerable record in these respects in Hungary, in Czechoslovakia and in other countries in Eastern Europe. My colleague from China could doubtless elaborate on this subject.

Let me assure the representative of the Soviet Union that the people of Hungary in 1956 and of Czechoslovakia in 1968 would have been only too delighted if the Soviet intervention had been to save a hundred hostages and had been of a duration not exceeding fifty-three minutes, as was the case at Entebbe. At that time the Soviet Union went to great pains to explain its position. Sergei Kovalev, in "Sovereignty and the International Duties of Socialist Countries," published in *Pravda* on September 26, 1968, explained the Soviet Union's justifications of such actions as follows: "Those who talk about the 'illegal' actions of the allied socialist countries in Czechoslovakia forget that in a class society there is not and there cannot be law that is independent of class."

In a civilized society there is not and cannot be law that is independent of the loftiest principles of man—namely, freedom and dignity of man. That, my colleague from the Soviet Union, was the principle that Israel was defending at Entebbe.

I can only reiterate what I said on Friday: Let us stop being selective. If terror is bad, it is bad everywhere, for everybody and on every occasion. It is bad whatever the color, race, creed or nationality of the terrorist. It is bad whatever the color, race, creed or nationality of the victim. That is the issue before us. That is the issue with which the United Nations has failed to deal. That is the issue which will plague the whole world until we deal with it.

I listened to the remarks of the representative of Pakistan. Frankly, I would have accorded them more respect if they had not come from the representative of a regime which has locked up its entire political opposition in jail. Here was the miserable apparition of the representative of a state whose own people were brutally driven out of Uganda by the racist regime of Idi Amin, falling over himself to ingratiate himself with the oppressors of his own kith and kin. How despicable can one be?

The representative of the Soviet Union asked me why we did not quote the documents of the United Nations banning aggression in international relations. The representative of the Soviet Union must be aware that the definition of aggression adopted by the General Assembly on December 15, 1974, has been widely criticized in all legal circles. It is not a binding statement of international law and does not, incidentally, rule out an act like that carried out by Israel.

When the representative of the Soviet Union asked why Israel did not file a complaint with the Security Council, I did not know whether he was naïve or he assumed that I was naïve. Let me assure him that at least in this respect I cannot be characterized as such, and I have no doubt that he is anything but naïve.

I ask the representative of the Soviet Union: Had we submitted a complaint, would the Soviet Union have supported us? Why was there no Soviet statement when the plane was hijacked? Why have they not condemned the terrorist acts of the PLO on many occasions in the past? Why did they not issue a statement or an appeal when the innocent hostages were being held in Entebbe? Why did not the representative of the Soviet Union have even one word to say about the fate of Mrs. Dora Bloch? Or one word of appeal directly to the representative of Uganda in this respect? After all, you have influence in Uganda.

Perhaps the more indicative of all in attitudes of governments was the document from Algeria circulated to members of this Council, which was mentioned favorably by the representative of the Soviet Union in the Security Council yesterday.

It is indeed appropriate that Algeria should speak out for the terrorists and hijackers, considering the fact that it was Algeria to which the first hijacked plane in operations against Israel in 1968 was directed. Algeria was directly involved in that operation and blazed the way for future terrorist exploits. One could hardly expect Algeria, which has played such a prominent part in the history of air hijacking, international kidnapping and the use of diplomatic immunity for terrorist purposes, to forfeit its place in the "hall of fame" of international terrorism. They had to get into the act. After all, what Amin did two weeks ago, they did in 1968.

In the course of all these discussions some delegations have tended to ignore the group which organized this hijacking—namely, the PLO. The PLO has issued a statement disassociating itself from this operation. This is a lie. The PFLP, to which the hijackers belonged, is a constituent member of the PLO. Members will recall that in the past the PLO denied any knowledge of the Black September organization, although Yassir Arafat's second-in-command actually commanded it. They were the group which, according to the President of Sudan, Yassir Arafat personally instructed to execute the American and Belgian diplomats in the Saudi Arabian embassy in Khartoum in 1973. . . .

These are the people who have brought misery, murder and assassination to the area of the Middle East and who have introduced terrorism as a form of international idiom—terrorism which affects innocent people wherever they may be. . . .

### Statement at conclusion of Entebbe debate, UN Security Council, July 13, 1976

Mr. President,

The weight of evidence to prove Ugandan complicity has been growing by the day as the detailed statements of the hostages are analyzed and new evidence becomes available. We now know from the debriefing of the passengers that the map in the hands of the leader of the hijacking group, Wilfred Böse, which he produced immediately after the plane took off from Athens, was already clearly marked with the route Athens–Benghazi–Entebbe. We know, too, as has indeed been published, that before the arrival of the plane at Entebbe, Idi Amin dispatched his personal plane to Somalia in order to pick up and bring to Entebbe the leader of the terrorists, who took control of the plane after it landed at Entebbe.

Furthermore, the members of the Council are fully aware by now that four terrorists hijacked the plane at Athens. The evidence which I have produced, and which other representatives have confirmed, shows that the plane was met at Entebbe Airport by reinforcements of terrorists, some five in number. Four terrorists hijacked the plane. Seven terrorists were accorded a state funeral with full military honors by the Ugandan government. In other words, by all accounts—including, impliedly, by Ugandan accounts—terrorist reinforcements appeared on the scene in Entebbe. In fact, we know that they were driven onto the scene in two official Ugandan cars, one driven by a soldier in uniform. . . .

I note too, as I am already discussing Arab compliance in terrorism, that the Egyptian government has co-sponsored the decision of the Organization of African Unity to bring this matter before the Council. Let me remind the Council that the Egyptian government released the cowardly assassins who shot Prime Minister Wasfi Tal of Jordan on the steps of the Sheraton Hotel in Cairo and then drank his blood. In 1970 the Egyptian government released the terrorists from the Black September organization who had landed the hijacked Pan American jumbo plane at Cairo Airport and had blown it up at that airport. . . .

I listened carefully to the long-drawn-out point of order made yesterday by the representative of Libya, and I must admit that I quite appreciate his concern—which he expressed again today. Who but the representative of Libya, a country which has been the paymaster and haven of international terrorism, would want to avoid a discussion in this Council on this evil—international terrorism? Libya's role in supporting international terrorism financially, militarily and politically and its involvement in attempts at the assassination of foreign leaders, including Arab heads of state, is known to all of us, and I need not repeat it here. . . .

In conclusion, may I express my appreciation to those representatives who have had the courage to take a stand clearly and unequivocally on the side of human decency and human freedom and against the scourge of international terror and those countries that support it, whether by commission or by omission.

The eloquent and moving statement by the representative of the United States of America, Mr. Scranton, and the call of all the other delegations that urged this body to take action, must evoke an echo throughout the world, regardless of political differences. I urge those countries that have already expressed their views on this issue at this table to join together to take action against hijackers and international terrorism.

I am sure that many will follow their lead. This series of meetings will decide in more ways than one whether the United Nations will continue its downward path in the grip of despots or will reassume its rightful role on behalf of humanity and international peace.

*Right of reply in response to statements made the same day (July 13):*

I fail to understand the statement made by the Libyan representative to the effect that I hate Libya. I never said so. Indeed, some of my best friends are Libyans.

But I should add that it is, perhaps, germane to quote President Gaafar Numeiry of Sudan, who only yesterday in a speech said that "the international community, as it is represented in the Security Council, must adopt resolutions which will put an end to the madness of the Libyan regime, a regime which threatens the security of the entire region, Arab and African." I did not say that; President Numeiry said it.

And President Sadat announced yesterday, "It is no secret that the notorious terrorist, Carlos, is now residing in Libya," and he went on at great length to describe Libya's implication. . . .

In reply to the Foreign Minister of Mauritius and to my colleague from Tanzania who asked me, "Would Israel have carried out similar rescue operations in Amsterdam, Paris, Athens or other European cities?," my reply is so obvious: none of the governments mentioned would ever have stooped so low as did the Ugandan government; they would never have become accomplices of international terrorism, and indeed, in two of the cases mentioned, in the past they have actively collaborated in action against terrorists when it occurred on their soil.

Finally, to the representative of the Soviet Union, let me remind him that the United Nations did not create Israel. Israel was created over three thousand years ago and was a nation dispensing moral values to the world thousands of years before the Soviet Union was ever dreamt of. The United Nations merely reaffirmed the debt owed to the Jewish people by history and by the world.

# Epilogue

# Negotiations for Peace

*The Egypt-Israel talks as of February 1978*

In discussing the Middle East today, even the most seasoned observers must exercise some modesty and restraint in their predictions for the future. Indeed, if all the top Middle Eastern experts from Washington, Jerusalem, Cairo, Harvard and elsewhere had been assembled under one roof just a few months ago, the chances are that not one of them would have predicted the scenario that in fact unfolded before our often unbelieving eyes.

As this book goes to press, strenuous efforts are being made towards a resumption of the Israel-Egypt negotiations which were broken off in January 1978 by President Sadat. A flurry of diplomatic activity has taken place since that historic day in November 1977 when the President of Egypt stepped off a plane at Ben-Gurion Airport and became the first Arab leader both to visit Israel and to open direct negotiations towards a peaceful settlement in the Middle East.

The drama of the moment deserved every bit of the attention and publicity lavished upon it. But the extensive media involvement that accompanied that event was not necessarily conducive to the success of the serious negotiations which followed. For three months every dramatic move had been so exposed to the media that not a step was taken without engendering an atmosphere of either wild euphoria or gloomy pessimism. It is therefore important at this juncture to examine the events of the first three months of this new situation in its proper perspective.

The first observation that must be made concerns the direct and human contact that has been established between Israel and its largest Arab neighbor. On November 20, 1977, the world watched spellbound as old suspicions and barriers were broken down, as rhetoric gave way to dialogue, and the limits of what seemed possible were suddenly expanded to new horizons. Most significantly, the visit to Israel by the President of the Arab Republic of Egypt and the subsequent Egyptian reaction to the Israeli delegates and press representatives in Cairo left no doubt that the common people of both countries profoundly desire peace. The joyful and tumultuous reception accorded to President Sadat in the streets of Jerusalem and Cairo bore witness to the people's yearnings and prayers for an end to war and suffering. It is clear that, given the chance, the common people of all countries in the region would express similar feelings.

The realists among us knew that peace would not be achieved in thirty-six hours. We were aware that long and perhaps arduous negotiations lay ahead before all the significant issues of the thirty-year-old conflict in the Middle East were resolved. But on November 20, the first step was taken; indeed, more than a step. It was an act of courage and imagination on both sides, and a challenge that transcended the rivalries and maneuverings of the past to create a new vista promising the first real hope for peace in our region.

For me personally, the true significance of the event hit home a week later, on November 27, when I sat on a couch with the Egyptian Ambassador to the United Nations, Dr. Esmat Abdel Meguid, and talked for over an hour. In retrospect it appears a disarmingly simple act, a cordial man-to-man conversation, but it took thirty years to happen. For until that moment not one Arab delegate or diplomat would to my knowledge speak with, greet or even acknowledge the presence of an Israeli representative. Ambassador Meguid and I did not agree on every issue, and we did not talk only about politics, but we dealt with each other as human beings.

The world quickly became accustomed to the sight of Egyptians and Israelis intermingling and interacting: Israel's Defense Minister Ezer Weizman went to Alexandria to meet with his Egyptian counterpart; Prime Minister Begin went to Ismailiya to talk with President Sadat; Egyptian Foreign Minister Ibrahim Kamel came to Jerusalem and met with Foreign Minister Moshe Dayan. While Egyptian-Israeli military and political committees began to discuss the substantive issues that have long separated the two peoples, Israelis visited the pyramids at Giza and Egyptian journalists visited the Wailing Wall in Jerusalem. The progress made by that human contact is irreversible.

The second observation is less positive and concerns President Sadat's relations with the other Arab states. While Israel welcomed the opening of negotiations, it could not ignore the ominous refusal of three of the states on its borders to participate in those discussions. Given that attitude, Israel must necessarily ask: Who will guarantee agreements made with Egypt concerning the eastern and northern frontiers, when the Arab states sitting along those borders have steadfastly refused to enter into a dialogue with Israel? In the United States it is often possible to lose sight of statements emanating from Damascus, Baghdad or Beirut. But Israel cannot afford that luxury, for its security is vitally linked to developments on *all* its frontiers.

It should be recalled that on the day of President Sadat's arrival in Israel, Syria declared a day of national mourning, Libya severed relations with Egypt, Iraq branded Sadat a traitor, and certain leaders of the PLO threatened openly to assassinate the Egyptian President. Two weeks later in Tripoli, Libya, the rejectionists cemented their alliance by harsh condemnations of the peace process, and warmongering vows to continue their struggle against Israel. The hysterical reactions of these states merely confirms Israel's legitimate concern for its security and the security of its citizens. Indeed, the Tripoli Conference vindicated Israel's insistence all along on direct face-to-face negotiations, for only such negotiations imply an end to the long-standing Arab denial of Israel's right to exist. The Tripoli participants—Syria, Iraq,

Libya, Algeria, South Yemen and the PLO—made very clear that they were not yet ready to abandon that position which has already led to four destructive wars in the Middle East.

But it is not only the pernicious and destructive influence of the so-called radicals with which President Sadat has had to deal. He appears to have been disappointed and dismayed also by the equivocal attitude of the moderates. Saudi Arabia withheld its support during the first three months of negotiations and was not even prepared to endorse a Jordanian federal solution for the West Bank and Gaza.

Perhaps the biggest blow to President Sadat was the attitude of Jordan's King Hussein. Sadat felt he had taken a bold step, gone out on a limb and already extracted major concessions from Israel. He felt he had actually been fighting Jordan's battle both against the PLO and against Israeli control of the West Bank. Yet Hussein did not have the courage to join in the process in those critical first three months.

An analysis of the events leading up to President Sadat's dramatic decision to suspend the political negotiations in Jerusalem in January 1978 and his subsequent visit to Washington in February 1978 must lead to the conclusion that President Sadat at a certain stage in the process realized that he had miscalculated at the outset what the Arab reaction would be. It is well to recall that Prime Minister Begin brought a plan to Washington which he presented to President Carter. This plan allowed for the return to Egyptian sovereignty of the whole of the Sinai peninsula, subject to special arrangements to be negotiated in respect of the Israeli settlements in Rafiah and at Sharm el-Sheikh and the Israeli airfields in the Sinai, arrangements which would be based on demilitarization, United Nations supervision and local Israeli police forces. In addition the plan called for the granting of self-rule to the Palestinian Arabs in the Judea and Samaria districts of the West Bank and the Gaza district, with a provision allowing for a review of the situation in five years time. This plan was characterized by President Carter at the time as showing "a great deal of flexibility" and as a "long step forward."

When it was brought to President Sadat by Mr. Begin his reaction too was encouraging. He subsequently remarked that "Begin brought a peace plan. For the first time they produced something specific. This time they moved a considerable distance more than expected. . . . We must desist from the policy of taking everything, for we have to take only what we can get. The road to peace is longer and more difficult than the road to war . . ." *

The political and military committees met respectively in Jerusalem and Cairo. The Jerusalem meetings took place with the participation of the Foreign Ministers of Israel and Egypt and the Secretary of State of the United States.

In less than forty-eight hours the Political Committee had resolved five of the seven issues dividing Israel and Egypt on a declaration of principles. There were good prospects to bridge the gap on the two remaining issues. Suddenly, without warning, the Egyptian delegation was recalled from Jerusalem to the utter amazement of all the participants, including the Egyptians.

There followed in the Egyptian press a spontaneous and inspired campaign of vilification of Israel and Prime Minister Begin in anti-Semitic terms which were disturbingly reminiscent to the Jewish people.

An analysis of these events supported by the subsequent explanation given by President Sadat reveals that the main problem for him became the pressure of the Arab world, particularly the so-called moderates.

It was evident to all participants in the negotiations that it would be possible to achieve an agreement between Egypt and Israel on all the outstanding bilateral issues. It was clear that the settlements issue was solvable and had nothing to do with Sadat's decision to break off the negotiations in the Political Committee. From President Sadat's remarks it is clear that he came to the conclusion at that stage that he had to harden his attitude in order to appease Arab public opinion outside Egypt.

It was by now obvious that even were Israel prepared to accede to all Egypt's proposals on a bilateral basis, President Sadat would not be prepared to move towards a separate peace at least until Jordan would become involved in the negotiations. In explaining the recalling of his delegation from the Political Committee in the midst of successful negotiations in January 1978, he explained in an abrupt change of attitude that what mattered to him was

* *October Magazine*, Cairo (January 1978).

not Sinai but the Golan Heights and the West Bank, in regard to which satisfactory progress was not being made. This statement indicated a sudden and unexpected major policy change on the part of President Sadat in the negotiations, for the Golan Heights and the West Bank could not be negotiated without the presence of Syria and Jordan. Syrian participation was out of the question, because Syria had aligned itself with the so-called rejectionist front. King Hussein of Jordan made his participation conditional on Israel's accepting in advance all his conditions before entering negotiations; in other words, Israel was presented with an ultimatum instead of an invitation to continue negotiations. President Sadat for his part indicated that he could not proceed without Jordanian participation. Thus a new and vicious circle had been created. Naturally, Israel was unwilling to accede to Jordan's ultimatum in advance of negotiations, maintaining that all issues raised by Jordan must be negotiated at the conference table.

Hence the holdup in negotiations is attributable to President Sadat's realization that he had initially miscalculated as to moderate Arab reaction to his peace initiative, and to his decision to change his approach and pander to inter-Arab opinion.

The issues were wrongly and falsely presented to the American people by much of the media as being that of Israeli settlements. That was at no time the main issue. If at all, it was a side issue. The problem was that President Sadat, at a certain point, decided he could not go it alone, for he realized that achieving an agreement with Israel in advance of an agreement with any other Arab country could prove to be an embarrassment. He therefore introduced a new element—namely, requiring Israel to agree in advance to all of Jordan's demands as a precondition for Jordan to enter the negotiations. Without Jordan, he maintained, he could not proceed. He thus placed a veto in the hands of King Hussein.

The third observation concerns the substance of the negotiations themselves. In this regard, two matters have received particular attention—Israel's settlements in Sinai, and the political future of the Palestinian Arabs in the West Bank and Gaza.

In order to appreciate Israel's security considerations in the south, it is only necessary to recall that the Sinai Peninsula was used in 1948, 1956 and 1967 as a base for attacking Israel. Indeed, as a bleak desert, it has served Egypt no purpose in the past other than as a deployment area for its troops. The trauma of May–June 1967 when Nasser moved a vast army into Sinai with the avowed purpose of annihilating Israel will not quickly be forgotten. That is why Israel insists on demilitarization of the peninsula. Similarly, the only use made by the Egyptians of Sharm el-Sheikh was to block Israeli shipping in the Straits of Tiran. That is why Israel asked for special arrangements at that point for the Jewish settlement which has been established there.

The area under dispute, however, is actually a tiny area in northeastern Sinai no larger than the proverbial postage stamp —100 square miles in the Rafiah salient, or just 2 percent of Sinai, or $1\frac{1}{50}$ of 1 percent of the area of Egypt. Israel has offered to return the entire Sinai Peninsula to Egyptian sovereignty, suggesting that special arrangements be negotiated in respect of the areas under discussion. What Israel is not prepared to do is return to a situation that would present an intolerable security threat.

The Rafiah salient, where several Jewish settlements have been established, is an empty sandy stretch which has served as a traditional highway for invading armies since Egyptian forces entered the land of the Philistines thousands of years ago. Today, a link between the 400,000 Arabs in the Gaza Strip and a potentially hostile army in Sinai would bring hostile forces, including modern missiles, within striking distance of Jerusalem and Tel Aviv. The issue is not, therefore, the settlements as such. The issue is security, and the special arrangements necessary for Rafiah would create a buffer against a potential future invasion.

Israel's concern over this tiny area of northern Sinai can be put into perspective by a simple comparison with American concern over the Panama Canal Treaty signed in September 1977. That treaty is currently one of the major issues in American public life with efforts being made to sway public opinion for and against the Administration's agreement with Panama. Until the year 2000, the United States will maintain bases in the Canal Zone, but Americans are deeply concerned about the security of the area after that date. James H. Scheuer, Democratic Representative from New York, put the issue this way:

Isn't it pious sanctimony for us to tell Israel that she cannot make national security judgments concerning lands contiguous to her border when we, the most powerful nation in the world, are currently preoccupied with the question of how we can maintain control and access to a 100-mile strip of water 1,500 miles from our shores after the year 2000? *

The second substantive issue over which major differences have arisen concerns the future of the Palestinian Arabs in Judea, Samaria and Gaza. Despite the refusal of Israel's eastern and northern neighbors to join the negotiations, Prime Minister Begin offered self-rule to a population that has never experienced political autonomy. For centuries the Arabs in those areas lived under Turkish-Ottoman rule, for thirty years they were under British rule and for nineteen years they lived under Jordanian and Egyptian occupation. For the first time they have been offered self-rule in a plan which had evoked initially favorable comment in the United States and in Egypt.

The Egyptian position, however, remains committed to the establishment of a Palestinian state in the West Bank and Gaza, a proposal which Israel views as a grave threat to its security. Self-determination, after all, has already been given to the Arab world in twenty-one independent states, and Palestinian Arabs already enjoy political sovereignty in the state of Jordan, which covers 80 percent of the territory of mandated Palestine. The concept of self-determination, in Israel's view, cannot be applied in a fragmented way to those Palestinian Arabs living in the West Bank any more than it can for example to the six million Mexicans in the United States.

Israel's proposal must, moreover, be seen in the context of the legal status of the Judea and Samaria districts of the West Bank and of the Gaza district, in which according to recognized international legal authorities Israel has better title than any other country (see Chapter 7). Despite this, Israel is offering a major concession in the form of autonomous self-rule.

One final observation on the current negotiations concerns the attitude of the United States of America. President Sadat directed his entire strategy primarily towards U.S. public opinion and with

---

* Washington *Post* (November 14, 1977).

an eye to the U.S. Administration. He concentrated on the U.S. media, his assumption being that as long as the resulting exposure continued, any holdup or difficulty would be solved by a parallel increase of American pressure on Israel.

When it was felt that President Carter regarded the Begin plan as a fair basis for negotiation and that the United States would not interfere in the quiet diplomacy that had evolved, President Sadat apparently decided to provoke a crisis. His withdrawal of the Egyptian delegation from Jerusalem in January 1978 may have been partly designed, therefore, in addition to the considerations already noted, to secure more active American involvement in the negotiations. Indeed, after this development he announced his intention of visiting President Carter in Washington and of taking his case to the American people, which he did in February 1978.

Clearly, President Sadat's purpose was to pressure the United States into pressuring Israel. However, the United States had become a part of the process of negotiation, with the Secretary of State serving as a member of the Political Committee. The American role has been and must continue to be one of an impartial honest broker, trusted by both sides, and assisting the parties to come to an agreement in conformity with both their national interests, which can and must be reconciled. The United States' role as a mediator in bridging the two apparently irreconcilable positions and bringing the parties again to the negotiating table has thus become an increasingly important and central one.

The peoples of the Middle East have gone through four wars that have left a legacy of distrust and suspicion. While the psychological barriers have been breached, the issues that divide them are still formidable. There will certainly be snags and difficulties, but the stakes are great and both sides know it. However, while the common goal remains peace and while an atmosphere of cooperation prevails, progress will continue to be made and peace can ultimately be achieved.

Israel is deeply committed to the negotiations which began in Jerusalem in November 1977, profoundly aware of the major breakthrough that has occurred and determined to break down the remaining barriers that have divided it from its neighbors for too long. Israel has taken and will continue to take risks for peace because it not only desires peace but, in common with our whole area, also needs peace. There is yet a long way to go till peace is achieved, and the most important step in that process is to extend the direct and constructive dialogue begun between Egypt and Israel to all Israel's neighbors. Israel has determined to forge ahead with the spirit created in Jerusalem on November 20 and to replace the decades of bloodshed and destruction with a new era of peace and cooperation.

# Appendix

# Chapter 1

*Declaration of the Establishment of the State of Israel, May 14, 1948* *

Eretz-Israel † was the birthplace of the Jewish people. Here their spiritual, religious and political identity was shaped. Here they first attained to statehood, created cultural values of national and universal significance and gave to the world the eternal book of books.

After being forcibly exiled from their land, the people kept faith with it throughout their dispersion and never ceased to pray and hope for their return to it and for the restoration in it of their political freedom.

Impelled by this historic and traditional attachment, Jews strove in every successive generation to re-establish themselves in their ancient homeland. In recent decades they returned in their masses. Pioneers,

---

* Published in the *Official Gazette*, No. 1 of the 5th Iyar, 5708 (May 14, 1948).
† Eretz-Israel (Hebrew)—the Land of Israel, Palestine.

ma'apilim * and defenders, they made deserts bloom, revived the Hebrew language, built villages and towns, and created a thriving community, controlling its own economy and culture, loving peace but knowing how to defend itself, bringing the blessings of progress to all the country's inhabitants, and aspiring towards independent nationhood.

In the year 5657 (1897), at the summons of the spiritual father of the Jewish state, Theodor Herzl, the first Zionist Congress convened and proclaimed the right of the Jewish people to national rebirth in its own country.

This right was recognized in the Balfour Declaration of the 2nd November, 1917, and re-affirmed in the mandate of the League of Nations which, in particular, gave international sanction to the historic connection between the Jewish people and Eretz-Israel and to the right of the Jewish people to rebuild its national home.

The catastrophe which recently befell the Jewish people—the massacre of millions of Jews in Europe—was another clear demonstration of the urgency of solving the problem of its homelessness by reestablishing in Eretz-Israel, the Jewish state, which would open the gates of the homeland wide to every Jew and confer upon the Jewish people the status of a fully privileged member of the comity of nations.

Survivors of the Nazi Holocaust in Europe, as well as Jews from other parts of the world, continued to migrate to Eretz-Israel, undaunted by difficulties, restrictions and dangers, and never ceased to assert their right to a life of dignity, freedom and honest toil in their national homeland.

In the Second World War, the Jewish community of this country contributed its full share to the struggle of the freedom and peace-loving nations against the forces of Nazi wickedness and, by the blood of its soldiers and its war effort, gained the right to be reckoned among the peoples who founded the United Nations.

On the 29th November, 1947, the United Nations General Assembly passed a resolution calling for the establishment of a Jewish state in Eretz-Israel. The General Assembly required the inhabitants of Eretz-Israel to take such steps as were necessary on their part for the implementation of that resolution. This recognition by the United Nations of the right of the Jewish people to establish their state is irrevocable.

---

* Ma'apilim (Hebrew)—immigrants coming to Eretz-Israel in defiance of restrictive legislation.

This right is the natural right of the Jewish people to be masters of their own fate, like all other nations, in their own sovereign state.

Accordingly we, members of the People's Council, representatives of the Jewish community of Eretz-Israel and of the Zionist movement, are here assembled on the day of the termination of the British Mandate over Eretz-Israel and, by virtue of our natural and historic right and on the strength of the resolution of the United Nations General Assembly, hereby declare the establishment of a Jewish state in Eretz-Israel, to be known as the State of Israel.

We declare that, with effect from the moment of the termination of the Mandate, being tonight, the eve of Sabbath, the 6th Iyar, 5708 (15th May, 1948). Until the establishment of the elected, regular authorities of the state in accordance with the constitution which shall be adopted by the elected Constituent Assembly not later than the 1st October 1948, the People's Council shall act as a provisional council of state, and its executive organ, the People's Administration, shall be the provisional government of the Jewish state, to be called "Israel."

The State of Israel will be open for Jewish immigration and for the ingathering of the exiles; it will foster the development of the country for the benefit of all its inhabitants; it will be based on freedom, justice and peace as envisaged by the Prophets of Israel; it will ensure complete equality of social and political rights to all its inhabitants irrespective of religion, race or sex; it will guarantee freedom of religion, conscience, language, education and culture; it will safeguard the Holy Places of all religions and it will be faithful to the principles of the Charter of the United Nations.

The State of Israel is prepared to cooperate with the agencies and representatives of the United Nations in implementing the resolution of the General Assembly of the 29th November, 1947, and will take steps to bring about the economic union of the whole of Eretz-Israel.

We appeal to the United Nations to assist the Jewish people in the building up of its state and to receive the State of Israel into the comity of nations.

We appeal—in the very midst of the onslaught launched against us now for months—to the Arab inhabitants of the State of Israel to preserve peace and participate in the upbuilding of the state on the basis of full and equal citizenship and due representation in all its provisional and permanent institutions.

We extend our hand to all neighbouring states and their peoples in an offer of peace and good neighbourliness, and appeal to them to establish bonds of cooperation and mutual help with the sovereign

Jewish people settled in its own land. The State of Israel is prepared to do its share in a common effort for the advancement of the entire Middle East.

We appeal to the Jewish people throughout the Diaspora to rally round the Jews of Eretz-Israel in the tasks of immigration and up-building and to stand by them in the great struggle for the realization of the age-old dream—the redemption of Israel.

Placing our trust in the Almighty, we affix our signatures to this proclamation at this session of the Provisional Council of state, on the soil of the homeland, in the city of Tel Aviv, on this Sabbath eve, the 5th day of Iyar, 5708 (14th May, 1948).

# CHAPTER 4

*Security Council Resolution 242 of 22 November 1967*

*The Security Council,*

*Expressing* its continuing concern with the grave situation in the Middle East,

*Emphasizing* the inadmissibility of the acquisition of territory by war and the need to work for a just and lasting peace in which every State in the area can live in security,

*Emphasizing further* that all Member States in their acceptance of the Charter of the United Nations have undertaken a commitment to act in accordance with Article 2 of the Charter,

1. *Affirms* that the fulfilment of Charter principles requires the establishment of a just and lasting peace in the Middle East which should include the application of both the following principles:

(i) Withdrawal of Israel armed forces from territories occupied in the recent conflict;

(ii) Termination of all claims or states of belligerency and respect for and acknowledgement of the sovereignty, territorial integrity and political independence of every State in the area and their right to live in peace within secure and recognized boundaries free from threats or acts of force;

2. *Affirms further* the necessity

(a) For guaranteeing freedom of navigation through international waterways in the area;

(b) For achieving a just settlement of the refugee problem;

(c) For guaranteeing the territorial inviolability and political independence of every State in the area, through measures including the establishment of demilitarized zones;

3. *Requests* the Secretary-General to designate a Special Representative to proceed to the Middle East to establish and maintain contacts with the States concerned in order to promote agreement and assist efforts to achieve a peaceful and accepted settlement in accordance with the provisions and principles in this resolution;

4. *Requests* the Secretary-General to report to the Security Council on the progress of the efforts of the Special Representative as soon as possible.

Adopted unanimously at the 1382nd meeting

### *Security Council Resolution 338 of 22 October 1973*

*The Security Council,*

1. *Calls upon* all parties to the present fighting to cease all firing and terminate all military activity immediately, no later than 12 hours after the moment of the adoption of this decision, in the positions they now occupy;

2. *Calls upon* the parties concerned to start immediately after the cease-fire the implementation of Security Council Resolution 242 (1967) in all of its parts;

3. *Decides that* immediately and concurrently with cease-fire, negotiations start between the parties concerned under appropriate auspices aimed at establishing a just and durable peace in the Middle East.

# Documents Relating to the Convening of the Geneva Peace Conference, December 1973

*Letter dated 18 December 1973 from the Secretary-General to the President of the Security Council*

I have received the attached letters from the Permanent Representatives of the Union of Soviet Socialist Republics and the United States of America concerning the forthcoming Conference on the Middle East. I should be grateful if you would communicate these letters to the members of the Security Council. It is my intention to proceed on the basis of these letters which I consider to be in accordance with Security Council resolution 344 (1973) of 15 December 1973.

*(signed)* Kurt Waldheim

*Letter dated 18 December 1973 from the Permanent Representative of the Union of Soviet Socialist Republics to the United Nations addressed to the Secretary-General*

On 22 October 1973, the Security Council adopted resolution 338 (1973) jointly sponsored by the Soviet Union and the United States which calls for negotiations to start between the parties concerned under appropriate auspices, aimed at establishing a just and durable peace in the Middle East. The Soviet Union and the United States have now been informed by the parties concerned of their readiness to participate in the Peace Conference, which will begin in Geneva on 21 December this year. The Conference will be convened under the auspices of the United Nations.

The parties have agreed that the Conference should proceed under the joint chairmanship of the Soviet Union and the United States. The parties have also agreed that the question of other participants from the Middle East area will be discussed during the first stage of the Conference.

We hope that you will find it possible to participate in the opening of the Conference at which it is hoped the Governments concerned will be represented by their respective Foreign Ministers and later by their specially appointed representatives with the rank of Ambassador.

We also hope that you will make available a representative who will keep you fully informed of the course of the work of the Conference. And finally, we should be grateful if the United Nations could provide the necessary facilities for the work of the Conference.

If, as we hope, you find it possible to participate, the Soviet Union and the United States, as co-chairmen, would be grateful if you would agree to act as convener of the Conference and to preside at its opening.

We request you to circulate this letter to the members of the Security Council for their information. We believe that it would be appropriate for the President of the Security Council to hold informal consultations with the members of the Council with a view to obtaining a favourable consensus in the Council.

> (*signed*) Y. MALIK
> Permanent Representative
> of the USSR
> to the United Nations

*Letter dated 18 December 1973 from the Acting Permanent Representative of the United States of America to the United Nations addressed to the Secretary-General*

I have the honour to transmit to you the following letter from Secretary Kissinger.

"Dear Mr. Secretary-General:

"On October 22, 1973, the Security Council adopted resolution 338 (1973) jointly sponsored by the Soviet Union and the United States, which calls for negotiations to start between the parties concerned under appropriate auspices, aimed at establishing a just and durable peace in the Middle East. The Soviet Union and the United States have now been informed by the parties concerned of their readiness to participate in the Peace Conference which will begin in Geneva on December 21. The Conference should be convened under the auspices of the United Nations.

"The parties have agreed that the Conference should be under the co-chairmanship of the Soviet Union and the United States. The parties have also agreed that the question of other participants from the Middle East area will be discussed during the first stage of the Conference.

"It is our hope that you will find it possible to participate in the opening phase of the Conference at which it is expected that the Governments concerned will be represented by their respective Foreign Ministers and, later, by their specially appointed representatives with ambassadorial rank. We also hope that you can make available a representative who would keep you fully informed as the Conference proceeds. Finally, we would also appreciate it if the United Nations could make appropriate arrangements for the necessary conference facilities.

"If as we hope you find it possible to participate, as co-chairmen the Soviet Union and the United States would appreciate it if you would agree to serve as convener of the Conference and preside in the opening phase.

"We request that you circulate this letter to members of the Security Council for their information. We believe it would be appropriate for the President of the Security Council to consult informally with the membership with a view to securing a favorable consensus of the Council."

> (*signed*) W. TAPLEY BENNETT, JR.
> Acting Permanent Representative
> of the United States of America
> to the United Nations

# The Disengagement Agreements

## I. Israel-Egypt

*Efforts to conclude an agreement on separation of forces between Israel and Egypt that were made at kilometre 101 in Sinai, and later in Geneva, initially failed. Secretary of State Dr. Kissinger arrived in the Middle East and was able to narrow the gap between the parties and bring about the conclusion of an agreement. Before the signing of the agreement, the Israel Government approved it and issued a statement. A day later, the agreement was signed at kilometre 101 by the Chiefs of Staff of the Israeli and Egyptian armies. Texts of the Cabinet statement and the agreement follow:*

a) Israel Government Statement on Separation of Forces Agreement, January 18, 1974:

Following the Cabinet session, which took place this afternoon, in which agreement on the separation of forces with Egypt was unanimously approved, the Government Secretary has issued the following announcement:

January 17, 1974                              2100 hours Israel-Egypt time
In accordance with the decision of the Geneva Conference, the
Governments of Israel and Egypt, with the assistance of the Government of the United States, have reached agreement on the disengagement and separation of their military forces.

The agreement is scheduled to be signed by the Chiefs of Staff of
Israel and Egypt at 1200 local time, Friday January 18, at kilometre
101 on the Cairo-Suez road. The Commander of the United Nations
Emergency Force, General Siilasvuo, has been asked by the parties to
witness the signing.


b) Egyptian-Israeli Agreement on Disengagement of Forces in pursuance of the Geneva Peace Conference

A. Egypt and Israel will scrupulously observe the cease-fire on land,
sea, and air called for by the UN Security Council and will refrain
from the time of the signing of this document from all military or
para-military actions against each other.

B. The military forces of Egypt and Israel will be separated in
accordance with the following principles:

1. All Egyptian forces on the east side of the Canal will be deployed
west of the line designated as Line A on the attached map. All Israeli
forces, including those west of the Suez Canal and the Bitter Lakes,
will be deployed east of the line designated as Line B on the attached
map.

2. The area between the Egyptian and Israeli lines will be a zone of
disengagement in which the United Nations Emergency Force
(UNEF) will be stationed. The UNEF will continue to consist of
units from countries that are not permanent members of the Security
Council.

3. The area between the Egyptian line and the Suez Canal will be
limited in armament and forces.

4. The area between the Israeli line (Line B on the attached map)
and the line designated as Line C on the attached map, which runs
along the western base of the mountains where the Gidi and Mitla
Passes are located, will be limited in armament and forces.

5. The limitations referred to in paragraphs 3 and 4 will be inspected
by UNEF. Existing procedures of the UNEF, including the attaching
of Egyptian and Israeli liaison officers to UNEF, will be continued.

6. Air forces of the two sides will be permitted to operate up to
their respective lines without interference from the other side.

C. The detailed implementation of the disengagement of forces will be worked out by military representatives of Egypt and Israel, who will agree on the stages of this process. These representatives will meet no later than 48 hours after the signature of this agreement at Kilometre 101 under the aegis of the United Nations for this purpose. They will complete this task within five days. Disengagement will begin within 48 hours after the completion of the work of the military representatives and in no event later than seven days after the signature of this agreement. The process of disengagement will be completed not later than 40 days after it begins.

D. This agreement is not regarded by Egypt and Israel as a final peace agreement. It constitutes a first step toward a final, just and durable peace according to the provisions of Security Council Resolution 338 and within the framework of the Geneva Conference.

> For Egypt
> General Abdul Gani al Gamasy
>
> For Israel
> David Elazar, Lt. Gen., Chief of Staff of I.D.F.

## II. Israel-Syria

a) Text of Agreement on Disengagement between Israeli and Syrian Forces Signed on 31 May, 1974

A. Israel and Syria will scrupulously observe the cease-fire on land, sea and air and will refrain from all military actions against each other, from the time of the signing of this document, in implementation of United Nations Security Council Resolution 338 dated 22 October, 1973.

B. The military forces of Israel and Syria will be separated in accordance with the following principles:

1. All Israeli military forces will be west of the line designated as Line A on the map attached hereto, except in the Kuneitra area, where they will be west of Line A-1.

2. All territory east of Line A will be under Syrian administration, and Syrian civilians will return to this territory.

3. The area between Line A and the Line designated as Line B on the attached map will be an area of separation. In this area will be stationed the United Nations Disengagement Observer Force established in accordance with the accompanying protocol.

4. All Syrian military forces will be east of the line designated as Line B on the attached map.

5. There will be two equal areas of limitation in armament and forces, one west of Line A and one east of Line B as agreed upon.

6. Air forces of the two sides will be permitted to operate up to their respective lines without interference from the other side.

C. In the area between Line A and Line A-1 on the attached map there shall be no military forces.

D. This agreement and the attached map will be signed by the military representatives of Israel and Syria in Geneva not later than 31 May, 1974, in the Egyptian-Israeli military working group of the Geneva Peace Conference under the aegis of the United Nations, after that group has been joined by a Syrian military representative, and with the participation of representatives of the United States and the Soviet Union. The precise delineation of a detailed map and a plan for the implementation of the disengagement of forces will be worked out by military representatives of Israel and Syria in the Egyptian-Israeli military working group who will agree on the stages of this process. The military working group described above will start their work for this purpose in Geneva under the aegis of the United Nations within 24 hours after the signing of this agreement. They will complete this task within five days. Disengagement will begin within 24 hours after the completion of the task of the military working group. The process of disengagement will be completed not later than twenty days after it begins.

E. The provisions of paragraphs A, B and C shall be inspected by personnel of the United Nations comprising the United Nations Disengagement Observer Force under this agreement.

F. Within 24 hours after the signing of this agreement in Geneva all wounded prisoners of war which each side holds of the other as certified by the ICRC will be repatriated. The morning after the completion of the task of the military working group, all remaining prisoners of war will be repatriated.

G. The bodies of all dead soldiers held by either side will be returned for burial in their respective countries within 10 days after the signing of this agreement.

H. This agreement is not a peace agreement. It is a step toward a just and durable peace on the basis of Security Council Resolution 338 dated 22 October, 1973.

b) Protocol to Agreement on Disengagement between Israeli and Syrian Forces Concerning the United Nations Disengagement Observer Force

Israel and Syria agree that:

The function of the United Nations Disengagement Observer Force (UNDOF) under the agreement will be to use its best efforts to maintain the cease-fire and to see that it is scrupulously observed. It will supervise the agreement and protocol thereto with regard to the areas of separation and limitation. In carrying out its mission, it will comply with generally applicable Syrian laws and regulations and will not hamper the functioning of local civil administration. It will enjoy freedom of movement and communication and other facilities that are necessary for its mission. It will be mobile and provided with personal weapons of a defensive character and shall use such weapons only in self-defense. The number of the UNDOF shall be about 1,250, who will be selected by the Secretary General of the United Nations in consultation with the parties from members of the United Nations who are not permanent members of the Security Council.

The UNDOF will be under the command of the United Nations, vested in the Secretary General, under the authority of the Security Council.

The UNDOF shall carry out inspections under the agreement, and report thereon to the parties, on a regular basis, not less often than once every fifteen days, and, in addition, when requested by either party. It shall mark on the site the respective lines shown on the map attached to the agreement.

Israel and Syria will support a resolution of the United Nations Security Council which will provide for the UNDOF contemplated by the agreement. The initial authorization will be for six months subject to renewal by further resolution of the Security Council.

## III. *Maps Illustrating Disengagement Agreements*

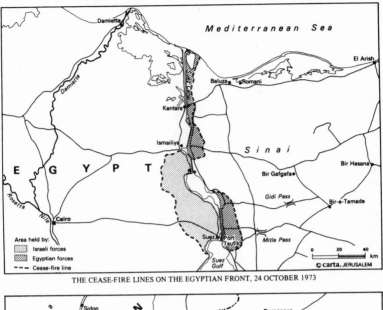

THE CEASE-FIRE LINES ON THE EGYPTIAN FRONT, 24 OCTOBER 1973

THE CEASE-FIRE LINES ON THE SYRIAN FRONT, 24 OCTOBER 1973

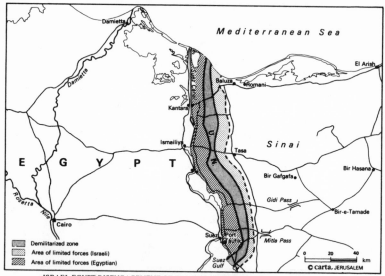

ISRAEL-EGYPT DISENGAGEMENT OF FORCES AGREEMENT LINES, 18 JANUARY 1974

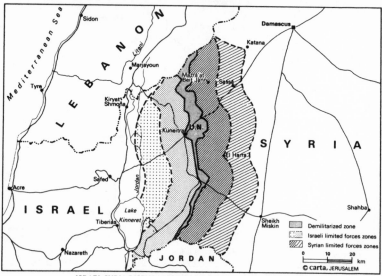

ISRAEL-SYRIA DISENGAGEMENT OF FORCES LINES, 30 MAY 1974

## Interim Agreement between Egypt and Israel, September 1, 1975

The Government of the Arab Republic of Egypt and the Government of Israel have agreed that:

### Article I

The conflict between them and in the Middle East shall not be resolved by military force but by peaceful means.

The agreement concluded by the parties Jan. 18, 1974, within the framework of the Geneva peace conference constituted a first step towards a just and durable peace, according to the provisions of Security Council Resolution 338 of Oct. 22, 1973, and they are determined to reach a final and just peace settlement by means of negotiations called for by Security Council Resolution 338, this agreement being a significant step towards that end.

### Article II

The parties hereby undertake not to resort to the threat or use of force or military blockade against each other.

## Article III

( 1 ) The parties shall continue scrupulously to observe the cease-fire on land, sea and air and to refrain from all military or paramilitary actions against each other.

( 2 ) The parties also confirm that the obligations contained in the annex and, when concluded, the protocol shall be an integral part of this agreement.

## Article IV

A. The military forces of the parties shall be deployed in accordance with the following principles:

( 1 ) All Israeli forces shall be deployed east of the lines designated as lines J and M on the attached map.

( 2 ) All Egyptian forces shall be deployed west of the line designated as line E on the attached map.

( 3 ) The area between the lines designated on the attached map as lines E and F and the area between the lines designated on the attached map as lines J and K shall be limited in armament and forces.

( 4 ) The limitations on armament and forces in the areas described by paragraph ( 3 ) above shall be agreed as described in the attached annex.

( 5 ) The zone between the lines designated on the attached map as lines E and J will be a buffer zone. On this zone the United Nations Emergency Force will continue to perform its functions as under the Egyptian-Israeli agreement of Jan. 18, 1974.

( 6 ) In the area south from line E and west from line M, as defined in the attached map, there will be no military forces, as specified in the attached annex.

B. The details concerning the new lines, the redeployment of the forces and its timing, the limitation of armaments and forces, aerial reconnaissance, the operation of the early warning and surveillance installations and the use of the roads, the U.N. functions and other arrangements will all be in accordance with the provisions of the annex and map which are an integral part of this agreement and of the protocol which is to result from negotiations pursuant to the annex and which, when concluded, shall become an integral part of this agreement.

## Article V

The United Nations Emergency Force is essential and shall continue its functions, and its mandate shall be extended annually.

### Article VI

The parties hereby establish a joint commission for the duration of this agreement. It will function under the aegis of the chief coordinator of the United Nations peace-keeping missions in the Middle East in order to consider any problem arising from this agreement and to assist the United Nations Emergency Force in the execution of its mandate. The joint commission shall function in accordance with procedures established in the protocol.

### Article VII

Nonmilitary cargoes destined for or coming from Israel shall be permitted through the Suez Canal.

### Article VIII

(1) This agreement is regarded by the parties as a significant step toward a just and lasting peace. It is not a final peace agreement.

(2) The parties shall continue their efforts to negotiate a final peace agreement within the framework of the Geneva peace conference in accordance with security council resolution 338.

### Article IX

This agreement shall enter into force upon signature of the protocol and remain in force until superseded by a new agreement.

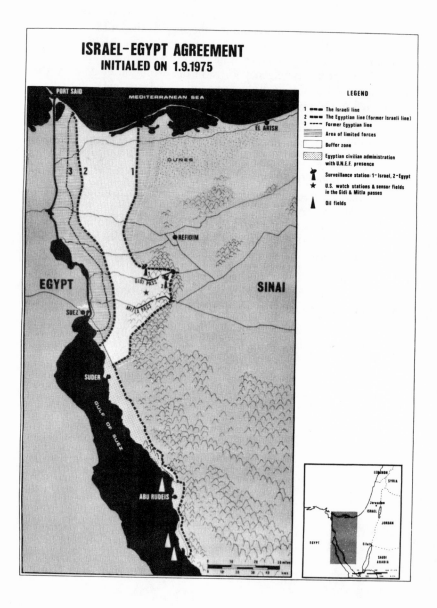

## ANNEX TO THE SINAI AGREEMENT

Within five days after the signature of the Egypt-Israel agreement, representatives of the two parties shall meet in the military working group of the Middle East peace conference at Geneva to begin preparation of a detailed protocol for the implementation of the agreement. In order to facilitate preparation of the protocol and implementation of the agreement, and to assist in maintaining the scrupulous observance of the cease-fire and other elements of the agreement, the two parties have agreed on the following principles, which are an integral part of the agreement, as guidelines for the working group.

### 1. Definitions of Lines and Areas

The deployment lines, areas of limited forces and armaments, buffer zones, the area south from line E and west from line M, other designated areas, road sections for common use and other features referred to in Article IV of the agreement shall be as indicated on the attached map (1:100,000—U.S. edition).

## 2. Buffer Zones

(a) Access to the buffer zones shall be controlled by the UNEF, according to procedures to be worked out by the working group and UNEF.

(b) Aircraft of either party will be permitted to fly freely up to the forward line of that party. Reconnaissance aircraft of either party may fly up to the middle line of the buffer zone between E and J on an agreed schedule.

(c) In the buffer zone, between line E and J, there will be established under Article IV of the agreement an early-warning system entrusted to United States civilian personnel as detailed in a separate proposal, which is a part of this agreement.

(d) Authorized personnel shall have access to the buffer zone for transit to and from the early-warning system; the manner in which this is carried out shall be worked out by the working group and UNEF.

## 3. Area South of Line E and West of Line M

(a) In this area, the United Nations Emergency Force will assure that there are no military or paramilitary forces of any kind, military fortifications and military installations; it will establish checkpoints and have the freedom of movement necessary to perform this function.

(b) Egyptian civilians and third-country civilian oil-field personnel shall have the right to enter, exit from, work and live in the above-indicated area, except for buffer zones 2A, 2B and the U.N. posts. Egyptian civilian police shall be allowed in the area to perform normal civil police functions among the civilian population in such numbers and with such weapons and equipment as shall be provided for in the protocol.

(c) Entry to and exit from the area, by land, by air or by sea, shall be only through UNEF checkpoints. UNEF shall also establish checkpoints along the road, the dividing line and at other points, with the precise locations and number to be included in the protocol.

(d) Access to the airspace and the coastal area shall be limited to unarmed Egyptian civilian vessels and unarmed civilian helicopters and transport planes involved in the civilian activities of the area, as agreed by the working group.

(e) Israel undertakes to leave intact all currently existing civilian installations and infrastructures.

(f) Procedures for use of the common sections of the coastal road along the Gulf of Suez shall be determined by the working group and detailed in the protocol.

### 4. Aerial Surveillance

There shall be a continuation of aerial reconnaissance missions by the U.S. over the areas covered by the agreement following the same procedures already in practice. The missions will ordinarily be carried out at a frequency of one mission every seven to 10 days, with either party or UNEF empowered to request an earlier mission. The U.S. will make the mission results available expeditiously to Israel, Egypt and the chief coordinator of the U.N. peace-keeping mission in the Middle East.

### 5. Limitation of Forces and Armaments

(a) Within the areas of limited forces and armaments the major limitations shall be as follows:

(1) Eight (8) standard infantry battalions.

(2) Seventy-five (75) tanks.

(3) Sixty (60) artillery pieces, including heavy mortars (i.e., with caliber larger than 120 mm.), whose range shall not exceed 12 km.

(4) The total number of personnel shall not exceed eight thousand (8,000).

(5) Both parties agree not to station or locate in the area weapons which can reach the line of the other side.

(6) Both parties agree that in the areas between lines J and K, and between line A (of the disengagement agreement of Jan. 18, 1974) and line E, they will construct no new fortifications or installations for forces of a size greater than that agreed herein.

(b) The major limitations beyond the areas of limited forces and armament will be:

(1) Neither side will station nor locate any weapon in areas from which they can reach the other line.

(2) The parties will not place antiaircraft missiles within an area of 10 kilometers east of line K and west of line F, respectively.

(c) The U.N. Force will conduct inspections in order to insure the maintenance of the agreed limitations within these areas.

### 6. Process of Implementation

The detailed implementation and timing of the redeployment of forces, turnover of oil fields and other arrangements called for by the agreement, annex and protocol shall be determined by the working group, which will agree on the stages of this process, including the phased movement of Egyptian troops to line E and Israeli troops to line J. The first phase will be the transfer of the oil fields and installations to Egypt. This process will begin within two weeks from the signature of the protocol with the introduction of the necessary technicians, and it will be completed no later than eight weeks after it begins. The details of the phasing will be worked out in the military working group.

Implementation of the redeployment shall be completed within five months after signature of the protocol.

# PROPOSAL FOR AN EARLY-WARNING SYSTEM

In connection with the early-warning system referred to in Article IV of the agreement between Egypt and Israel concluded on this date and as an integral part of that agreement (hereafter referred to as the basic agreement), the United States proposes the following:

1. The early-warning system to be established in accordance with Article IV in the area shown on the attached map will be entrusted to the United States. It shall have the following elements:

A. There shall be two surveillance stations to provide strategic early warning, one operated by Egyptian and one operated by Israeli personnel. Their locations are shown on the map attached to the basic agreement. Each station shall be manned by not more than 250 technical and administrative personnel. They shall perform the functions of visual and electronic surveillance only within their stations.

B. In support of these stations, to provide tactical early warning and to verify access to them, three watch stations shall be established by the United States in the Mitla and Gidi Passes as will be shown on the agreed map.

These stations shall be operated by United States civilian personnel. In support of these stations, there shall be established three unmanned electronic-sensor fields at both ends of each pass and in the general vicinity of each station and the roads leading to and from those stations.

2. The United States civilian personnel shall perform the following duties in connection with the operation and maintenance of these stations:

A. At the two surveillance stations described in paragraph 1A, above, United States personnel will verify the nature of the operations of the stations and all movement into and out of each station and will immediately report any detected divergency from its authorized role of visual and electronic surveillance to the parties to the basic agreement and the UNEF.

B. At each watch station described in paragraph 1B above, the United States personnel will immediately report to the parties to the basic agreement and to UNEF any movement of armed forces, other than the UNEF, into either pass and any observed preparations for such movement.

C. The total number of United States civilian personnel assigned to functions under these proposals shall not exceed 200. Only civilian personnel shall be assigned to functions under these proposals.

3. No arms shall be maintained at the stations and other facilities covered by these proposals, except for small arms required for their protection.

4. The United States personnel serving the early-warning system shall be allowed to move freely within the area of the system.

5. The United States and its personnel shall be entitled to have such support facilities as are reasonably necessary to perform their functions.

6. The United States personnel shall be immune from local criminal, civil, tax and customs jurisdiction and may be accorded any other specific privileges and immunities provided for in the UNEF agreement of Feb. 13, 1957.

7. The United States affirms that it will continue to perform the functions described above for the duration of the basic agreement.

8. Notwithstanding any other provision of these proposals, the United States may withdraw its personnel only if it concludes that their safety is jeopardized or that continuation of their role is no longer necessary. In the latter case the parties to the basic agreement will be informed in advance in order to give them the opportunity to make alternative arrangements. If both parties to the basic agreement request the United States to conclude its role under this proposal, the United States will consider such requests conclusive.

9. Technical problems including the location of the watch stations will be worked out through consultation with the United States.

## *Memorandum of Agreement between the Governments of Israel and the United States October 7, 1975* *

The United States recognizes that the Egypt-Israel Agreement initialed on September 1, 1975 (hereinafter referred to as the Agreement), entailing the withdrawal from vital areas in Sinai, constitutes an act of great significance on Israel's part in the pursuit of final peace. That Agreement has full United States support.

United States–Israeli Assurances

1. The United States Government will make every effort to be fully responsive within the limits of its resources and Congressional authorization and appropriation, on an on going and long-term basis to Israel's military equipment and other defense requirements, to its energy requirements and to its economic needs. The needs specified in paragraphs 2, 3 and 4 below shall be deemed eligible for inclusion within the annual total to be requested in FY76 and later fiscal years.

2. Israel's long-term military supply needs from the United States shall be the subject of periodic consultations between representatives of the United States and Israeli defense establishments, with agreement reached on specific items to be included in a separate United States–Israeli memorandum. To this end, a joint study by military experts will be undertaken within 3 weeks. In conducting this study, which will include Israel's 1976 needs, the United States will view Israel's requests sympathetically, including its request for advanced and sophisticated weapons.

3. Israel will make its own independent arrangements for oil supply to meet its requirements through normal procedures. In the event Israel is unable to secure its needs in this way, the United States Government, upon notification of this fact by the Government of Israel, will act as follows for five years, at the end of which period either side can terminate this arrangement on one-year's notice.

(a) If the oil Israel needs to meet all its normal requirements for domestic consumption is unavailable for purchase in circumstances where no quantitative restrictions exist on the ability of the United States to procure oil to meet its normal requirements, the

---

* Sen. Rep. Appendix on Israel-U.S. Agreements (10/7/75), 1219.

United States Government will promptly make oil available for purchase by Israel to meet all of the aforementioned normal requirements of Israel. If Israel is unable to secure the necessary means to transport such oil to Israel, the United States Government will make every effort to help Israel secure the necessary means of transport.

(b) If the oil Israel needs to meet all of its normal requirements for domestic consumption is unavailable for purchase in circumstances where quantitative restrictions through embargo or otherwise also prevent the United States from procuring oil to meet its normal requirements, the United States Government will promptly make oil available for purchase by Israel in accordance with the International Energy Agency conservation and allocation formula as applied by the United States Government, in order to meet Israel's essential requirements. If Israel is unable to secure the necessary means to transport such oil to Israel, the United States Government will make every effort to help Israel secure the necessary means of transport.

Israeli and United States experts will meet annually or more frequently at the request of either party, to review Israel's continuing oil requirement.

4. In order to help Israel meet its energy needs, and as part of the overall annual figure in paragraph 1 above, the United States agrees:

(a) In determining the overall annual figure which will be requested from Congress, the United States Government will give special attention to Israel's oil import requirements and, for a period as determined by Article 3 above, will take into account in calculating that figure Israel's additional expenditures for the import of oil to replace that which would have ordinarily come from Abu Rodeis and Ras Sudar (1.5 million tons in 1975).

(b) To ask Congress to make available funds, the amount to be determined by mutual agreement, to the Government of Israel necessary for a project for the construction and stocking of the oil reserves to be stored in Israel, bringing storage reserve capacity and reserve stocks now standing at approximately six months, up to one-year's need at the time of the completion of the project. The project will be implemented within four years. The construction, operation and financing and other relevant questions of the project will be the subject of early and detailed talks between the two Governments.

5. The United States Government will not expect Israel to begin to implement the Agreement before Egypt fulfils its undertaking under the January 1974 Disengagement Agreement to permit passage of all Israeli cargoes to and from Israeli ports through the Suez Canal.

6. The United States Government agrees with Israel that the next agreement with Egypt should be a final peace agreement.

7. In case of an Egyptian violation of any of the provisions of the Agreement, the United States Government is prepared to consult with Israel as to the significance of the violation and possible remedial action by the United States Government.

8. The United States Government will vote against any Security Council resolution which in its judgment affects or alters adversely the Agreement.

9. The United States Government will not join in and will seek to prevent efforts by others to bring about consideration of proposals which it and Israel agree are detrimental to the interests of Israel.

10. In view of the longstanding United States commitment to the survival and security of Israel, the United States Government will view with particular gravity threats to Israel's security or sovereignty by a world power. In support of this objective, the United States Government will in the event of such threat consult promptly with the Government of Israel with respect to what support, diplomatic or otherwise, or assistance it can lend to Israel in accordance with its constitutional practices.

11. The United States Government and the Government of Israel will at the earliest possible time, and if possible, within two months after the signature of this document, conclude the contingency plan for a military supply operation to Israel in an emergency situation.

12. It is the United States Government's position that Egyptian commitments under the Egypt-Israel Agreement, its implementation, validity and duration are not conditional upon any act or developments between the other Arab states and Israel. The United States Government regards the Agreement as standing on its own.

13. The United States Government shares the Israel position that under existing political circumstances negotiations with Jordan will be directed toward an overall peace settlement.

14. In accordance with the principle of freedom of navigation on the high seas and free and unimpeded passage through and over straits connecting international waters, the United States Government regards the Straits of Bab-el-Mandeb and the Strait of Gibraltar as international waterways. It will support Israel's right to free and unimpeded passage through such straits. Similarly, the United States Government recognizes Israel's right to freedom of flights over the Red Sea and such straits and will support diplomatically the exercise of that right.

15. In the event that the United Nations Emergency Force or any

other United Nations organ is withdrawn without the prior agreement of both Parties to the Egypt-Israel Agreement and the United States before this Agreement is superseded by another agreement, it is the United States view that the Agreement shall remain binding in all its parts.

16. The United States and Israel agree that signature of the Protocol of the Egypt-Israel Agreement and its full entry into effect shall not take place before approval by the United States Congress of the United States role in connection with the surveillance and observation functions described in the Agreement and its Annex. The United States has informed the Government of Israel that it has obtained the Government of Egypt agreement to the above.

> YIGAL ALLON
> Deputy Prime Minister and
> Minister of Foreign Affairs
> (For the Government of Israel)
>
> HENRY A. KISSINGER
> Secretary of State
> (For the Government of the United States)

### Memorandum of Agreement between the Governments of Israel and the United States

The Geneva Peace Conference

1. The Geneva Peace Conference will be reconvened at a time coordinate between the United States and Israel.

2. The United States will continue to adhere to its present policy with respect to the Palestine Liberation Organization, whereby it will not recognize or negotiate with the Palestine Liberation Organization so long as the Palestine Liberation Organization does not recognize Israel's right to exist and does not accept Security Council Resolutions 242 and 338. The United States Government will consult fully and seek to concert its position and strategy at the Geneva Peace Conference on this issue with the Government of Israel. Similarly, the United States will consult fully and seek to concert its position and strategy with Israel with regard to the participation of any other additional states. It is understood that the participation at a subsequent phase of the Conference of any possible additional state, group or organization will require the agreement of all the initial participants.

3. The United States will make every effort to ensure at the Conference that all the substantive negotiations will be on a bilateral basis.

4. The United States will oppose and, if necessary, vote against any initiative in the Security Council to alter adversely the terms of reference of the Geneva Peace Conference or to change Resolutions 242 and 338 in ways which are incompatible with their original purpose.

5. The United States will seek to ensure that the role of the co-sponsors will be consistent with what was agreed in the Memorandum of Understanding between the United States Government and the Government of Israel of December 20, 1973.

6. The United States and Israel will concert action to assure that the Conference will be conducted in a manner consonant with the objectives of this document and with the declared purpose of the Conference, namely the advancement of a negotiated peace between Israel and each one of its neighbors.

> YIGAL ALLON
> Deputy Prime Minister and
> Minister of Foreign Affairs
> (For the Government of Israel)
>
> HENRY A. KISSINGER
> Secretary of State
> (For the Government of the United States)

---

### Assurances from USG to Israel

On the question of military and economic assistance to Israel, the following conveyed by the U.S. to Israel augments what the Memorandum of Agreement states.

The United States is resolved to continue to maintain Israel's defensive strength through the supply of advanced types of equipment, such as the F-16 aircraft. The United States Government agrees to an early meeting to undertake a joint study of high technology and sophisticated items, including the Pershing ground-to-ground missiles with conventional warheads, with the view to giving a positive response. The U.S. Administration will submit annually for approval by the U.S. Congress a request for military and economic assistance in order to help meet Israel's economic and military needs.

---

## Assurances from USG to Egypt

1. The United States intends to make a serious effort to help bring about further negotiations between Syria and Israel, in the first instance through diplomatic channels.

2. In the event of an Israeli violation of the Agreement, the United States is prepared to consult with Egypt as to the significance of the violation and possible remedial action by the United States.

3. The United States will provide technical assistance to Egypt for the Egyptian Early Warning Station.

4. The U.S. reaffirms its policy of assisting Egypt in its economic development, the specific amount to be subject to Congressional authorization and appropriation.

# Chapter 5

### The Covenant against Israel *

The Palestinian National Council, comprised of representatives of Palestinian organizations throughout the Arab world, met in Cairo in July 1968 to draft and adopt a "Palestinian National Covenant." Terrorist organizations had at least 47 representatives in the 100-member Council. The use of the word "covenant" rather than "charter" reflects the national sanctity of the document. (Underscore ours)

### Excerpts from the Covenant

Article 1: Palestine is the homeland of the Palestinian Arab people and an integral part of the great Arab homeland, and the people of Palestine is a part of the Arab nation.

Article 2: Palestine with its boundaries that existed at the time of the British Mandate is an integral regional unit.

* Comments are by Professor Yehoshafat Harkabi of the Hebrew University, Jerusalem.

Comment: This suggests that Palestine should not be separated into a Jewish and an Arab state, but rather should be one regional unit. This would include the West Bank and the Gaza Strip, as well as the states of Jordan and Israel.

Article 3: The Palestinian Arab people possesses the legal right to its homeland, and when the liberation of its homeland is completed, it will exercise self-determination solely according to its own will and choice.

Comment: This may explain why the PLO has not yet declared a government-in-exile—it will wait until the "liberation of the homeland is completed." The article claims that only the Palestinian Arabs possess a legal right to self-determination, not the Jews.

Article 4: The Palestinian personality is an innate, persistent characteristic that does not disappear, and it is transferred from fathers to sons. The Zionist occupation, and the dispersal of the Palestinian Arab people as a result of the disasters which came over it, do not deprive it of its Palestinian personality and affiliation and do not nullify them.

Article 5: The Palestinians are the Arab citizens who were living permanently in Palestine until 1947, whether they were expelled from there or remained. Whoever is born to a Palestinian Arab father after this date, within Palestine or outside it, is a Palestinian.

Article 6: Jews who were living permanently in Palestine until the beginning of the Zionist invasion will be considered Palestinians.

Comment: This is a crucial article. Arab literature marks the "Zionist invasion" as the year of the Balfour Declaration—1917. It is, therefore, unclear whether Jews born in Israel after 1917 would be allowed to remain. Jews who arrived in Israel after 1917, including the survivors of Hitler's tortures, would certainly have to go—one way or the other.

Article 7: The Palestinian affiliation and the material, spiritual and historical tie with Palestine are permanent realities. The upbringing of the Palestinian individual in an Arab and revolutionary fashion, the undertaking of all means of forging consciousness and training the Palestinian, in order to acquaint him profoundly with his homeland, spiritually and materially, and preparing him for the conflict and the armed struggle, as well as for the sacrifice of his property and his life to restore his homeland, until the liberation—all this is a national duty.

Article 9: Armed struggle is the only way to liberate Palestine and is therefore a strategy and not tactics. The Palestinian Arab people affirms its absolute resolution and abiding determination to pursue the armed struggle and to march forward toward the armed popular revolution, to liberate its homeland and return to it [to maintain] its right to a natural life in it, and to exercise its right of self-determination in it and sovereignty over it.

Comment: This precludes any negotiated peace or compromise with Israel. There exists only one way to liberate Palestine—armed struggle to eliminate the State of Israel.

Article 10: Fedayeen action forms the nucleus of the popular Palestinian war of liberation. This demands its promotion, extension and protection, and the mobilization of all the mass and scientific capacities of the Palestinians, their organization and involvement in the armed Palestinian revolution, and cohesion in the national (*watani*) struggle among the various groups of the people of Palestine, and between them and the Arab masses, to guarantee the continuation of the revolution, its advancement and victory.

Article 13: Arab unity and the liberation of Palestine are two complementary aims. Each one paves the way for realization of the other. Arab unity leads to the liberation of Palestine, and the liberation of Palestine leads to Arab unity. Working for both goes hand in hand.

Article 14: The destiny of the Arab nation, indeed the very Arab existence, depends upon the destiny of the Palestine issue. The endeavor and effort of the Arab nation to liberate Palestine follows from this connection. The people of Palestine assumes its vanguard role in realizing this sacred national (*qawmi*) aim.

Article 15: The liberation of Palestine, from an Arab viewpoint, is a national (*qawmi*) duty to repulse the Zionist, imperialist invasion from the great Arab homeland and to purge the Zionist presence from Palestine. Its full responsibilities fall upon the Arab nation, peoples and governments, with the Palestinian Arab people at their head.

For this purpose, the Arab nation must mobilize all its military, human, material and spiritual capacities to participate actively with the people of Palestine in the liberation of Palestine. They must, especially in the present stage of armed Palestinian revolution, grant and offer the people of Palestine all possible help and every material and human support, and afford it every sure means and opportunity enabling it to continue to assume its vanguard role in pursuing its armed revolution until the liberation of its homeland.

Article 16: The liberation of Palestine, from a spiritual viewpoint, will prepare an atmosphere of tranquility and peace for the Holy Land, in the shade of which all the holy places will be safeguarded, and freedom of worship and visitation to all will be guaranteed, without distinction or discrimination of race, color, language or religion. For this reason, the people of Palestine looks to the support of all the spiritual forces in the world.

Comment: This sets forth the goal of a "democratic Palestinian state" with freedom for all religions. The Sixth Congress of the Palestinian National Council, meeting in Cairo in 1965; adopted this slogan for propaganda purposes only because it "met with remarkable world response." The Council decided to drop "the slogan of 'throwing the Jews into the sea' which has done grave damage to the Arab position in the past" (minutes from the Congress).

Article 17: The liberation of Palestine, from a human viewpoint, will restore to the Palestinian man his dignity, glory and freedom. For this, the Palestinian Arab people looks to the support of those in the world who believe in the dignity and freedom of man.

Comment: According to Arab literature, the very existence of Israel cosmically prevents the Arabs from achieving their true national destiny. Israel's existence flaws the Palestinian's personality.

Article 19: The partitioning of Palestine in 1947 and the establishment of Israel are fundamentally null and void, whatever time has elapsed, because they were contrary to the wish of the people of Palestine and its natural right to its homeland, and contradict the principles embodied in the Charter of the United Nations, the first of which is the right of self-determination.

Comment: This reiterates rejection of Jewish self-determination. In truth, the armies of Arab nations voided the United Nations partition when they invaded Israel in 1948.

Article 20: The Balfour Declaration, the Mandate Document, and what has been based upon them are considered null and void. The claim of an historical or spiritual tie between Jews and Palestine does not tally with historical realities nor with the constituents or statehood in their true sense. Judaism, in its character as a religion of revelation, is not a nationality with an independent existence. Likewise, the Jews are not one people with an independent personality. They are rather citizens of the states to which they belong.

Comment: Palestinian chauvinism denies the very rights of self-determination for Jews that Palestinians claim for themselves. Unlike Palestinians, Jews are not a people, but members of a religion.

Article 21: The Palestinian Arab people, in expressing itself through the armed Palestinian revolution, rejects every solution that is a substitute for a complete liberation of Palestine, and rejects all plans that aim at the settlement of the Palestine issue or its internationalization.

Article 22: Zionism is a political movement organically related to world imperialism and hostile to all movements of liberation and progress in the world. It is a racist and fanatical movement in its formation; aggressive, expansionist and colonialist in its aims, and fascist and nazi in its means. Israel is the tool of the Zionist movement and a human and geographical base for world imperialism. It is a concentration and jumping-off point for imperialism in the heart of the Arab homeland, to strike at the hopes of the Arab nation for liberation, unity and progress.

Israel is a constant threat to peace in the Middle East and the entire world. Since the liberation of Palestine will liquidate the Zionist and imperialist presence and bring about the stabilization of peace in the Middle East, the people of Palestine looks to the support of all liberal men of the world and all the forces of good, progress and peace; and implores all of them, regardless of their different leanings and orientations, to offer all help and support to the people of Palestine in its just and legal struggle to liberate its homeland.

Comment: Zionism here is castigated as an enemy of the world, not just of the Arabs or the Palestinians. Arab literature frequently portrays Israel as a member of an imperialist plot to subjugate the Third World and Israelis as followers of the *Protocols of the Elders of Zion.*

Article 23: The demands of security and peace and the requirements of truth and justice oblige all states that preserve friendly relations among peoples and maintain the loyalty of citizens to their homelands to consider Zionism an illegitimate movement and to prohibit its existence and activity.

Comment: This article calls on Third World nations to support the Palestinian battle against "illegitimate" Israel. The PLO has received support, in one form or another, from the People's Republic of China, the Viet Cong, North Viet Nam, Cuba, and terrorist groups such as the Baader-Meinhof gang and the Japanese Red Army.

Article 24: The Palestinian Arab people believes in the principles of justice, freedom, sovereignty, self-determination, human dignity and the right of peoples to exercise them.

Article 26: The Palestine Liberation Organization, which represents the forces of the Palestine revolution, is responsible for the movement of the Palestinian Arab people in its struggle to restore its homeland, liberate it, return to it and exercise the right of self-determination in it. This responsibility extends to all military, political and financial matters, and all else that the Palestine issue requires in the Arab and international spheres.

Comment: The Palestine Liberation Organization assumes leadership as the umbrella organization for all Palestine terrorist groups engaged in the struggle against Israel.

Article 27: The Palestine Liberation Organization will cooperate with all Arab States, each according to its capacities, and will maintain neutrality in their mutual relations in the light of, and on the basis of, requirements of the battle of liberation, and will not interfere in the internal affairs of any Arab state.

Article 28: The Palestinian Arab people insists upon the originality and independence of its national (*wataniyya*) revolution and rejects every manner of interference, guardianship and subordination.

Comment: The Palestinian liberation movement professes that it does not serve as a tool for Arab governments. The PLO, however, has not refused the largesse of Arab governments in the form of arms, money, and logistical support.

Article 29: The Palestinian Arab people possess the prior and original right in liberating and restoring its homeland and will define its position with reference to all states and powers on the basis of their positions with reference to the issue [of Palestine] and the extent of their support for [the Palestinian Arab people] in its revolution to realize its aims.

Comment: This legitimizes Palestinian terror attacks on countries friendly to Israel. Surrendering to this blatant threat, European governments have freed virtually all Arab terrorists caught in their countries.

Article 30: The fighters and bearers of arms in the battle of liberation are the nucleus of the popular army, which will be the protecting arm of the gains of the Palestinian Arab people.

Article 32: To this covenant is attached a law known as the fundamental law of the Palestine Liberation Organization, in which is determined the manner of the organization's formation, its committees, its institutions, the special functions of every one of them and all the requisite duties associated with them in accordance with this covenant.

### *Ten Points for War*

On June 8, 1974, the Palestine National Council met in Cairo to draft the political principles to be followed in the PLO's present political offensive. Reprinted here is the text of the Ten Point Program. (Underscore ours)

Preamble:
Proceeding from the Palestinian National Charter and the PLO's political program which was approved during the 11th session of the PNC held from 3 to 12 January 1973, believing in the impossibility of the establishment of a durable and just peace in the area without the restoration to our Palestinian people of all their national rights, foremost of which is their right to return to and determine their fate on all their national soil, and in the light of the study of the political circumstances which arose during the period between the Council's previous and current sessions, the Council decides the following . . .

Comment: It is important to note the use of the word all—"all their national soil." This means that, contrary to some press interpretations, the PLO will not be satisfied with a separate Palestinian state to include merely the West Bank and Gaza but will insist on a state including all of what is now Israel.

The Ten Points
1. The assertion of the PLO position regarding Resolution 242 is that it obliterates the patriotic and national rights of our people and deals with our people's cause as a refugee problem. Therefore, dealing

with this resolution on this basis is rejected on any level of Arab and international dealings, including the Geneva conference.

Comment: The PLO has always rejected Security Council Resolution 242. Now that Arab governments have accepted it, the PLO wants the language of that resolution changed so that it may participate in Geneva on its own terms. Unable to establish itself as a genuine government-in-exile, the PLO seeks a *fait accompli*. It proposes to win international recognition and a windfall of power and influence by semantics.

2. The PLO will struggle by all means, foremost of which is armed struggle, to liberate Palestinian land and to establish the people's national, independent and fighting authority on every part of Palestinian land to be liberated. This necessitates making more changes in the balance of power in favor of our people and their struggle.

3. The PLO will struggle against any plan for the establishment of a Palestinian entity, the price of which is recognition, conciliation, secure borders, renunciation of the national right, and our people's deprivation of their right to return and their right to determine the fate of their national soil.

Comment: Articles 2 and 3 are the heart of the document. The PLO is determined to continue the armed struggle to liberate every part of the "Palestinian land"—a threat to both Israel and Jordan.

4. Any liberation step that is achieved constitutes a step for continuing to achieve the PLO strategy for the establishment of the Palestinian democratic state that is stipulated in the resolutions of the previous national councils.

Comment: This is construed as an attempt by Yassir Arafat to obtain discretion to maneuver and improvise as long as he does not depart from the major PLO objectives. But Arafat's freedom to maneuver is curtailed by the addendum to paragraph 10 (see below).

5. To struggle with the Jordanian national forces for the establishment of a Jordanian-Palestinian national front whose aim is the establishment of a national democratic government in Jordan—a government that will cohere with the Palestinian entity to be established as a result of the struggle.

Comment: Thus, the PLO swears not only to liquidate Israel but also to overthrow Hussein and eliminate the ruling groups in Jordan.

It should be noted that the Council debated its language for 10 days. Palestinians, more than any other Arab people, have fought among themselves in the name of unity. Until now, the PLO has not managed to establish a constituency in the areas administered by Israel and in Jordan, although these are the areas in which they propose to establish their state.

6. The PLO will strive to establish a unity of struggle between the two peoples [Palestinian and Jordanian] and among all the Arab liberation movement forces that agree on this program.

Comment: The document contains the phrase "all the Arab liberation movement forces that agree on this program." Thus, some guerrilla factions, jealous of their own power, will still not submit to any assertion of central authority.

7. In the light of this program, the PLO will struggle to strengthen national unity and elevate it to a level that will enable it to carry out its duties and its patriotic and national tasks.

8. The Palestinian national authority, after its establishment, will struggle for the unity of the confrontation states for the sake of completing the liberation of all Palestinian soil and as a step on the path of comprehensive Arab unity.

Comment: Once again, the Arab states are reminded that they must struggle for the liberation of "all Palestinian soil." This may also be a nod to the Syrian, Iraqi, and Libyan proponents of the guerrillas' cause.

9. The PLO will struggle to strengthen its solidarity with the socialist countries and the world forces of liberation and progress to foil all Zionist, reactionary and imperialist schemes.

Comment: This is a sop to African states, other Third World and Communist countries. The PLO will take allies wherever they can be found.

10. In the light of this program, the revolution command will work out the tactics that will serve and lead to the achievement of these aims.

A recommendation has been added to the political program. The recommendation stipulates that the Executive Committee implement this program. Should a fateful situation connected with the future of the Palestinian people arise, the Council will be called to hold a special session to decide on it.

Comment: Article 10 and its attached addendum almost destroyed the Council meetings. Arafat tried to change his own wording, seeking to add a mandate for "the leadership of the revolution to use the necessary tactic" for "the liberation of Palestine." The PFLP, PFLP-GC and ALF revolted against what they perceived as Arafat's attempt to secure freedom and total executive power.

## *Resolutions of the 13th Palestine National Council*

There has never been a session of the Palestine National Council (PNC) whose resolutions were so eagerly awaited in many circles as the one which convened in Cairo from March 12 to 20, 1977.

The fifteen resolutions express the views of the mainstream of the PLO which is mistakenly referred to as moderate. The extremity of the resolutions demonstrates the inherent difficulties of moderating the PLO position even tactically, despite Arab governments' pleas and persistent pressures. This resilience stems from the absolutism and totalism which characterize the PLO position of laying claim to Palestine in its *entirety*. Hence, moderating its position implies relinquishment of the PLO's central idea or the core value of its ideology. The cohesiveness of this ideology as one integral system renders a partial, incremental or gradual change almost impossible. The PLO cannot be transformed to become the PPLO—"Part of Palestine Liberation Organization."

The text of the resolutions (a revised UPI English version) with annotations [by Professor Harkabi] follows:

Preamble:

On the basis of the Palestinian National Charter and the resolutions adopted by previous National Council Sessions, motivated by a keen desire to preserve the political gains achieved by the PLO on Arab and international levels during the period that followed the 12th session of the PNC, after having studied and discussed the latest development of the Palestine problem, and reaffirming the necessity to strengthen the forward march of the Palestinian national struggle in Arab and international forums, the Palestine National Council affirms the following:

Comment: Had the Covenant or Charter been an onerous burden of which the PLO wished to rid itself, the PNC could have refrained from referring to it, for consigning a revered ideological document to oblivion can serve as a means of *de facto* abrogating it. Here, on the contrary, the PNC categorically declares its allegiance to the Covenant and to the resolutions of the previous PNCs, as a source for its own resolutions. Thus the authority of the Covenant is reconfirmed as are the Ten Points of the last PNC (the 12th).

Reverential references to the Covenant are not mandatory in PNC resolutions. They did not occur at all in Shukeiri's days. After him, the PLO became a coalition of fedayeen organizations disputing and competing amongst themselves. The Covenant acquired functional importance providing a common denominator which linked them together and assured the coherence of the movement. The reference to the Covenant in the preamble is doubly important as a deliberate rebuttal of the prognostications from various sources that it would be changed and of demands addressed to the Council to amend it.

The frequency of references to the Covenant by Palestinian spokesmen has greatly increased in recent months which also bears evidence to the vitality of this document.

The Covenant and the previous PNC resolutions are presented as an integral unit and as the source of inspiration for the present Council. However, there is a difference between them. A new resolution promulgated by a majority vote of a PNC can replace an old resolution, whereas an amendment of the Covenant, which has been elevated to the status of a constitution, has to be voted by a two-thirds majority in a council especially convened for this purpose.

Article 1. The PNC affirms that the Palestine problem is the essence of the Arab-Zionist conflict and that UN Security Council Resolution 242 ignores the Palestinian People and its inalienable rights. Consequently, the Council reaffirms its rejection of this resolution and its refusal to negotiate on its basis, on Arab and international levels.

Comment: The 4th PNC (July 1968) rejected Resolution 242 for a host of reasons, first and foremost because of its stipulation of recognition and a settlement of the conflict including secure and recognized borders. The 12th PNC covered up these reasons, which are the genuine ones, making it seem as if the only flaw in the 242 Resolution was its failure to mention the Palestinian people. (Its demand for "a just solution for the refugee problem" can, as Arabs have rightly noted, apply also to the Jews who found refuge in Israel from the Arab countries.)

Here another fault in the 242 Resolution is brandished, namely its ignoring the inalienable rights of the Palestinian people which, in the PLO conception, imply its right to the entire territory of Palestine, based on an axiomatic truth, as it were, that Palestine belongs to the Palestinians by definition. Thus such "an inalienable right" is an indirect, euphemistic expression for the liquidation of Israel. Hence Resolution 242 is rejected as it is incompatible with the demand for the demise of Israel. Article 1 in the resolution follows a similar article in the 12th PNC's resolution, except for the omission of an explicit mention of a rejection of the Geneva conference.

The conflict is referred to as "Arab-Zionist," rather than as Arab-Israeli, its usual name. Such an appellation falls within a tendency in PLO parlance to shun the mention of "Israelis," calling them Jews, as any acknowledgement that Israelis exist implies that they have some collective quality besides their religion and that they are, thus, at least a nation in the making, contradicting the PLO basic conception that the Jews constitute a religion only.

In Arab political literature, the hatred of Zionism is much greater than that of Israel as a state. The depravity of Israel flows from its being, first and foremost, the creation of Zionism. Zionism is defined as Jewish nationalism, which is an aberration, as the Jews are not a nation. Thus describing the conflict as between a normal group—the Arabs—and a depraved movement such as Zionism which has been internationally condemned, predisposes the judgment in favour of the Arabs.

Article 2. The Council affirms the PLO's determination to continue the armed struggle and other accompanying forms of political and mass struggle to achieve the inalienable national rights of the Palestinian People.

Comment: The PLO's resolutions have repeatedly stipulated that the armed struggle is the main form of struggle and that other forms are secondary and ancillary. The "mass struggle," which is added here, refers to protests and civil disobedience in the occupied territories. The importance of such activities has recently been given greater prominence in the PLO arsenal as other venues of action from Jordan, Syria and Lebanon have been closed to them. The importance of this issue is reflected in the fact that another article is allotted to it.

Article 3. The PNC affirms that the struggle in the occupied territory in all its military, political and mass forms, constitutes the central link in its programme of struggle. On this basis, the PLO is exerting itself to escalate the armed struggle in the occupied territory, to intensify all other forms of struggle and to extend all forms of material and moral support to the masses of our people in the occupied territory so that they can escalate the struggle and increase their resolve to persevere, defeat and liquidate the occupation.

Comment: The passing of the onus of struggle to the population of the occupied territories calls for expression of support and sympathy towards it. The "occupied territory" can refer also to Israel within the green line as was its common appellation in Arab political rhetoric.

Article 4. The PNC affirms the PLO's position in rejecting all forms of American capitulationist settlements and all plans for liquidation (of the Palestinian cause). It also affirms the PLO's determination to resist and thwart any settlement achieved at the expense of the inalienable national rights of the Palestinian people. It calls on the Arab nation to fulfil its national responsibility and mobilize all its resources to confront the imperialist and Zionist designs.

Comment: "Liquidation plans" refer to plans for the settlement of the conflict through compromise, without full realization of the PLO demands for the whole of Palestine. Any compromise is condemned as "surrender," thus stigmatizing it both intellectually and emotionally. The "liquidation of the Palestinian problem" and the "liquidation of Israel" are juxtaposed as mutually exclusive and exhaustive alternatives. Insuring the existence of Israel in any size is tantamount to the liquidation of the Palestinian problem. Such statements of position depict PLO absolutism which does not recognize partial satisfaction of its claims.

Article 5. The PNC affirms the importance and necessity of national unity, both military and political, among all fighting units of the Palestinian revolution within the framework of the PLO because this is a fundamental condition for victory. Therefore, it is our duty to strengthen national unity at all levels on the basis of commitment to those resolutions and programmes and to implement them.

Comment: This is an organizational article calling for unity. Similar articles have been common in PLO resolutions. The weakening of various organizations may facilitate steps towards unification, at least their coming closer together, as the spectrum of views which separated them has recently narrowed.

Article 6. The PNC affirms its determination to maintain the right of the Palestinian revolution to be present on sister Lebanon soil within the framework of the Cairo Agreement and its protocols, concluded between the PLO and the Lebanese authorities. It also affirms its insistence on the implementation of these agreements in letter and spirit, including preservation of the position of the revolution in Lebanon and the maintenance of the security of the camps.

The Council rejects any unilateral interpretation of this agreement and its protocols, while expressing its keen desire for the maintenance of Lebanon's sovereignty and security.

Comment: The "Palestine Revolution" is an honourific term for the Palestinian struggle against Israel. The right to continue the incursions into Israel and the right to operate in Lebanon should be preserved, against developments within Lebanon, including the Syrian take-over which may further restrict PLO freedom of action. This article embodies two contradictory elements: Lebanese sovereignty and Palestinian freedom of action. However, as demonstrated through experience, the latter infringes upon the former.

The PLO invokes the agreement with Lebanon of November 3, 1969, which allowed Palestinian action from Lebanon albeit within limitations which were specified in it and in its annexes (protocols). Rejection of "unilateral interpretation" of the Cairo agreement refers to the conclusion of the Arab League "Four-party Commission" that the Palestinian population in Lebanon should be reduced numerically to the level it had been at the time of the conclusion of the Cairo agreement.

Article 7. The PNC hails the heroic Lebanese people and affirms the PLO's interest in preserving Lebanon's integrity, unity, security, independence and sovereignty. It expresses its appreciation of the support given by this heroic people to the PLO, which is struggling for the recovery of our people's right to its homeland and the right of return. It strongly affirms the necessity of deepening the union between all Lebanese nationalist forces and the Palestinian revolution.

Comment: Lebanese support of the Palestinians in the previous article is complemented by support of the Palestinians for Lebanese sovereignty which, in practice, fell short of the commitment as expressed in this article. The "nationalist forces" probably refer to the leftists as the others are branded as "isolationists." Preserving Lebanon's integrity implies opposition to partition and moreover an assurance that the Palestinians do not aspire to take a region in Lebanon for themselves as an "alternative homeland," as some Lebanese circles have accused them.

Article 8. The Council affirms the necessity of strengthening the Arab front participating in the Palestinian revolution and intensifying cohesion with all the forces participating in it all over the Arab world. It also stresses the necessity of escalating the joint Arab struggle and boosting support for the Palestinian revolution to resist imperialist and Zionist designs.

Comment: The "participating front" is a framework of organizations and parties organized in order to support the PLO by exerting pressure on Arab Governments to prevent them from taking action against the PLO. The need for such an organization was a lesson learned from the PLO debacle in Jordan in 1970–1971. Once established, Kamal Jumblatt headed it. Organizing such a front meant intervention in the internal affairs of Arab states.

The Lebanese catastrophe does not discourage the PLO from continuing the same policy. The "participating front" was originally established for internal purposes. However, this article implies its use in the field of external affairs—as a bulwark against foreign pressures.

Article 9. The PNC decides to strengthen Arab solidarity and struggle on the basis of the fight against imperialism and Zionism, action to liberate all occupied Arab territory and commitment to support the Palestinian revolution for the recovery of the Palestinian Arab people's permanent national rights without a peace (sulh) or recognition.

Comment: The need to strengthen Arab solidarity is a recurring theme in Arab meetings. The solidarity described here is not rooted positively in a social and ideological common approach, but negatively in participation in the struggle against external foreign forces. The second half of this article states that whatever the political settlement may be, recognition of Israel and peace with it are categorically proscribed. The permanent (thabita) or historical rights of the Palestinian people are their rights to the entire territory in distinction with "current rights" (rahina) which has a more restrictive meaning, namely what can be achieved at the present stage.

Article 10. The Council affirms the right of the PLO to discharge its responsibilities in the struggle at the Arab national level and across any Arab territory for the sake of liberating the occupied lands.

Comment: Hence the PLO right to operate in any Arab country and through it against Israel. This claim is directed now in the main towards Jordan, but also to Syria and Lebanon. The PLO has the right to act in the international arena, mainly the U.N.

Article 11. The Council decides to continue the struggle for recovery of the national rights of the Palestinian people, foremost among them the right to return and the right of self determination and the establishment of an independent national state on its national soil.

Comment: In the 12th PNC, the state in the West Bank was called "an authority," so calling it a "state" is not a major change though it does signify greater acceptance of such a state. The merit of this article is its ambiguity. Internally it may be understood as applying to Palestine in its entirety, as the traditional PLO objective calls for. Externally it may also be interpreted as referring to a small Palestinian state. Foreign protagonists of the PLO may make use of the second version, as a proof of PLO moderation.

What the true intention of these two versions is can be learned from the tenor of the whole resolution and from the Political Statement published by the Council accompanying its resolutions in which the objective of setting up the Palestinian Democratic State is explicitly stated. The right to return includes the right to get back all former Arab landed property, the return of which will cause the mass eviction of Israelis from Jaffa, Nazareth, Ramle, etc. "The return" is thus both a strategic objective and a principle in the Palestinian programme of action leading towards the demise of Israel.

Article 12. The Council emphasizes the importance of strengthening cooperation and solidarity with the socialist, non-aligned, Islamic and African countries and with all national liberation movements in the world.

Comment: Ever since its inception, the PLO has expressed orientation towards the Eastern Bloc and the developing countries. The West, including Europe, is branded as imperialistic.

Article 13. The Council hails the attitudes and struggles of all democratic countries and forces which have opposed Zionism as a form of racism and opposed its aggressive practices.

Comment: The Council thanks all nations who supported the General Assembly November 10, 1975 resolution condemning Zionism, thus undermining the ideological foundation on which Israel as a state was established.

Article 14. The Council affirms the importance of relations and coordination with democratic and progressive Jewish forces, both inside and outside the occupied homeland, which are struggling against

Zionism as an ideology and a practice. It calls on all freedom, justice and peace-loving countries and forces to cut off all forms of assistance to and cooperation with the Zionist racist regime and to refuse to have any contact with it or its tools.

Comment: The possibility of a progressive movement developing in an inherently aggressive and reactionary state such as Israel, and whether such forces could acquire power and change Israel's nature have occupied the attention of Arab intellectuals. The agreement of May 6, 1970 between all the Fedayeen groups marking the start of the joint action stated: "Israel, by virtue of its structure, is a closed racialist society linked with imperialism and, also by virtue of its structure, the limited progressive forces that exist in it are incapable of bringing about any radical change in the character of Israel as a Zionist racialist state linked with imperialism. Therefore the aim of the Palestinian revolution is to liquidate this entity in all its aspects, political, military, social, trades union and cultural, and to liberate Palestine completely." (Walid Khadduri (ed.), *International Document on Palestine* 1970, Beirut, The Institute for Palestine Studies and the University of Kuwait, 1973, p. 796.)

The circles with which some PLO personalities have had contacts are described or praised as anti-Zionist. The connection between progressiveness, support of the PLO and anti-Zionism it seems is inherent. Zionism in Arab political thinking is described as Jewish (or Israeli) nationalism. Anti-Zionism means opposition to the establishment of a Jewish state and advocating its dismantlement now that it exists. Thus the purpose of anti-Zionism is to eradicate the Zionist character from Israel. Then Israel's uniqueness as a Jewish state will fade out and it will become like all other countries in the region and dissolve in it, that is, cease to exist.

Article 15. The PNC, having taken into account the important achievements made on the Arab and international levels since the 12th session of the council, and having studied the political report submitted by the PLO executive committee, decides the following:

a. It affirms the right of the PLO to participate on an independent, equal footing in all international conferences, forums and efforts concerned with the Palestinian question and with the Arab-Zionist conflict with the aim of achieving our inalienable rights—which have been approved by the U.S. General Assembly in 1974, in particular, in General Assembly Resolution 3236.

b. It declares any settlement or agreement affecting the rights of the Palestinian people and made in its absence as null and void.

Comment: This is perhaps the most important operative article. The PLO claims the right to participate in any international conference, first and foremost presumably, Geneva, although this is not mentioned explicitly. Such participation would be on the basis of the General Assembly resolution of November 22, 1974, which granted the PLO international recognition and status and stated that "the Palestinian people are indispensable for the solution of the question of Palestine," and "a principal party in the establishment of a just and durable peace in the Middle East." Using this resolution, the Council tries to circumvent Resolution 242 which constitutes the basis for the Geneva conference.

The second part of the article is directed against the Arab states, threatening rejection of any settlement achieved without the participation of the PLO. Thus the Arab states had better refrain from any conference from which the PLO is excluded. The PLO claims veto power over a settlement concerning the Palestinian problem. Such a resolution presents a challenge to a state like Egypt. Thus Egypt presses emphatically for PLO participation in the Geneva conference, irrespective of its rejection of Resolution 242.

# Index

# About the Author

CHAIM HERZOG, Israel's Ambassador to the United Nations, emigrated from Ireland to Israel as a boy and was educated at the universities of London and Cambridge. He served in World War II in the British Army, and in various command and staff posts in the Israel Defense Forces, concluding his service with the rank of major-general. His appointments included two periods as Director of Israeli Military Intelligence, and he served as the first Military Governor of the West Bank of Jordan in 1967.

Ambassador Herzog has headed an industrial investment group in Israel and a law firm. He has established himself as Israel's leading military and political commentator, broadcasting regularly in Israel, in Europe and in the United States.

He is the author of *Israel's Finest Hour* (1967), *Days of Awe* (1973) and *The War of Atonement* (1975), a best seller in several countries.

He was awarded a knighthood (K.B.E.) in 1970.